Combatting Cyber Terrorism

A guide to understanding the cyber threat landscape and incident response planning

Combatting Cyber Terrorism

A guide to understanding the cyber threat landscape and incident response planning

RICHARD BINGLEY

IT Governance Publishing

IT Governance Publishing Ltd
Unit 3, Clive Court
Bartholomew's Walk
Cambridgeshire Business Park
Ely, Cambridgeshire
CB7 4EA
United Kingdom
www.itgovernancepublishing.co.uk

First published in the United Kingdom in 2024 by IT Governance Publishing.

ISBN 978-1-78778-519-9

Cover image originally sourced from Shutterstock®.

Dedicated to Milena.

Thank you for everything.

ABOUT THE AUTHOR

Richard Bingley has led and operated a number of vital security projects including the London 2012 Olympics and Sochi 2014, as well as serving as executive director of London First's security and resilience division. He's the co-founder and director of the business security briefing service CSARN.org.

His book publications to date include:

- *The Security Consultant's Handbook* (ITGP: 2015);
- *Terrorism: Just the Facts* (Heinemann: 2003); and
- *Arms Trade: Just the Facts* (Heinemann: 2003).

Richard was senior lecturer for security and resilience at Buckinghamshire New University (2012–15) and director of the BNU Business School. He is CEO and principal of the CSARN Global Cyber Academy and a frequent media commentator on cyber security and future technology issues, including recently for the *London Evening Standard* and *Sunday Express*.

CONTENTS

Contents

FOREWORD

If you're anything like me as a reader, the first couple of questions you have before (or after!) purchasing a non-fiction book is *who wrote this and why?* After all, it takes a rather large amount of time for any individual to research, write and arrange the content you find before you.

Probably the first explanation to provide is that I've spent more than two decades in a range of job roles that either directly related to undertaking terrorism research or overlapped significantly into having to consider terrorist threat actors as a meaningful risk to one's own organisations and personnel. During a diverse career, I've been an IT manager, governmental spin doctor, cabinet minister events co-ordinator, close protection operative (CPO) and British armed forces member. For more than a decade, I've also served as a senior university lecturer and security risk management instructor to a wide array of agencies, military establishments and high-profile business sector clients. Each of these roles has provided me with the privilege to learn and develop from some of the best security management thinkers and organisational leaders out there. I hope that by writing this guide I can contribute something of purpose back to those who work so tirelessly (and often anonymously) behind the scenes to keep us all safe and well.

A couple of quirks of fate also led me to write this book and focus on the specific content that I did. I narrowly missed the 7 July 2005 Al-Qaeda London transport bombings. That morning, heading into work in Westminster (planning to take a half-day as it was my thirtieth birthday), I fortuitously ran late into Liverpool Street station. I missed the Circle Line tube explosion near Aldgate by four or five minutes. Many years later, as Plymouth City Council leader, I was part-responsible for the city's crisis recovery programme, put in place after spree killings conducted by an irate incel chat forum user. These and other life events sometimes force us to think existentially as well as plan much better to 'expect the unexpected'. Also, to corral those around us into action! I don't think that I'm unusual in being ever-so-slightly impacted by perpetrators of terrorism. And I've certainly never been physically harmed, unlike so many others less fortunate. Nonetheless, attempting to prevent terrorism, or helping others to counter it, has been a consistent theme in much of my work. This book, I guess, is the product of that desire to raise awareness and offer guidance in relation to risk management and incident response.

I originally arrived at the idea for producing a 'cyber terrorism' manuscript after feeling – despite a complete lack of science to back my hunch up – that many contemporary terror cases bore so much dependency upon Internet-enabled computer systems. Social media and the roll-out of interactive web 2.0 platforms since the millennium became ubiquitous, not just in the US and wealthier economies. Several countries moved swiftly to wrap controls around public use and placed direct responsibility for content transmission squarely onto the shoulders of Internet service providers. Most others didn't – and, for better or for worse – it's this unregulated legacy, fifty years after the Internet's inception, that so many countries and companies are challenged by today.

When social media spawned effectively, offering unvetted end users 24/7 availability and functionality, a glorious 'genie' escaped from bottle, for those considering active political extremism. Violent non-state actors – no matter how geographically remote, politically insignificant, or ideologically warped – could now easily interact with audiences well beyond their hitherto limited theatres of operation. Fringe figures from anywhere, prone to promoting violent discrimination and sectarianism – often shunned by civil society within their home jurisdictions – now had prime access to an intoxicatingly reliable instrument of international publicity and bilateral audience engagement.

Better still (for the terrorist), picture-driven content could be tailored for, and literally hand-delivered directly to, digitally-addicted mass audiences. Violent extremists conducting the most awful atrocities found that they could bypass mainstream news organisations and set viewing agendas themselves. At the same time, mainstream media editors were effectively pressurised to cover the perpetrator's grisly insider view. If some news agencies tried to do the right thing by not always following the maxim 'if it bleeds, it leads' and not offering the low-end clickbait, they risked sinking into obscurity and riling their shareholders.

For extremist orators and terror recruiters, cleverly-worded manipulations, defamations and damnations began appearing routinely on our smartphone and tablet screens. These home-brewed radical news feeds, packaged reportage and scripted comment with catchy soundbites, arrived just as quickly, authoritatively and slickly as productions broadcast by mainstream news anchors and documentary makers. Advanced tech certainly ushered in 'information democratisation'. But alongside that gain sat a significant degree of anarchy too. It is rather paradoxical, it seems, that as much of the world came together to better coordinate international counterterrorism after the 9/11 atrocities in America, such obvious human security challenges posed by information communication technology (ICT) advance were left almost entirely unaddressed in the US, EU and beyond.

This book will demonstrate that cyber terrorism gained significant – some might say, unhampered – traction from the early 2000s. The notion of 'cyber terrorism' became of primary importance in understanding so much of the necessary detail that really lies within the phenomenon of contemporary terrorism. Nowadays, because of widespread access to advanced communications and robot technologies, terrorism activities are so much more diffuse, randomised, unpredictable. And, one might plausibly argue, unaccountable. (Some terror groups and politically extremist organisations appear to have lost complete centralised control of operations conducted under their banner.) Such evidence pointing to the digitally-enabled decentralisation of violent extremism has recently been borne out in many formal investigations, inquests and judicial reports. Computer forensics evidence presented by prosecutors in court demonstrate that digital media platforms have often become the *single most important reason* why an individual 'activated' and moved forward along an emotional continuum towards carrying out a physical terrorist attack.

Since the early 1800s, a panoply of terrorism scholars, authoritative news organisations and governmental institutions have come to define terrorism as pre-meditated political violence carried out by *non-state actors*. (Although, the term hailed from the bloodthirsty actions taken during 1793/4 by France's post-revolutionary 'government': the *Reign of Terror* or *Règne de la Terreur*.) Confusion has reigned a little when it comes to discussing 'cyber terrorism'. When I scoped out writing this book, I couldn't understand why so many news references to cyber terrorism were not applying this elegantly simple *non-state* definitional criteria.

Especially because, as I felt, so much cyber terrorism is being perpetrated by non-state actors; many of whom are distinctly *anti-government* in worldview.

Indeed, the biggest difficulty I faced in writing about cyber terrorism was in deciding which cases and aspects to omit and why. For the reader's benefit, I wished to safeguard twin goals: keep it brief and deliver an overview. This book could easily have been three or four times the size. Examples and case studies presented are only a snippet of what's going on out there. Thus, this book is principally an overview and guide, laced with case studies and useful signposting. I hope it prompts further, much more detailed, research. (Please get in touch if you take up this challenge!)

Therefore, this book does not *per se* cover state-sponsored cyber terrorism. Namely, cyber attacks or the facilitation of physical attacks either directly authorised and implemented by government or by a 'plausibly deniable' proxy. There are a couple of exceptional case studies and references where the chain of responsibility is sufficiently hazy, or attack methods have been shown to be of documented interest to terror groups. However, most threat intelligence analysts would likely understand that government-directed or sanctioned cyber attacks – designed to terrorise or kill human targets – tend to fall within the *cyber warfare* or *warfare* definitional domain. I leave that very fertile and expansive research territory to be harvested by other authors.

Following the COVID-19 Pandemic, a drive to hybrid working, the physical fall of ISIS on the battlefield, and the 2021 Capitol Hill riots, still no dedicated cyber terrorism guide for business appeared readily available. Security risk managers and chief information security officers (CISOs) also still eagerly awaited the publication of peer-reviewed industry standards that could shed light on the best approaches to identify and mitigate the security risks posed by advanced technology. For example, an artificial intelligence (AI) security risk management standard was not due out until 2025. In this book – as part of addressing imminent advanced tech cyber terrorism concerns – we therefore describe and excavate tools and products found in the domains of AI, chatbots, drones and cryptocurrency. We explain how these powerful capabilities are being exploited by terrorist entities. We explore risk management frameworks that might be quite traditional but explain how they can be applied to our contemporary, advanced digital ICT world.

A personal note now. This is my fourth published book. It has been, by far, the most difficult to complete. In part, because the target topic is so potentially vast and the exploitation possibilities within the cybersphere are characterised by a level of speed and complexity that few human beings can easily cope with! The strain of writing any book is physical and mental. It's a long, drawn-out, emotionally grinding process. You spend a lot of time working alone to maintain focus and grip the issue at hand. This uber-focused psychological mode soon begins to feel like punishing austerity. A little like voluntarily locking your mind into solitary confinement for a year or longer. Outside of your day job (mine's teaching), you can't read much beyond related books and articles. (Many are referenced throughout and at the end: approximately 360 in total.) Exciting new books and films pass by unobserved. Professional frustration lurks beneath the surface too. News reports seemingly break every day, related to 'your topic'. But if you move to comment upon, or study them in any depth, you have ultimately become distracted...prolonging the torment of failing to finish that manuscript! Then arrive various stages of review and edit. But we (and I say 'we' because it's not just me) got there in the end.

I would therefore like to record very important 'thank yous'. Firstly, to my publisher, ITGP, and Publications Manager, Nicola Day, for her Confucian patience during the writing process. I would like to thank Kirsty Ridge, Copy Editor at GRC International Group PLC, for her help copy editing the material in this book. I completely underestimated the size and scale of research and content required. I'd also like to thank the book's two reviewers. Firstly, Simon King, formerly senior lecturer in security and resilience at Buckinghamshire New University; a good colleague back in our university teaching days. I'm pleased to say that nowadays we both discuss cricket far more than security dilemmas. His forensic feedback massively enhanced the first draft. Our second reviewer, Ze'ev Portner, serves as a university lecturer in law. Ze'ev possesses a rich pre-academia career background having worked at the Houses of Parliament as a chief of staff. Ze'ev was also employed at various stadia within the UK security industry. He started his legal career with law firms in Israel and London. Ze'ev's positivity about this book's relevancy for non-technical readers really helped shape our approach to structuring and fine-tuning the finished product.

Thanks also to Marshall Kent, former counterterrorism coordinator at London's Metropolitan Police. Marshall kindly granted an interview and I've also found our recent conversations really insightful and valuable in pushing cyber terrorism considerations forward to officials and policymakers. 'Thank you' similarly to the following: Helen Prendergast, who so ably and patiently supported me in my *other world* during 2022/23. David Evans (founder and chairman) and Andy Williams (deputy chair) at the Global Terrorism Information Network (TINYg); in my view the best public-private sector partnership for counter-terrorism discussions out there. The late Graeme McGowan – formerly at GCHQ and the Home Office – for his inspiring and tireless support, energy and positivity. (GMG sadly passed away shortly before this book's publication.) Finally, much love and thanks to my wife, Milena, for her consistent support and belief in me.

It seemed to me by 2021 – after two decades in and around the security world – that all my conference talks, course writing, teaching and pub-bar warnings, counted for zero…unless I could successfully encapsulate the issue at hand: cyber terrorism. Then, explain coherently, the critical importance of preventing some of its devastating impacts. For me personally, it was time to 'put up or shut up'. To bring the security sector's thoughts, research outputs and media commentary together. As Arnold Schwarzenegger famously said: *"You can have results or excuses."* I've tried here to deliver a basic overview and snapshot of cyber terrorism. Anything beyond that – such as our readers' updating their security plans, or recommending this ITGP book to others – would clearly be a positive result!

Richard Bingley.

London, 2024.

CHAPTER 1: INTRODUCTION

Security practitioners are increasingly confronted with a chilling phrase: *cyber terrorism*. For many, such as me, it conveys a sense of fear and hopelessness at the same time. What is this thing called 'cyber terrorism'? Moreover, what can we begin to do about it? Until it hits us, the impact feels a million miles away. Another person's nightmare. Another organisation's problem. Another country's war.

For the purposes of precisely understanding cyber terrorism throughout this book, we have borrowed and applied the National Cyber Security Centre's core two principles used to define and characterise a cyber crime:

1. **Cyber-dependent crimes** – crimes that can be committed only through the use of information and communications technology (ICT) devices, where the devices are both the tool for committing the crime, and the target of the crime.
2. **Cyber-enabled crimes** – traditional crimes that can be increased in scale or reach by the use of computers, computer networks or other forms of ICT. (CPS: 2019)

We will demonstrate how terrorists intentionally use computer systems to attack and harm human beings and property. They also use computer systems to diversify, complicate and increase terrorist attack impacts, including body counts and escalated public panic. Or to provide **disinformation** and **misinformation** to target audiences, including the emergency services and/or investigators, to sabotage aid, medical assistance and evidence. Nefarious ICT users, programmers and programs (including much AI-powered software) have all been instrumental in recruiting, inspiring, training, executing and amplifying acts of terrorism, which has resulted in the loss of life and/or lifechanging physical injuries that could never have occurred without cybersphere support and facilitation, whether by inanimate technology or others on the network using it. All of the above can be encapsulated by the phrase 'cyber terrorism'.

The issue at hand

The Internet is an integral part of everyday life for the vast majority of businesses and individuals. According to the Department for Digital, Culture, Media & Sport, even before the homeworking revolution prompted by the COVID-19 pandemic, nine out of ten adults live (and sometimes breathe) our lives online. We use the Internet in many ways to enrich and transform our lives. For instance, billions of us use the Internet for free lessons for leisure, formal education or to improve our professional prospects. But here's the downside: *"In the wrong hands the internet can be used to spread terrorist and other illegal or harmful content"* (DCMS: 2019).

This government warning is particularly foreboding given that access to the Internet is becoming less voluntary. Web access has become viewed as an existential human right, a pre-requisite of citizenship and societal belonging. In some jurisdictions, and during some public safety incident scenarios (such as pandemic management and military curfews), using online public services is the *mandated* method for contacting public sector support and accessing critical national infrastructure. (A lot of companies and public bodies have completely junked customer telephone lines and other routes to informal support.) Ergo, like it or not, it seems we must all be online.

This state of play is not just applicable to adults who are supposedly more life-experienced and threat-savvy. In most advanced industrial economies, 99% of 12 to 15 year olds regularly use the Internet too. In most cases, children travel about cyberspace with relatively unfettered limitations. And just like their elders, they've experienced little if any cyber security awareness training. The flip side to such joyous online libertarianism is now becoming apparent. According to British and European police forces, we are witnessing record numbers of children radicalised and prosecuted for online extremism (Counter Terrorism Policing: 2021). **During chapters 2 and 3** and elsewhere – using some cases in point – we confront cyber security vulnerabilities related to digital netizens who are underage or in their early teens. Similar to adults who experience behavioural mental illnesses, underdeveloped younger brains are at an additional risk from becoming attracted to and sucked into an online whirlpool of physical self-harm as well as public disorder and violence.

Despite well-meaning interventions by a range of influential stakeholders (tech firms, governments, police and academia alike), our computer networks remain riddled with easily-accessible horror images, violence-inspiring proclamations and instructional *how to* videos guiding the weak and angry into executing acts of terrorism. For billions of end users, such vivid, violent material is plastered over social networking sites by way of pop-ups, short URLs and preview videos. Social media forums, including gaming forums, boast monthly active audience sizes that are comparable to the world's most populous nation states or continents.

Therefore, accessing terrorism content does not require much in the way of research skills, technical ability or patience. AI-powered search engine prompts, hashtag funnels and slick terrorist-operated digital marketing strategies fuse together, preying upon end users and hooking into those most psychologically receptive. Out of the many millions who might catch a glimpse of such a pop-up image, or click through into an extremist website, either in error or innocent curiosity, it only takes a tiny fraction to become hooked for us all to have a major problem. Because a tiny fraction of a million views translates into a new legion of recruits to yet another terror network. In **chapters 2 and 3,** we learn how it is not just Al-Qaeda and ISIS that attempt to stimulate and nurture a 'cyber caliphate'. But that emerging terror networks across Europe and America – including the extreme far right and affiliated teenage hacktivists – are conducting copycat operations and have come to define themselves proudly as 'generation terror'.

According to Tech Against Terrorism (TAT), the non-governmental organisation (NGO) formed by big tech firms to help counter terrorism, the organisation tracked 45,000 URLs from 2016 to 2019 that led to numerous websites hosting terrorist material. This number was just a snapshot (read, massive underestimation), the group felt. Some 330 digital media platforms were used by terror groups for broadcasting, communications and file sharing. Of these, half were small or micro-platforms (Tech Against Terrorism: 2019). Nonetheless, during the span of this book's research (2022–24), the preponderance of terrorist material with mass reach, and arguably greater impact, was hosted on the super-sized social media platforms. Therefore, throughout **chapter 3,** we closely examine the role of several of the largest social media platforms. We also demonstrate and affirm TAT's findings that terror activists and material are fast moving onto the anonymously run decentralised web (DWeb). Although, because the DWeb reaches far lower audiences, terror groups still tend to use the pre-eminent digital platforms for signature event communications while retaining and deploying DWeb forums for niche discussions and/or for business continuity backup solutions following various waves of government/tech-industry takedowns.

Meanwhile, for those more technically adept, the DWeb (which we cover at the back-end of **chapter 3**) offers a technical playground where warfare fantasies and dark operations can be enjoyed. It remains relatively easy for tech-savvy netizens to quickly become an integral part of online terror communities, including the push for #online jihad, a hashtag phrase increasingly used beyond ISIS and Al-Qaeda domains. The thrill and attraction for programmers and software developers in carrying out core technical tasks on behalf of a terror organisation and its ringleaders, and building bespoke platforms (mainly for gaming and training), is observable across countless decentralised web programming forums. At the lower technical level, tasks for online terror supporters tend to include collaborative assistance in helping to build **click farms** and fake social media accounts. Meanwhile, more advanced technical assistance can involve shared project work between programmers and software engineers to design and distribute malware for direct cyber attacks. Or more subtle requirements to help with technical eavesdropping and technical surveillance (including spyware injections and development), **honeypot** exploits, or even enticing the enemy into physical or online honeytraps. Most tech support terrorists work from home, commit to office hours, have a boss, follow orders and collaborate online. Hybrid working at its most malignant.

As this book came to be researched, terrorism causation data began to noticeably shift. Although we should remain circumspect and not pre-judge pattern analysis in mid-flight, there appears to have been a tangible increase in politically motivated terror incidents within North America, Europe and Oceania. According to the Global Terrorism Index (GTI), politically motivated terrorist attacks came to outnumber religious-inspired attacks by the early 2020s (Global Terrorism Index: 2022). If this is correct, it appears to be that the pendulum of terrorism activity within most 'western hemisphere' political environments has swung back at least slightly towards violent political extremism related more to policy rejection than religious mission.

Data from Europol and European police agencies also shows a clear uptick in extreme far right terrorism activity across much of the Western hemisphere. With a sense of foreboding, this book's research points towards politically motivated domestic terrorists – including violently radicalised children – being shepherded into terrorism by the same cyber-enabled features that stoked and sustained two decades (and counting) of jihadist attacks. Perhaps a central lesson that all terror groups have learned from ISIS is best summarised by the Washington Post's **Joby Warwick**: *"In the [shrunken] life cycle of news — normal, breaking news — things tend to disappear quickly anyway [...] If the Islamic State can extend the news cycle to 30 hours before being shut down, they've succeeded"* (Washington Post: 2018).

Furthermore, due to Web 2.0's democratisation of content production, which empowers any end user to broadcast video material, terrorists can circumvent the media almost entirely.

1: Introduction

According to Professor Hagai Segal at New York University: *"Today anybody can be a journalist [. . .] Terrorists are journalists and they recognise their capacity to generate news but also to drive the news agenda [. . .] in a way that is designed to create that psychological impact."* Segal cites the three days of terror attacks in Mumbai, India, during 2008, as a pivotal news event whereby terrorists came to realise that by attacking civilians in key tourist centres, they could also significantly influence the lives of massive video audiences; viewers who found themselves unable to switch off from the sequence of atrocities. (Vimeo: 2015). In his paper *ISIS and Innovative Propaganda*, digital media expert Dylan Gerstel observes: *"ISIS propaganda in the West targets 16-25 year olds who are isolated from their societies and who do not have a strong sense of identity or purpose"* (Gerstel: 2016).

Several years later, and much depleted by military defeat in Syria and much of Iraq, Washington-based terrorism monitoring service, MEMRI, argues that *"ISIS media dissemination [is the] most important means of support"* (MEMRI: 2022b). It seems that such vividly successful cyber warfare lessons – which directly transformed ISIS's recruitment strength way beyond Al-Qaeda's limited reach – has now been researched and processed by other violent extremist groups. What this means for public safety is beyond this book's scope. Nevertheless, throughout **chapter 2,** we examine the dominant cyber terrorism ideologies or lines of thinking (idealisations). The book will reflect upon several cases in point from each ideological categorisation.

In **chapter 4,** we look at the use of cyber terrorism against industry and infrastructure while also considering potential exploits of advanced technologies. A little more than a decade ago, former CIA Director and US Secretary of

Defense, Leon Panetta, suggested that the world was *"facing the possibility of a 'cyber-Pearl Harbor'"* that could *"dismantle the nation's power grid, transportation system, financial networks and government"* (Bumiller and Shanker: 2012). While, to our knowledge, this near-apocalyptic threat hasn't quite materialised to date, we examine how, *inter alia*, AI, chatbots, cryptocurrency, drones and GPS eavesdropping and sabotage can become (or may already have become) weaponised tools within the modern terrorist armoury.

As we confront the terrorists' use of tools, tactics, ideologies and responses within cyber-enabled domains, it is refreshing to note that this book has a rare advantage over most other security-dilemma-related fact books. Namely, the burden of proof as to whether tech firms and policymakers need to deliver far more tangible outcomes in combatting cyber terrorism seems already to have been proven beyond all reasonable doubt within the court of public opinion. Opinion polls across America found that the public views cyber terrorism as the third-most critical threat over the next decade – ranked ahead of fears about China's military power or conflict in the Middle East (McCarthy 2016; Norman 2018). Consistently throughout this book, we provide commentary and guidance as to the nature of the threat and how individuals, families and businesses can recognise the symptoms and do something about them! **Chapter 5** – our final chapter – is therefore dedicated to security planning and incident response.

Finally, we point you to this book's closing pages that provide an alphabetical list of 'Key organisations and digital platforms' cited, an alphabetical list of and 'Description of terrorist organisations' cited, links to online summaries of terrorist attacks, and a glossary of terms used within this publication. We also provide Appendix E – kindly reproduced from the UK Crown Prosecution Service – that defines and characterises each UK cyber crime and legislation that it can be prosecuted under. Some key organisations, platforms and groups described are highlighted in bold at the first point of reference when reading through this publication.

1.1 Definitions and criteria

At the time of writing, there is no universally accepted definition of 'cyber terrorism'. Determining a definition for terrorism has been problematic for law enforcement agencies, policymakers and academics alike. According to the US **FBI**, cyber terrorism is any *"premeditated, politically motivated attack against information, computer systems, computer programs, and data, which results in violence against non-combatant targets by subnational groups or clandestine agents"* (Dataconomy.com: 2022). A concrete definition is also provided by a local authority in the UK. Wigan Council's cyber team summarises cyber terrorism – also known as 'digital terrorism' – as: *"Disruptive attacks by recognised terrorist organisations against computer systems with the intent of generating alarm, panic, or the physical disruption of the information system."* The council goes on to identify several potential methods of attack that can be fairly construed as cyber terrorism: *"The internet can be used by terrorists to finance their operations, train other terrorists, and plan terror attacks. The more mainstream idea of cyber terrorism is the hacking of government or private servers to access sensitive information or even siphon funds for use in terror activities"* (Wigan Council: 2023).

The UK Terrorism Act 2000 defines terrorism as the use or threat of one or more of the actions bullet-pointed below:

Specific actions included are:

- Serious violence against a person;
- Serious damage to property;
- Endangering a person's life (other than that of the person committing the action);
- Creating a serious risk to the health or safety of the public or a section of the public; and
- Action designed to seriously interfere with or seriously disrupt an electronic system.

The Act supposes that these actions are designed to influence the government, or an international governmental organisation, or to intimidate the public. For terrorism to have occurred, the action or threat must be for the purpose of advancing a political, religious, racial or ideological cause. Actions or threats that become investigated and prosecuted can occur outside the UK.

The use or threat of action, as set out above, which involves the use of firearms or explosives, is terrorism regardless of whether the action is designed to influence the government or an international governmental organisation, or to intimidate the public or a section of the public (CPS: 2023). The Act also extends into support and planning terrorist activities. According to terrorism guidance issued publicly by the Crown Prosecution Service: *"It is important to note that, in order to be convicted of a terrorism offence, a person doesn't actually have to commit what could be considered a terrorist attack. Planning, assisting and even collecting information on how to commit terrorist acts are all crimes under UK terrorism legislation"* (CPS: 2023). Given the complexity, criticality and heavy-duty security requirements involved in processing (or not) terrorism prosecutions, the

CPS operates a dedicated Special Crime and Counter Terrorism Division (SCCTD). This department provides *"early investigative advice to the police, make charging decisions and prosecute individuals accused of committing an offence"* (CPS: 2023).

Beyond the UK, (although London is a key member) a grouping of 57 nations form the Organization for Security and Cooperation in Europe (OSCE). This international body conducts and supports an impressive range of conflict prevention and counter-extremism work across its purview territories straddling North America, Europe and Central Asia. Several years ago, following mass casualty terror attacks inside the US, UK, Europe and Russia, the OSCE identified a "typology of terrorism"; highly useful because so many countries could not agree upon a definition and therefore formal international partnership working and guidance development was tricky. The OSCE's timely typology drew together many common and agreed strands from each country that define an act of terrorism. The typology that an act of terrorism was:

- Of an organised nature, whether the organisation involved is large or small;
- A danger to human life, limb or property;
- An attempt to intentionally undermine democratic government. In particular, by trying to influence policy and lawmakers; and
- Characterised by randomness and consequential spreading of fear/terror among a population (OSCE and ODIHR: 2007).

Government analysts and practitioners across the UK and US have coalesced around asserting four key indicators within the planning stage that point towards defining a major security incident as a "terrorist" event:

1. Planned beforehand – in 'cold blood'.

2. Carried out to achieve political change.

3. Aimed at non-combatants/civilians.

4. Usually the work of a group (not necessarily a group setting).

(Source: CIA's Paul Pillar cited in Bingley (2003).)

Leading academic scholars within terrorism domains appreciate strict definitions, typologies and categorisation because it enables them to conduct research within clear parameters. Terrorism definitions from such scholars are also very useful because they bypass internal diplomatic sensitivities and governmental definitional preferences, which can often be perceived as biased within territories suffering from civil war or polarised social and ethnic conflicts. Therefore, identifying a definition of 'terrorism' acceptable to most sides and parties may be too complex or lengthy an issue to revolve. For this reason, we now include a terrorism definition provided by leading academic experts, including psychiatrist **Jerrold Post:**

> *"Premeditated, politically motivated violence – or the threat of violence – against noncombatants or property by subnational groups or clandestine agents to influence, coerce, or intimidate an audience extending beyond the immediate target of the attack"*

(Post, Ruby & Shaw, 2000).

1: Introduction

The leading researcher behind criminal aggression theorisation as well as group identity and dynamics, **Albert Bandura**, states: *"Terrorism is usually defined as a strategy of violence designed to promote desired outcomes by instilling fear in the public at large"* (Bandura: 162). Award-winning US journalist and author **Ron Suskind** wrote in his insightful book *The One Per Cent Doctrine: Deep Inside America's Pursuit of its Enemies Since 9/11* that: *"People will do all sorts of things to make fear stop – so creating fear is a goal of the terrorist"* (Suskind: 2006). Such motivation by some individuals and groups to coerce and control large target audiences, in essence, partly explains why cyber terrorism spawned so speedily and omnipotently across very many digital media platforms during the tech sector's somewhat unregulated formative years. But this conundrum also takes national policymakers and advisers (and, indeed, organisational leaders) into challenging intellectual territory. Namely, to what extent can they or should they seek to intervene in, or even impede, information communication technologies that function (as neutral data package carriers) across their jurisdictions? In many states, terrorism incitement and glorification offences have been instituted that typically require a substantial burden of proof before prosecutors present a case before court. In turn, jurors and/or judges should only convict upon the evidence being presented as being so compelling that the defendant's guilt is factual "beyond all reasonable doubt". Such offences – primarily based upon the defendant's use of communication tools and techniques – are incredibly difficult to fairly prove and, therefore, rarely successful. It's worth recalling that the introduction of such laws were strongly resisted by policymakers beforehand, due principally to fears that law enforcement agencies would become enmeshed in policing 'thought' or that those who were radicalised (or suffering mental health difficulties), but whom were non-violent, could be prosecuted or imprisoned. Nevertheless, democratic societies – particularly across Europe – have broadly accepted that incitement and glorification statutes within counter-terror legislation have had to be introduced and/or strengthened.

However, the perceived spread of cyber terrorism has now pushed policymakers, tech firm chiefs, and other organisational leaders, into discussing levels of ICT intrusion that potentially move the scales further towards significant mass monitoring and intervention capabilities. A hypothesis emerging within counter-terrorism analysis fields called 'Stochastic terrorism' refers to influential media figures, including political leaders, that publicly demonise or vilify others in such a forceful manner that acts of political violence could be inspired against the target within the speech. Such language and rhetoric may not cross the legal threshold to be considered in breach of incitement laws. However, techniques could include the use of demeaning personalised jokes, coded or vague references, or a crude 'dog whistle' remark (for example, naming a sole individual as responsible for an unpopular political outcome). Such rhetoric, whereby the instigator can plausibly deny responsibility for any tangible outcome, would fall short of incitement laws in many jurisdictions. For example, in the UK and US, legal incitement is generally understood to mean speech that is intended to produce *"imminent lawless action"* (Amman and Meloy: 2022).

1.2 Laws and regulations

UK

The **Terrorism Act of 2006** established offences that in effect relate to the government's ongoing 'Prevent' terrorism strategy. They include, in particular, the offence of encouraging terrorism or disseminating publications that seek to encourage political violence. Such offences of incitement to terrorism are sometimes known as *glorification* offences. The legal framework for this provision is provided by Sections 1 and 2 of the Terrorism Act 2006 (TACT), which create the offences of encouragement of terrorism (s.1) and the dissemination of terrorist publications (s.2). Section 3 of TACT provides that those served with notices who fail to remove, without reasonable excuse, the material that is unlawful and terrorism-related within a specified period, are treated as endorsing it. (HMG Prevent Strategy: 2011: 77).

The **Counter-Terrorism and Security Act 2015** determines that schools and universities must help divert students from recruitment into terrorist groups, as part of Prevent. Educators are expected to report students suspected of terrorist or extremist sympathies to a local government body, and vet the remarks of visiting speakers, among other obligations (Freedom House: 2022).

The **Counter-Terrorism and Border Security Act**, which received royal assent in 2019, included provisions related to online behaviour. Individuals can receive prison sentences of up to 15 years for viewing and accessing material that is useful or likely to be useful in preparing or committing a terrorist act. The law provides for exceptions for journalists or academics who access such materials in the course of their work but does not sufficiently explain other possible circumstances in which access might be legitimate (Freedom House: 2023).

The **Counter-Terrorism and Sentencing Act (2021)** has made provisions for jail sentences of up to 14 years for anyone who *"supports a proscribed terrorist organisation"* (HMG Legislation: 2023). In addition, the Act materially ends the likely prospect of early release for anyone convicted of a serious terror offence and forces them to spend their whole term in jail. The maximum penalty for membership of a proscribed terror organisation increased from 10 to 14 years under this Act (GOV.UK: 2021).

A proposed **Online Safety Bill**, initially tabled before the Houses of Parliament during 2021, still had not passed all the legislative committee stages at the time of writing. Scuppered by internal political changes within the government, as well as uncertainty as to the level of content intervention expected of Internet service providers (ISPs), the bill's proposals are sanctions-based. They include giving power to Ofcom, the regulator, to fine online services the greater of £18 million or 10% of global turnover, if they do not comply with the bill's provisions. According to some reports, social media giants would be required to quickly remove illegal content such as hate speech or *"face hefty penalties and even potential criminal prosecutions for tech executives who fail to act"* (Politico: 2023).

Draft Terrorism (Protection of Premises) Bill: This proposed law is also known as 'Martyn's Law' in memory of Martyn Hett, one of 22 people killed in the 2017 Manchester Arena bombing attack conducted by a Manchester-born **Al-Qaeda** operative. The subsequent formal inquest by **Sir John Saunders** found that several key aspects of security planning, threat identification and incident response failed before, during and after the attack. The proposed bill focuses mainly on mandating security risk assessments and implementing basic security controls at publicly accessible locations and/or events hosting more than one hundred people. The bill was lightly criticised by the Home Affairs Select Committee in July 2023 for proposing requirements that could potentially over-burden businesses, while not actually preventing further mass casualty attacks. Whatever happens to this piece of legislation, the lessons for cyber security risk managers are clear. Data owners should be aware that the secure ownership, storage and distribution of personal data is a fundamental counter-terrorism requirement (see CCTV case study later). Likewise, sensitive site security documents (including site, evacuation incident response, crisis management and training plans) must be kept securely and safely away from access by would-be terrorists or witting and unwitting accomplices. Employee naivety in relation to publishing very useful advance information, including site photos, staff and planning details – is a recurring feature running throughout so many post-incident reports into terrorism. Such data breaches and privacy indiscretions could come with real legal sanctions if Martyn's Law or other pieces of future counter-terrorism legislation ever catch up with the cybersphere.

Case study: CCTV, data storage and the law

Proposed new counter-terrorism legislation potentially enacted by the aforementioned Draft Terrorism (Protection of Premises) Bill is likely to enshrine a *Protect Duty* whereby organisations must better plan for and secure their locations. Within this law, organisational incident response policies and practices, including expectations of training a cadre of counter-terrorism 'competent persons', are all expected to become mandated. This proposed statute and variations of it are being closely looked at by many other jurisdictions around the world. (Even if the UK Premises Bill stalls, the following good practice can be considered *the right thing to do*, as well as very much legally advisable!)

One of the key challenges of countering cyber terrorism is understanding precisely how laws impacting the physical security space will be implemented and operationalised, within any business. Genetec's Steve Green observes that gathering most digital evidence, including CCTV images, was hitherto largely dependent upon *"manual processes such as sharing footage on USB sticks or burning it to DVDs"*. Green advises that *"the Cloud offers much better options for a faster, safer and more accountable means of providing access to digital evidence"* (City Security Magazine: 2023: 9). According to the National Counter Terrorism Office (NACTSO) guidance on Publicly Accessible Locations, *"If an incident occurs, the [CCTV] images should be copied onto removable media. A record should be kept of movement of the CD or CDR disk, SD card, or other media showing an identification number, times, dates and names of those handling the media. All used media should be destroyed or disposed of securely"* (PALs Guidance: 2023).

When deploying a surveillance camera system, you must have a clear understanding of your organisation's responsibilities under data protection laws. The General Data Protection Regulation (GDPR or EU GDPR across Europe) and the Data Protection Act 2018 are formal laws backed up by heavy sanctions including significant fines and breaches that attract negative media coverage. The Information Commissioner or equivalent offices in many other countries have published detailed guidance on how to create data protection impact assessments (DPIAs). If you are making decisions around capturing personal data captured as a controller, or joint controllers, you are responsible for compliance with data protection law, including the requirement to carry out a DPIA. It is recommended that DPIAs are carried out when:

- New systems are installed;
- Cameras are added or removed from systems;
- Cameras are moved or change position;
- Whole or parts of systems are upgraded; and
- Where systems that include biometrics capabilities such as automatic facial recognition are in use.

During and after cyber terrorism events, organisations remain legally responsible for data and privacy breaches within the UK, EU, USA and elsewhere. The fact that an organisation and its staff suffered a severe shock (read 'disruption' in business continuity parlance) does not reduce or remove this 24/7 legal obligation. Moreover, following major security incidents, organisations and individuals – including their electronic devices – caught up in the event are prone to attract unwanted attention from all manner of hackers. There is also a likelihood that communications data and all CCTV-related data could be seized or subpoenaed by investigative agencies, regulatory bodies and/or formal inquests. Therefore, if CCTV or other personally identifiable information (PII) is stored within Cloud services, do ensure that strong security settings including **multifactor authentication (MFA)**, firewalls, further backup solutions and decent encryption are consistently applied in and around your Cloud. Cyber attacks on organisational Cloud storage backup solutions, conducted by a mix of hostile state actors and pro-extremist hacktivist groups, are exponentially rising.

UK cyber crime laws

Computer Misuse Act (1990): According to the government, *"the Computer Misuse Act 1990 (CMA) is the main legislation that criminalises unauthorised access to computer systems and data, and the damaging or destroying of these. The Act has the intention of protecting the integrity and security of computer systems and data through criminalising access to them which has not been authorised by the owner of the system or data"* (Home Office: 2023a). In May 2021, the Home Secretary announced a review of the CMA because law enforcement and industry felt that malicious acts on computer systems, and areas necessary for effective incident response, were not adequately addressed by the current laws. In some scenarios, cyber investigators faced prosecution for unauthorised access into external computer systems. Proposed areas for legal enhancement include: providing extra legal powers for authorities or other agreed bodies to take down domain names and **IP addresses** used for clearly criminal activity, the takeover of IP and domain names, powers to ensure data preservation, unauthorised data copying becoming treated as 'theft', as well as new powers to launch cyber investigations overseas (Home Office: 2023a).

Data Protection Act (2018) – DPA: UK only. Replaces the Data Protection Act (1998) and incorporates the EU GDPR into British law. DPA installs the Information Commissioner's Office (ICO) as the enforcement authority. The 2018 Act establishes the importance of organisations to be more *responsible* with personal data as well as to improve and safeguard data *confidentiality*. Suspected data breaches must be reported to the ICO within 72 hours and data subjects must be informed. DPA has seven parts, including the processing of data by competent bodies and the intelligence services, which falls beyond the GDPR.

One requirement under the DPA/GDPR is that an organisation undertakes a **Data Protection Impact Assessment (DPIA):** According to the ICO, a DPIA is a process to help you identify and minimise the data protection risks of a project. You must do a DPIA for processing personal data that is likely to result in a high risk to individuals. Your DPIA must:

- Describe the nature, scope, context and purposes of the processing;
- Assess necessity, proportionality and compliance measures;
- Identify and assess risks to individuals; and
- Identify any additional measures to mitigate those risks.

A full list of all cyber crime and prosecutor's guidance is produced by the Crown Prosecution Service (CPS). Some of these laws may be very useful for businesses and/or police forces that could conduct investigations, or seek to make other forms of early interventions, to prevent politically violent radicalisation or physical attacks. The online guide covers areas ranging from online harassment, unlawful eavesdropping and surveillance, economic crime and fraud, and cyber attacks, *inter alia*. The CPS's tabularised summary of all criminal laws related to cyber crime is provided in this book's Appendix E.

US

The First Amendment of the United States Constitution determines that Congress makes no law respecting an establishment of religion or prohibiting its free exercise. It protects freedom of speech, the press, assembly, and the right to petition the government for a redress of grievances. Thus, the US body politic has been cautious to regulate any form of freedom of speech although the PATRIOT Act (described below) fundamentally shifted power into Federal government security agencies and national law-enforcement forces.

PATRIOT Act: The *Uniting and Strengthening America by Providing Appropriate Tools Required to Intercept and Obstruct Terrorism Act* became signed into law during 2001 by President George W. Bush after the 9/11 terrorist atrocities and subsequent anthrax attacks within the US. The legislation sought to bolster US national security, particularly against foreign-related acts of terrorism. The PATRIOT Act is expansive and wide-ranging, increasing surveillance (including phone-tapping), easing interagency communications and increasing sentences for terrorism-related offences.

For instance, Section 505 authorises government agencies to seize financial, Internet, credit and telephone records without prior judicial review and without articulable suspicion that the target is a terrorist or a spy. Another area that strengthened powers for ICT monitoring was published under Section 901. This section permits the US intelligence community head (CIA director) to set *"requirements and priorities"* for domestic intelligence-gathering, which could include domestic communications surveillance and monitoring (American Civil Liberties Union: 2023).

In 2012, President Barack Obama signed the PATRIOT Sunset Extensions Act into law, providing for roving wiretaps, business-record searches and conducting surveillance on lone wolves. According to the US Office of Justice Programmes: *"The Act also expands the list of situations in which the Secret Service may participate in the investigation of computer crimes and authorizes the U.S. Attorney General to establish regional computer forensic laboratories to train Federal, State, and local law enforcement in investigating computer crimes"*. More specifically for cyber-related concerns, including terrorism financing: *"the [PATRIOT] Act expands the scope of key money laundering statutes; includes computer fraud and abuse as part of the grounds for charges of terrorism; and modifies the computer fraud statute, including permitting extraterritorial jurisdiction"* (Office of Justice Programs: 2002).

US cyber crime laws

Computer Fraud and Abuse Act (CFAA): Passed in 1984 as an amendment to the rather weak Comprehensive Crime Control Act (1984). CFAA came from a strong concern that federal and other governmental networks were being targeted by skilled hackers. Specifically, the CFAA prohibits the following:

- Knowingly accessing a computer without authorisation to obtain national security or other government-restricted data.
- Intentionally accessing a computer without authorisation to obtain certain information from:
  ○ A financial institution or consumer reporting agency;
  ○ The federal government; or
  ○ A protected computer.
- Intentionally accessing and affecting the use of a government computer.
- Knowingly accessing a protected computer to defraud and obtain anything of value.
- Causing damages specified in the statute by knowingly transmitting harmful items or intentionally accessing a protected computer.
- Knowingly trafficking in computer passwords.
- Extortion involving threats to damage a protected computer.

"In certain circumstances," say legal experts, *"the CFAA permits an individual who suffers damages to bring a civil action for damages or injunctive relief against a violator"* (Thomson Reuters Practical Law website: 2023). The Act's

network security provisions (drafted pre-World Wide Web) have been amended and strengthened several times, including by the PATRIOT Act. In the wake of computer researcher Aaron Swartz's suicide, some US legislators sought to amend and limit some CFAA provisions so that it would not inadvertently capture most white or grey hat hacking activities. Aaron Swartz, a computer programmer and Internet hacktivist, had been charged by federal prosecutors on two counts of wire fraud and eleven violations of the CFAA. Unhappy that his plea bargain for a lighter sentence had been rejected, Swartz took his own life in 2013.

Health Insurance Portability and Accountability Act (HIPAA): Signed into law by President Bill Clinton during August 1996. HIPAA modernised health data processing laws to protect the data subject and the transmission of healthcare information. It stipulates how personally identifiable information (PII) acquired, stored and disseminated by the healthcare and healthcare insurance industries should be protected from fraud and theft. Fines and sanctions find their way to organisations that are found to be responsible for lax security and breaches.

North American Electric Reliability Corporation Critical Infrastructure Protection (NERC CIP): This sector partnership was originally established during the 1960s out of concerns about preventing power blackouts in the US and Canada. Now it is very much engaged in assisting its members to prevent cyber terrorism. According to industrial power experts, Verve: *"Discussions around the consideration of the creation of a set of cyber security standards for the industry began when the catalyzing events of 9/11/2001 occurred and provided an increased sense of urgency to the effort"* (Verve: 2022). The NERC CIP standards are now mandatory security standards that apply to all entities that own or manage facilities forming part of the Canada and US electric power grid. These standards were initially approved by the Federal Energy Regulatory Commission (FERC) in 2008. According to TechTarget's Rahul Awati and Ben Cole: *"These standards carry the force of regulations, meaning they are required by law [...] All entities that fall under the purview of NERC CIP must comply with these standards"* (TechTarget: 2023). The following graphic illustrates NERC CIP's nine golden rules to safeguard cyber security:

9 rules imposed by NERC CIP standards

CIP-001 Sabotage reporting

CIP-002 Critical cyber asset identification

CIP-003 Security management controls

CIP-004 Personnel and training

CIP-005 Electronic security perimeters

CIP-006 Physical security of critical cyber assets

CIP-007 Systems security management

CIP-008 Incident reporting and response planning

CIP-009 Recovery plans for critical cyber assets

Figure 1: NERC's Nine Rules[1]

---

[1] Figure 1 sourced from the TechTarget website:
https://www.techtarget.com/searchsecurity/definition/North-American-Electric-Reliability-Corporation-Critical-Infrastructure-Protection-NERC-CIP.

Federal Information Security Modernization Act (FISMA) :S. 2521. Signed into Federal law in December 2014 by President Barack Obama. Commonly referred to as FISMA Reform, this legislation was passed in response to an increasing amount of significantly impactful cyber attacks on federal government systems. FISMA changed existing laws to enable the federal government to more effectively respond to cyber attacks on departments and agencies.

Communications Decency Act: Following the January 2021 crowd attack on Congress in Washington DC, we may well be about to witness *"a new era of social media regulation"* argues *Harvard Business Review* columnist, Dipayan Ghosh (2021). In an incident that rocked America, and shocked much of the world, seven people were killed and 140 police officers injured. Afterwards, social media companies participated in a relatively synchronised takedown of around 70,000 QAnon conspiracy theory group members' social media accounts. Tech firms moved swiftly and controversially. Donald Trump's Twitter (now X) feed was shut down and Snapchat imposed a temporary lockout for the former president. In addition, YouTube removed what it considered to be a handful of community guideline-breaching videos, citing their inflammatory nature. Stripe's online payment platform ceased processing Trump campaign website payments.

Since this historic incident, a groundswell of senior figures across US government and both Houses of Congress have moved to strengthen or remove Section 230 of the Communications Decency Act (CDA 1996). This is the federal law provision that grants Internet service providers protection from liability (aka immunity) for user-generated content, hosted and disseminated on their platforms (Ghosh: 2021). In the US and across Europe, ISPs including Google,

Twitter, AOL, Grindr and Facebook enjoyed their legal immunity being upheld, seeing cases against them dismissed, although their servers and services carried undoubtedly inflammatory, dangerous and brazenly false or conspiratorial communications.

The Force v. Facebook Inc., 934 F.3d 53 (2nd Cir. 2019) second appeals court decision held that Section 230 bars civil terrorism claims against social media companies and Internet service providers despite expert testimony asserting that: *"Mounting evidence suggests that providers designed their algorithms to drive users toward content and people the users agreed with — and that they have done it too well, nudging susceptible souls ever further down dark paths"* (McCabe: 2021). The case against Facebook had been brought under the US Anti-Terrorism Act by families and friends of several killed by terrorists in Israel. Hamas had reportedly used the social media platform to coordinate activities.

(Proposed) Social Media Child Protection Act: At the time of writing, the US Congress 2023–24 session were discussing passing legislation *"To require providers of social media platforms to prohibit children under the age of 16 from accessing such social media platforms, and for other purposes"* (Congress.gov: 2023). If passed, the Social Media Child Protection Act will very much supersede existing provisions under the Children Online Privacy Protection Act (1998) that curb marketing directly to minors and acquiring children's personal data without parental consent.

Europe and EU

In major European economies, successful cases have been brought – albeit rarely – against directors of tech companies whose systems and platforms have published words and/or images that breach criminal or libel-related laws. Although in these exceptional cases costly appeals have sometimes been won, there is a clear political/governance trajectory moving towards more regulation and liability placed on the shoulders of ISPs and social media platforms. One successful appeal was brought by business leader, Felix Somm, former managing director of CompuServe Germany. Somm became charged with violating child pornography laws because of content being carried on CompuServe's servers stored within Germany. In the initial criminal case (1998), Somm was convicted and sentenced to two years' probation (Kuner 1998). Somm was cleared on appeal the following year. In the original case, the judge appeared unimpressed by the technical defence that content filtering was impossible when he declared that CompuServe had let *"protecting the young ... take second place to maximizing profits"* (Internet Archive Wayback Machine: 2023). Legal interpretations can appear fickle with devastating consequences for business owners and security managers that are slow to address potential criminal activities hosted on their networks.

EU General Data Protection Regulation (EU GDPR): Adopted by the EU in 2016 and enforceable since 2018. A key component to the GDPR is that informed consent must have been acquired by the user from the data subject, for the subject's data to be used. The regulation applies if the data controller (an organisation that collects information about living people, whether they are in the EU or not), or processor (an organisation that processes data on behalf of a data controller like Cloud service providers), or the data subject (person) is based in the EU. Under certain circumstances, the regulation also applies to organisations based outside the EU if they collect or process personal data of individuals located inside the EU. The regulation does not apply to the processing of data by a person for a *"purely personal or household activity and thus with no connection to a professional or commercial activity"*. Similar or mirror legislation has been passed in several non-EU states and territories including the UK, California (The California Privacy Rights Act (CPRA), Turkey, Japan, Kenya, Brazil, Argentina and South Korea.

Network and Information Systems (NIS) 2: Critical infrastructure within the EU is supposed to conform to the **Network and Information Systems (NIS) 2** Directive. Published in 2022 and repealing the first NIS directive (2016), NIS 2 imposes stricter legal requirements for operating information systems within the EU by introducing legal obligations for cyber security risk management measures and reporting requirements. In addition to requiring organisations to achieve a level of managed **security posture** maturity, and addressing supply chain risks, NIS 2 will capture 160,000 organisations within a new information exchange network called The Network and Information Systems Cooperation Group. NIS 2 seeks to create a *"culture of security" across seven core sectors vital for economic and critical infrastructure: banking, finance, digital, energy, healthcare, transport and water"* (DataGuard: 2023). This reflects the EU's overarching Cybersecurity Strategy (2020) that has driven forward proposals for an EU-wide Cyber Resilience Act (CRA). Passed by the European Parliament in 2024, the CRA seeks to harmonise digital and software development rules and create *"an obligation to provide duty of care for the entire* lifecycle of such products" (EU Cyber Resilience Act).

International law

Council of Europe, Budapest Convention (2001): The convention was the first international treaty on crimes committed via the Internet and other computer networks, dealing particularly with infringements of copyright, computer-related fraud, child pornography and violations of network security. It also contains a series of powers and procedures such as the search of computer networks and interception. The Convention's "Action Against Cybercrime" page can be accessed on its website, and the relevant URL is provided in the references chapter at the end of this book.

UN Security Council Resolution (SCR) 1624 (2005) calls for member states to take necessary and appropriate actions *"to prohibit by law incitement to commit a terrorist act and prevent such conduct"* (UN CTED: 2021). **UN SCR 2341** (2017) reaffirmed that nation states were to address cyber security within wider counter-terrorism planning and responsibilities. **UN SCR 2354** (2017) sets out guidelines for a "comprehensive international framework" in "developing counter-narratives" and "public-private partnerships" while safeguarding human rights to freedom and privacy. This resolution and others that year were key catalysts in the UN's support and involvement in forming **Tech Against Terrorism** and **Global Internet Forum to Counter Terrorism (GIFCT),** founded by Facebook, Microsoft, YouTube and Twitter in 2017.

UN SCR 2462 (2019) notes the use of emerging easy-access and unaccountable payment systems, including crowdfunding sources, virtual assets (cryptocurrency) and mobile-phone-hosted transactions.

1.3 Terrorist mindset and motivations

We have seen in that there are some clear dimensions that enable us to define terrorism. Two clear dimensions supporting an act of terrorism definition are offered by **Alex Schmid** at Case Western Reserve University: (1) that terrorism involves aggression against noncombatants and (2) that the terrorist action in itself is not expected by its perpetrator to accomplish a political goal but instead to influence a target audience and change that audience's behaviour in a way that will serve the interests of the terrorist (Schmid: 2004). Eminent terrorist psychiatrist **Jerrold Post** usefully divided political motivations for sub-state terrorism actors into:

1. Social revolutionary terrorism;
2. Right-wing terrorism;
3. Nationalist-separatist terrorism;
4. Religious extremist terrorism; and
5. Single-issue (e.g. Animal rights) terrorism.

He proposed that each type tends to be associated with its own social-psychological dynamics (Post: 1998). The predominant content in this book reflects that the overwhelming majority of the most serious cyber terrorism cases recorded since the millennium emanate principally from three ideological precincts: extreme right-wing terrorism, religious fanaticism and politically-motivated misogynistic attacks.

Given that there is such a different range of causes and tactics driving terrorist behaviour, is it possible to identify common characteristics that might provide clues or cues for law enforcement, or indeed wider society, to identify terrorism-in-the-making? And, if so, prevent some terror attacks occurring? When considering this, it's worth keeping at the forefront of our mind that the origins of terrorist mindset and behaviour begin with a single, identifiable, individual. Carrying out a terrorist act, or materially assisting an extremely violent political action, is extremely unusual human behaviour. Indeed, shock-and-awe terrorism acts are so unusual that they have been described by one psychologist as comparable to a lethal shark attack: horrific but rare.

On average, four to five thousand significant terrorism attacks, spread across more than one hundred countries, are committed every year. Some 200,000 since 1970, when the much heralded **START** Global Terrorism Database based in Maryland, US, drew its first line of composition from (START GTD: 2023). Given this volume, psychosocial theorists advise that counter-terrorism analysts may be able to establish human characteristics or behavioural patterns prevalent in terrorist actors. After all, there are many millions of politically radicalised individuals who are not violent. Therefore, what occurs within the human mind to move an individual from radical or troubled thoughts into committing an act of terrorism? Prominent contemporary counter-terrorism academics, **Hamm and Spaaj,** feel that *"Such insight may provide investigators with a sort of detection system, or 'signatures'—as minimal as they may appear— that an individual with a terrorist intent will demonstrate in preparing for an attack"* (Hamm, and Spaaj: 2015). Another leading academic researcher **Jeff Victoroff** asserts: *"Improved modeling of markers of psychological subtypes may enhance the prediction of terrorist behaviors"* (Victoroff: 2005). Terrorist-turned-British-government agent **Aimen Dean** commented in his book *Nine Lives* about the draw into Al-Qaeda's terror operations for Islamist radicals:

1: Introduction

"As I came from jihadis across different backgrounds, I became fascinated by what had brought them to Al-Qaeda's camps. Some had come to believe in jihad after years of thought and argument. Some – often less stable – had been radicalized almost overnight, perhaps as a reaction against a form of addiction or in seeking redemption for some terrible sin. They were escaping demons or the tedium of a mundane existence. Still others [...] were told by preachers that they were needed: hooked and drawn in like helpless fish by a silver-tongued imam. There were many personal journeys, but all sought one end: martyrdom [...] There was a bloodlust among some fighters[...]" (Dean: 2018: 112).

A substantial amount of academic and governmental research has already enriched – or possibly complicated – our knowledge about terrorism perpetrators. Leading terrorism analysts, including **Martha Crenshaw,** to posit that, in general, terrorists tend to reason, think rationally, and follow psycho-logic processes in pursuit of a life strategy. Within the conduct of supporting and carrying out extremism, terrorists are following rational strategic choices to achieve their aims (Crenshaw: 1998). Crenshaw observes that *"terrorism may follow logical processes that can be discovered and explained"* (Crenshaw: 1998: 7). Terrorist behaviour is not so much a psychological force but resorting to violence *"is a wilful choice made by an organization for political and strategic reasons, rather than as the unintended outcome of psychological or social factors"* (Crenshaw: 1998: 7–8).

Similarly, in his post 9/11 study of convicted jihadist terrorists, **Marc Sageman** (a career US intelligence analyst and long-serving professional psychologist) found few clues from either the social or psychological backstories of Al-Qaeda and Egyptian Islamic Jihad terror convicts to indicate anything other than cognitive normalcy. Indeed, a distinct lack of childhood trauma or 'injured self' complaints were recorded across Sageman's sample of 172 convicted terrorists. The injured-self hypothesis is associated with 'narcissistic harm', causing the subject to belittle and attack others while also possessing an inflated sense of self-importance. Sageman's research therefore seems to imply that rational choice theory principally explains terrorist psychosocial approaches radicalised within jihadist networks at the very least (Sageman: 2017).

However, beyond jihadist domains, and before the digital media revolution, several terrorism analysts with psychological research backgrounds were able to identify clearer psycho-social aspects in research subjects that they vaunted merited further research. This was because discernible patterns, if not firm conclusions, about underlying psychological behavioural drivers, had been found. For example, Interior Ministry terrorism psychology research conducted around 1980 in West Germany delved mainly into violent extreme left Red Army Faction militants. Analysing some 227 convicts, the sample size is historically significant by terrorism psychological research standards. Researchers found that subjects experienced much higher instances of serious parental relationship schisms, sexual identity conflict, college dropout rates and weapons fetishes (Jager, Schmidtchen and Sullwold: 1981). **Jerrold Post** also documented from his research that many violent extremists had identifiable personality disorders.

Interestingly, other digital-revolution studies into terrorist personalities generate a clearer pattern of discernible psychosocial characteristics. **Ferracuti and Bruno's** cavernous research into Italy's far-right political extremism through the 1970s and 1980s involved a sample size of 908 convicted terrorists. Drawing lots of this research together more recently, psychiatrist and neurologist, **Jeff Victoroff**, observed that the following personality traits and characteristics were widespread among offenders:

1. Ambivalence towards authority.

2. Defective insight.

3. Adherence to convention.

4. Emotional detachment from the consequences of their actions.

5. Sexual role uncertainties.

6. Magical thinking.

7. Destructiveness.

8. Low education.

9. Adherence to violent subculture norms and weapons fetishes. (Victoroff: 2005)

Similar personality traits have been cited in court evidence presented at many contemporary grievance and terrorism murder trials, sentencing hearings and parole boards. Examples of the troubled psychological state of many prominent homophobic terrorists include **David Copeland** (1999), **Anders Breivik** (2011), **Thomas Mair** (2016), **Brenton Harrison Tarrant** (2019), and many others that will be highlighted in this book's "Extreme right wing" section (chapter 2). It could be plausibly argued that aspects of these subject profiles chime uncannily with Ferracuti and Bruno's findings. Researching and intervening much more regularly and obtrusively with those who demonstrate clear psychosocial extremism behaviours, as well as with those who conduct online engagement with dominant terrorism causes and entities, may well be one of the most purposeful changes that national and local jurisdictions can make in tackling future cyber terrorism. Because it's clear – at present – that various prevention programmes around the world lack resources and operational teeth. According to forensic psychiatrist, **Gwen Adshead**, when the social conditions are ripe, and personality defects align, a "bicycle lock" combination effect can trigger desperate, often final, acts of explosive violence (Adshead and Horne: 2022).

An added complication to identifying potential perpetrators online is the technical ability of supposed lone actors to mask their own identity and encrypt and firewall communications from those who may support or sympathise with them. According to Hamm and Spaaj's comprehensive research on US-based lone terror actors since 9/11: *"Four out of every 10 [...] lone wolves demonstrated an affinity with extremist organizations, but affinities are an exception to the rule that lone wolf terrorists are becoming increasingly independent. At the root of this change is technology. With the rise of Internet chat rooms, conspiracy websites, Facebook and Twitter, online activists can connect scattered people who are worried about everything from drone strikes to a one-world government and the pending imposition of martial law in the US and tell them that they do not worry in isolation. Moreover, radicalization is caused by an affinity with online sympathizers"* (Hamm and Spaaj: 2015: 11). Glimpses for intervention exist but often arrive too late: *"76% broadcasted their intent, often more than once. The broadcastings were made through e-mails, text messages, Facebook postings and Twitter feeds, PowerPoint presentations and Podcasts"* (Hamm and Spaaj: 2015: 9).

In closing this section, it should be noted that a very useful overview of terrorist mindset was published by market research company Quantum in 2015. Television research interviews were conducted with 49 ISIS fighters in Syria (and defectors) at the height of ISIS's insurgency in that region. Quantum's content analysis research chimes with two other major contributions to understanding the ISIS-fighter mindset. These are produced by Stern and Berger in their book *ISIS: The State of Terror.* Followed up by comprehensive academic research into 4,000 fighter backgrounds researched by Evans, Milton and Young (Stern and Berger: 2015) (Oxford University Press: 2020). The headline findings are summarised within the case study below.

Case study: Why join ISIS?

Quantum Communications (2015) identified nine principal motivations behind joining ISIS:

- **Status seekers:** *"Intent on improving "their social standing" these people are driven primarily by money "and a certain recognition by others around them."*

- **Identity seekers:** *"Prone to feeling isolated or alienated, these individuals "often feel like outsiders in their initial unfamiliar/unintelligible environment and seek to identify with another group."* Islam, for many of these, provides *"a pre-packaged*

---

transnational identity."

- **Revenge seekers:** *"They consider themselves part of a group that is being repressed by a community or someone else."*
- **Redemption seekers:** *"They joined ISIS because they believe it vindicates them or atones for previous sinfulness."*
- **Responsibility seekers:** *"Basically, people who have joined or support ISIS because it provides some material or financial support for their family."*
- **Thrill seekers:** *"Joined ISIS for adventure."*
- **Ideology seekers:** *"These want to impose their view of Islam on others."*
- **Justice seekers:** *"They respond to what they perceive as injustice. "The justice seekers' 'raison d'être' ceases to exist once the perceived injustice stops," the report says."*
- **Death seekers:** *"These people "have most probably suffered from a significant trauma/loss in their lives and consider death the only way out with a reputation of martyr instead of someone who has committed suicide.""*

(Source: Quantum Communications Ltd. Cited in *The Atlantic*: 2015)

CHAPTER 2: CYBER TERRORISM – IDEOLOGIES AND IDEALISATIONS

2.1 Incel and misogynist

In many countries, extremist 'incel' activity is seen as an emerging and expanding terrorism threat. A shortening of the phrase 'involuntary celibate', incel terrorism is also known as 'misogynist' or 'male supremacist' violent extremism. Dozens of lethal attacks have been launched that have distinct misogynist motivations perpetrated principally by males who contain a deep-seated hatred for women. Shootings at Cleveland public library during 1984 conducted by Kent Malcolm were perhaps the first such killing spree attack acknowledged explicitly as 'misogynist' motivated in contemporary US history (Web Archive: 1985). Many tragic instances have followed since, including a shooting massacre at Montreal's Ecole Polytechnique in 1989 where 14 women were killed after the suicidal attacker, who blamed feminism for ruining his life, separated a mechanical engineering class by gender and began shooting female targets.

Many analysts point to a marked increase in violent incel and misogynist attacks since social media became a mainstream communications form (see list below). To such an extent, that a nexus of academics, politicians and government officials advocate formal categorisation and **securitisation** of incel "ideology", as has occurred with other designated terrorism typologies (Tomkinson et al: 2020). By 2022, UK counter-terrorism officers recorded that some 77 (around 1%) referrals into the government's anti-radicalisation programme, Prevent, possessed women-hating 'incel' views. UK police refer to incel material online as "propaganda", so far resisting incel's categorisation as a terrorist "ideology" (*The Guardian*: 2023). In North America, a Secret Service report spanning research throughout the last decade found that the incel terrorism threat is growing within the USA (CBS News: 2022). The US National Threat Assessment Center's deep dive into misogynist terrorism was prompted by a series of spree killings and massacres by incels and male supremacists, including a mass shooting by a 40-year-old ex-teacher and military veteran who shot six women (two died) at Tallahassee Hot Yoga studio in 2018. YouTube videos posted by the killer four years before the killings showed that he identified as involuntary celibate and sympathised with the 2014 Isla Vista incel mass murderer, **Elliot Rodger**. Both posted misogynist music onto their SoundCloud accounts (CNN: 2018).

According to a European Commission Home Affairs department report (2021), *"Incel-created websites and forums, such as incels.is, are the most high-risk platforms in the ecosystem where discussion of all [levels of] violence can be found."* The report concludes that there appear to be subtle differences in the way that various social media platforms are used and exploited. For example, *"Communities on popular social media platforms, such as YouTube and Twitter, represent lower-risk platforms where discourse tends to focus on personal-level violence, however, discussion of interpersonal- and societal-level violence can also occur."* Meanwhile, the EU Commission report finds that *"**Reddit** was historically a high-risk incel platform, but a series of bans of incel **subreddits** in 2017 and 2018 has reduced the amount of incel content on Reddit"* (EU Commission: 2021: 7).

Suicidal ideation discussions and the promoting of self-harming body modifications are extremely common across the incel ecosystem (EU Commission: 2021: 4). Interest in suicide and discussions around methods of suicide and encouragement to take one's own life are regular and dominant discourse among incel chat forums. Suicide notes are commonly posted. Suicidal individuals are often encouraged to "go ER", which is an explicit reference to the 2014 Isla Vista massacre and suicide of incel "hero" Elliot Rodger (EU Commission: 2021: 7). Some incel chat users refer to Rodger as a "martyr". Other online encouragement to "go Minassian" or "go Sodini" is explicit referencing and encouragement for other incel chat members to follow in the footsteps of two other high-profile misogynist spree killers (EU Commission: 2021: pp7-8)

Incel ideology

Before we take a look at contemporary cases of misogynist terrorism, it is useful to for those tasked to prevent and mitigate terrorism to establish key terms and philosophical tenets emerging from 'inceldom'. The US Secret Service Report *Hot Yoga Tallahassee: A Case Study of Misogynistic Extremism* found that an emerging 'incel' movement operated as a subculture within a wider 'manosphere'. The manosphere can be broken down into four categories, suggest researchers, characterisable as: (1) pickup artists; (2) men's rights activists; (3) men going their own way; and (4) incels. This cauldron of rhetoric (not always inhabited by males; there are also females in manosphere and inceldom chats) serves as a largely self-reaffirming online male supremacist ecosystem. This subculture is supported and interconnected by many thousands of blogs and discussion forums that can cover anything from parental rights to suicide method selection. Just like the jihadist and extreme right-wing chats, an underlying ideological flooring reflects a rather suffocating ideology of omnipotent victimhood. Just as politicised victimhood narratives are propelled into jihadist and extreme far-right chat forums, increasingly systems-theory critiques pour into incel forums. (These can be understood most simply as *"it's the system's fault, not me!"*. *Within this narrative, of course, any individual who is not part of inceldom becomes an insignificant blur, indistinguishable from others. 'Outside' individuals are depersonalised, and thoughts of attacking outsiders become legitimised. Threats become targets and those in the way become 'fair game'.) "Although these groups are known to promote male-dominant views,"* states the report, *"some members express extreme ideologies involving anti-woman hate, sexual objectification of women, and calls for violence targeting women"* (US Secret Service: 2022).

Extremism researcher **Florence Keen**, from the International Centre for the Study of Radicalisation at King's College London, found that one of the biggest incel forums has 13,000 active members and around 200,000 threads. *"The caveat I would always give is that we can't say that the whole of the incel subculture is violent,"* Keen told the BBC after the August 2021 incel-related lethal spree shooting in Plymouth, UK. *"It really varies. Some will glorify violence while others [in these forums] will say 'this is not what we are'"* (BBC News: 2021). Analysts from the Council on Foreign Relations and Georgetown University found that *"as new online incel forums proliferated on sites such as 4chan and Reddit, they also became more extreme: either ending or drowning out many of the previous discussions and debates about inceldom"* (Hoffman, Shapiro and Ware: 2022). Incels often make reference to taking a red or black pill – a metaphor extracted from science-fiction movie series, *The Matrix*, whereby individuals taking the red pill experience a harsh awakening to truthful world realities. There is no black pill in *The Matrix*, just a blue one that enables folk to live in illusion/delusion. But incels refer to taking a 'black pill' that delivers an even harsher reality, whereby women are inherently prejudiced against unattractive males, nurturing a socially-nihilistic, yet self-hating mindset that embraces self-isolation, sexual marginalisation, and compounds inceldom's prevailing idea that women are shallow and discriminatory (Stijelja and Mishara: 2022). A cul-de-sac mindset summarised as follows by leading counter-terrorism scholar Bruce Hoffman et al:

"The incel worldview is grounded in two ineluctably intertwined beliefs: their understanding of society as a hierarchy where one's place is determined mostly by physical characteristics, and their identification of women as the primary culprit for this hierarchy. Accordingly, at the top of this structure are the idealized men and women respectively referred to as "Chads" and "Stacys." So-called "normies" are in the middle, with the lowly incels languishing at the bottom. In incel lore, a small number of Chads attracts the majority of women, leaving only the apparently unattractive women for the normies, and none for incels . . . if one did not 'win' the genetic lottery, they are destined for mediocrity, social isolation, and abject loneliness."

(Hoffman, Shapiro and Ware: 2022: 5).

Cases in point: Internet-inspired incel and misogynist attacks

2009: George Sodini (aged 48). Collier Township, Pennsylvania, US. Maintained and published extremist website. Mass shooting with pistols at public gym. Kills four (including self), injures nine.

2011: Jared Loughner (aged 23). Political rally. Tuscon, Arizona, US. Shoots congresswoman Gabby Giffords at close range in the head. Conducts spree shooting, killing six (including a nine-year-old girl) and wounding 13, including Giffords with lifechanging injuries. Increasingly erratic after drug abuse, Loughner's teachers, family and classmates were worried he would conduct a school shooting after being excluded from college. A YouTube conspiracy theorist broadcaster, handwritten notes found afterwards saying *"die bitch"* and *"assassination plans have been made"* were documented by investigators (CNN: 2011). Loughner was a participant on conspiracy theorist message board *Above Top Secret*, where it is thought his marijuana-infused psychosis advanced.

2014: Elliot Rodger (22). Isla Vista, California, US. Uploaded YouTube video 'Elliot Rodger's Retribution' during spree killings conducted with pistols, knives and vehicle ramming. Kills seven (including self), comprising three males by stabbing, and injures 14. Maintained a disturbing YouTube channel and emailed 107,000-word extremist manifesto midway through his sequence of attacks. Often referred to as "The Supreme Gentleman" and "Saint Elliot" by incels on chat forums.

2014: Ben Moynihan (18). Portsmouth, UK. In three separate incidents, stabbed three women, citing extreme misogynist views and requesting arrest before a fourth planned attack. Found guilty of attempted murder in 2015.

2015: Chris Harper-Mercer (26). Umpqua Community College, Oregon, US. Mass shooting and suicide in college building. Motivations cited include satanism, racism and social/sexual rejection by females. Kills ten (including self) and injures eight. Maintained a MySpace profile and several other accounts where he published homages to firearms, IRA fighters and mass shootings. On another website called KickAss Torrents, Harper-Mercer uploaded videos about school massacres and celebrated fame achieved by the perpetrator responsible for shooting dead two WDBJ reporters during a live broadcast.

2018: Alek Minassian (30). Toronto, Canada. Vehicle ramming. 10 killed and 16 injured. Identified on Facebook and **4chan** chats as incel and published posts eulogising the 2014 Isla Vista perpetrator and calling for incel revolution. Jailed for life in 2022.

2018: Scott Paul Beierle (40). Hot Yoga, Tallahassee, Florida, US. Mass shooting and suicide in yoga studio. Kills three (including self) and injures five. YouTube videos posted by Beierle from 2014 reveal he self-identifies as Incel and sympathises with Isla Vista murderer, Elliot Rodger. Many videos, including one titled 'Dangers of Diversity', show him ranting against inter-racial relationships, African Americans and immigration (CNN: 2018).

2020: Unnamed male teenager (17). Toronto, Canada. Machete attack at erotic bar. One female killed, two people injured (including attacker). Perpetrator's video game profile on Steam platform called for "incel rebellion" and web searches targeted leading incel terror figures including Alek Minassian.

2020: Armando Hernandez Junior (20). Westgate Entertainment District, Arizona, US. Mass shooting, reportedly targeting couples. Three injured. Attack conducted soon after Toronto (above).

2020: Tobias Rathjen (43). Shisha bar, Hanau, Frankfurt, Germany. Mass shooting, suicide and matricide. Kills 11 (including self and mother at home after event) and injures 5. Ultra-nationalist and racist motivations behind attack; perpetrator cites sexual frustration as driver behind violence. Maintained a personal website, published a racist manifesto months before the attack, promoted eugenics, and stated that voices in his head frustrated his success in relationships with women.

2021: Jake Davison (22). Home and street attack, Plymouth, Devon, UK. Six killed (including self and mother) and two injured. Published YouTube videos as 'Professor Waffle' reflecting a black pill worldview and referencing "inceldom". Subscribed and participated in Reddit and subreddit incel chat forums before his accounts were suspended for inappropriate online comments to a 16-year-old girl. Davison carried out his massacre the following day after shooting his mother.

2.2 Extreme right wing

UK

It's helpful to briefly set the ideological bearings for what we're about to cover here. The extreme right wing, as opposed to the radical right wing, is, generally speaking, anti-democratic and supportive of direct action, including violence, to achieve its goals. (Rose and AC: 2022: 8). I frame the following encapsulation for far right terrorism upon the basis of manifold court documents and press cuttings: Extreme right wing terror actors have almost without exception explicitly embraced totalitarian political solutions, supported ultra-nationalist and racialist policy 'solutions' (including racial separation/apartheid), and touched base with groups that have suggested support of Hitlerism and its murderous policy programmes against ethnic groups, LGBT+, dissenters and dissidents.

In February 2016, **National Action (NA)** released a recruitment video called *Inside The White Jihad*, which included images of its members engaged in martial art training. Those who attended its training camps are also reported to have been shown ISIS videos. NA used the hashtag #WhiteJihad on **Twitter** – most notably when, following the murder of MP Jo Cox in June 2016, it posted: *"Only 649 MPs to go #WhiteJihad"* (CST: 2020: 12). Members of NA praised the assassin of Jo Cox MP, perpetrated by 53-year-old Thomas Mair. From post-incident digital forensics investigations, it became clear that Mair was a prolific supporter of politically violent far-right groups, including the British National Front, South Africa apartheid propogandists, and America's white supremacist **Ku Klux Klan (KKK)**. Mair had a penchant for Internet searches about Nazi war crime operations, as well as white supremacist terrorist, Anders Breivik, about whom he also collected physical news clippings. This behaviour only became apparent after the Yorkshire-based Member of Parliament for Batley and Spen was slain. Prior to Mair's conviction, NA became the 71st violent political organisation to become proscribed by the UK government. Then Home Secretary, Amber Rudd MP, stated at the time: *"National Action is a racist, antisemitic and homophobic organisation which stirs up hatred, glorifies violence and promotes a vile* *ideology [...] Proscribing it will prevent its membership from growing, stop the spread of poisonous propaganda and protect vulnerable young people at risk of radicalisation from its toxic views"* (Home Office: 2016). According to counter-extremism analysts within the London-based Community Security Trust (CST) research team: *"Compared to other British groups, their [National Action] online activism was relatively slick and daring, and it was accompanied by street activities that directly targeted the Jewish community. Most strikingly of all, they consciously copied the language and imagery of jihadist propaganda from ISIS and other terrorist organisations"* (CST Blog: 2020).

One avid follower, aged 20, was stopped and arrested by counter terrorism police as he prepared for a machete attack at a pub hosting a gay pride event in Barrow, Cumbria, during June 2017. The terrorist told a far-right message app that he was "going to war" and planned to "slaughter". In a dilemma about his own bisexuality, he posted extremist comments on Facebook to supposedly impress neo-Nazi groups. As a teenager, this individual had been reportedly diagnosed with an autism spectrum disorder (BBC News: 2018). During the same month on 19 June 2017 **Darren Osborne** was charged with terrorism-related murder and attempted murder for deliberately vehicle ramming Finsbury Park mosque attendees after Tarawih nighttime prayers. Osborne killed one person and wounded at least nine others and cited the ISIS-inspired (3 June 2017) London Bridge terror attacks for his motivation. Osborne became fixated on the London Bridge attacks (vehicle ramming and stabbing) via prolonged watching of Twitter-hosted video clips, and also sending and receiving politically-charged emails from a founder of the English Defence League. The UK's most senior counter-terrorism police officer at the time, **Mark Rowley,** stated that there was "no doubt" that material posted online by people including [said politician] drove the Finsbury Park terror attacker to targeting Muslims (*The Independent*: 2018).

Significant cases demonstrating neo-Nazi terrorist use of a diverse eco-system of VoIP and instant messaging platforms continue to be reported and processed by the UK criminal justice system. In July 2023, Teesside Crown Court convicted a 20-year-old man for planning an act of terrorism: the bombing of Forth Bank police station, Newcastle. The individual conducted his plans to accelerate a race war by conducting a combination of physical hostile reconnaissance alongside online research into napalm, Molotov cocktail construction and other forms of bombmaking. The former college student was aged 17 as he advanced his plans. He adopted the username "Adolf Hitler" on a chat forum hosted on the **Discord** IM/VoIP platform, into which he posted racist, misogynistic, antisemitic and transphobic comments. The defendant's legal team pleaded in mitigation that their client possessed an autism spectrum disorder and low IQ. In summing up, the recorder stated that the defendant had also *"openly expressed attacking multiple minority groups"* and *"made heroes of those who carry out atrocities in the name of fascism"* (BBC: 2023). One day before, two London-based neo-Nazi podcasters were convicted at Kingston Crown Court for encouraging acts of terrorism. Their broadcasts – including segments that explicitly incited physical terrorism – were viewed more than 152,000 times and attracted around 1,000 subscribers. In addition, one podcaster operated a neo-Nazi online library that *"held more than 500 videos of extreme right-wing-related speeches and propaganda documents"* (Homeland Security US: 2023).

Young people

In September 2021, Metropolitan Police Commissioner Cressida Dick stated that the number of terror suspects who were children had tripled in the last year. (Rose and AC: 2022: 3) (UK Counter Terrorism Policing statement 09/09/2021). According to the Community Security Trust research team: *"Young people – politicised, active and highly connected – are no longer just passive consumers of online terrorist content by adult groomers but are themselves propaganda creators, group organisers, peer recruiters, extremist financers and terrorist convicts"* (Rose and AC: 2022: 3). The report's authors dub this process as *"youth-on-youth radicalisation"*, whereby they emphasise squarely the initiative and agency that young people possess *"in a digital era in which the information hierarchy is increasingly flattened"* (Rose and AC: 2022: 3). Young wannabe terrorists are often far more experienced online – including in skills of identity masking – than older Internet users. According to CST, younger extremists are adept at using different platforms for different purposes, *"dedicating themselves to maintaining presence on mainstream platforms through second accounts and circumventing platforms' content moderation algorithms. As such, they 'funnel' users to accounts on platforms with increasingly extreme content and ecosystems"* (Rose and AC: 2022: 3).

A couple of cases we now mention serve merely as a 'tip of the iceberg' experienced by UK authorities and referrals into counter-terrorism Prevent channels. A teenager from Cornwall discussed online about *"gassing"* Jewish people, hanging gay people and *"wanting to shoot up their parades"*. He also commissioned a "Nuke London" poster adorned with the caption: *"Sterilise the cesspit that you call London"*. This active member of **Feuerkrieg Division**

group was awarded a non-custodial sentence in 2021 at London's Old Bailey criminal court. Another UK terror offender – aged 14 – sent encrypted chat messages instructing an Australian jihadist to bomb police attending an ANZAC day parade in 2015. The individual was jailed for 'life' in 2015 but subsequently released by UK authorities in 2021 (Dearden, 2021).

Another teenager left the BNP around 2014 and an organisation called **National Strike Force.** The organisation morphed variously to describe itself as *"fervently anti-Jewish"* branch called 'North West Infidels', its ringleaders reportedly formed part of **National Action (NA),** a far-right terror group that overtly celebrates attacks upon and the extermination of Jewish people. Proscribed in 2016 under the Terrorism Act 2000, NA is the first far-right group to become banned in the UK since the Second World War. Descending towards extreme radicalisation, CST reported that *"photographs show [Jack] Renshaw performing the raised finger gesture that has become associated with jihadists. Not only did he intend to die carrying out a suicide terrorism plot to murder an MP and a police officer, but he also suggested to his fellow neo-Nazis that he could film a 'jihadi-style' propaganda video to be shown posthumously"* (CST: 2020: 12). Renshaw was eventually sentenced to life imprisonment during 2018 for his attempt to murder a female UK Member of Parliament as well as a female police detective. The latter had successfully prosecuted Renshaw for child sex offences some months earlier.

Threat identification and decent cyber defences including firewalls, network monitoring, digital media filtering and acceptable use policies, can all help companies prevent and deter access to extremist websites and ISPs. But terrorism awareness among as many employees as possible is key to generating the most effective method to combat dangerous threats. According to UK Counter Terrorism Policing, reporting on those close to you *"is a difficult thing to do"*. Yet, *"Every year thousands of reports from the public help police tackle the terrorist threat. If you see or hear something that doesn't seem right, trust your instincts and contact **[Action Counters Terrorism]** ACT by reporting to police in confidence at gov.uk/ACT"* (Counter Terrorism Policing: 2020).

Case study: Child A

Child A first triggered the law-enforcement radar while barely a teenager. During 2020, her mother reported her into Prevent, the UK government anti-radicalisation programme. According to Child A's mother, her autistic daughter behaved secretly online, became obsessed with neo-Nazism and was soaking up extremist, racist views *"like a sponge"*. Following a police investigation, the 14-year-old was charged in April 2021 with possession of instructions to make firearms and explosives and stood accused of writing instructions and videos to produce 3D guns. She was charged with the *"commission, preparation of instigation of an act of terrorism"*. Child A was a member of an American neo-Nazi group. She had carved a swastika into her own forehead.

Investigators assert that Child A initially experienced recruitment and grooming from her mother's boyfriend, a white supremacist and active member of Arizona's **Aryan Brotherhood (AB)**. Child A then became subjected to systematic and sexualised online exploitation from an AB ringleader in the US. This included the exchange of sexualised content via Telegram, potentially leaving the

---

child open to manipulation and blackmail. These messages were retrieved by the FBI from devices owned by the AB ringleader. Terrorism charges against Child A were eventually dropped in December 2021.

Steps had been taken by the family and local authorities to reduce the risk posed to Child A. She had been moved from her home and placed into a local council residential home. But she remained extremely anxious about AB Telegram users trolling and threatening her. Following several incidents of self-harm and suicide, and another care home move, Child A was found dead by hanging, aged 16, in her bedroom. Child A's progress was praised by the care homeowner: *"She had come with a swastika on her forehead but she had attempted to gouge it out."* Child A *"came to us from a radicalised background and we took her to the point where she was taking GCSEs"* (Press Reader: 2022).

International

On 15 March 2019, Australian-born Brenton Harrison Tarrant, aged 28, attacked two Mosques by mass shooting in Christchurch, New Zealand, murdering 51 people and injuring 40. Shortly beforehand, the perpetrator announced onto an **8chan** forum *"I will carry out an attack against the invaders"* then published links on 8chan and Twitter to his manifesto and Facebook livestreaming of the attack. One respondent replied: *"Good luck shitposter. Rolling for many dead chinks and niggers"* (Baele et al: 2021). Tarrant also emailed a 74-page manifesto titled *The Great Replacement* to 30 recipients including media outlets and the Prime Minister's office. Tarrant was intercepted by armed police while driving on his way to attack another Mosque outside Christchurch (in Ashburton) and was captured alive. Tarrant had been an active user of many chat forums advocating xenophobia and political violence for several years. In the months that followed, similar terrorist incidents occurred around the world that cited Tarrant as the inspiration behind violent action. For example, two American-based mass shooters (John Earnest and Patrick Crusius) followed Tarrant's modus operandi by announcing imminent racist attacks then posting onto 8chan social media links to virulent anti-immigration manifestos. (Related cases are outlined at this section's end.)

8chan was finally closed in August 2019 but many replacement 'chan' iterations were established or existing chans attracted migration from 8chan's dispossessed anonymous (anon) chat users. In effect, this cyber *"constellation"* is a myriad of imageboards dedicated *"to hosting 'politically incorrect' (a euphemism for racist and anti-Semitic) conversations"* argue researchers published by the Terrorism Research Institute. Researchers identify preferred, specific chans used by extremists as: 8kun (8chan's direct replacement), 9chan, 16chan, ShitChan, EndChan or NeinChan (Baele et al: 2021). Most chans operate on the open Internet although some operate at a dark web or semi-dark-web level. In several neo-Nazi chat groups, Tarrant is often referred to as "The Saint" or "Saint Tarrant" (Bellingcat: 2019).

Chat group users on the German language imageboard 'Kohlchan' favourably disseminated Stephan Balliet's Halle synagogue shooting video links; the live video was originally published on **Twitch**, a popular US-based video gaming live streaming platform. In **October 2019,** Balliet shot and killed two and injured three other synagogue worshippers, blaming

Germany's Jewish residents for promoting feminism and mass immigration. He uploaded his manifesto beforehand onto Facebook before live streaming the attacks for 35 minutes (Ziegele: 2019). Kohlchan users also hosted and distributed terrorist Tobias Rathjen's video and manifesto almost immediately after his lethal **February 2020** shooting attack at two shisha bars in Hanau, Germany.

At this point, it's worth re-emphasising why video content can enable (train and educate) and inspire (encourage and motivate) acts of terrorism. Including as a potential performance denouement within the mind of a suicide-interested human being. **Stuart Bender** of Curtin University, Australia, observed that the use of live video as an integral part of the attacks *"makes [them] a form of 'performance crime' where the act of video recording and/or streaming the violence by the perpetrator is a central component of the violence itself, rather than being incidental"* (Stevenson and Anthony: 2019). Moreover, another senior academic, Missouri University's **Benjamin Warner**, points to the power of digital media's ideological reinforcement. In his work on political extremism, Warner wrote, *"If individuals are only in contact with people they already agree with, there is a danger that their opinions will polarize and become increasingly radical"* (Warner: 2010: 431).

In other Internet-inspired attacks, I will now refer to two incidents that reflect the nature of hate-crime terrorism in our truly globalised media age. Moreover, both cases below represent the daunting diversity of targets identified by neo-Nazi, white supremacist attackers, that over the past decade or more have also shifted their range of attack targets to encompass political figures, movements generally supportive of immigration and the police. The latter being perceived as treacherous 'state agents' that prop up supposed 'liberal elites' – a fusion of politicians, media personalities and bankers – that *intentionally* implement 'great replacement theories' and white genocide. Genocidaires such as Tarrant and Norway's Anders Breivik, *"commit terrorist acts with genocidal intent as – in their own mind – preventative self-defence; not as acts of aggression but, as he writes, 'a partisan action against an occupying force'"*, observes award-winning genocide scholar, Dirk Moses (Moses: 2019). Digital media-era extreme right-wing idealisation is not necessarily confined to racism, supremacy and identitarian defence against cultural and economic invasion. Quite noticeable is the worldview overlap between the cases in point outlined within this book's Incel/Misogyny section, and so many of the cases outlined within this section focusing on extreme right-wing terrorism (ERW) perpetrators. Many investigations demonstrate that ERW terrorists have sprawled into terrains of virulently attacking feminism, women's rights and elections results (Associated Press: 2022). Such a diverse attack surface imagined and created by ERW terrorists means that several national counter-terrorism strategies around the world have been re-engineered and refreshed to deal with the "internationalisation" of ERW. For example, the UK's updated CONTEST strategy was published in July 2023 providing an explicit explanation: *"We now face a domestic terror threat which is less predictable, harder to detect and investigate"* (Home Office: 2023).

On 2 June 2019 a widely-respected **Christian Democratic Union (CDU)** regional leader, Walter Lubcke, Kassel district president, was shot dead by neo-Nazi extremist, Stephan Ernst. Ernst cited Lubcke's pro-immigration comments about welcoming refugees' escaping Middle

Eastern warzones, as his reason for murdering an elected politician on his home doorstep. Ernst was actively linked to a German branch of Combat 18, a violent UK neo-Nazi group, originally founded decades ago to serve as the British National Party's internal physical security unit. Another linked group to Ernst, prepper network Nordkreuz ('Northern Cross') reportedly possessed ammunition, firearms, and body bags, as well as 'kill lists' for politicians after compiling or acquiring a database of 25,000 names, that they allegedly disseminated via the messaging app Telegram.

Several years earlier, on 22 July 2011, Norway's Anders Breivik exploded a car bomb near to the Prime Minister's apartment block in Oslo (killing eight people and wounding 209) before travelling two hours away to Utøya Island, where he shot and killed dozens of young Labour Party summer camp activists. A total of 77 people were killed in the attacks. The Utøya attack is the deadliest known mass shooting by a lone individual in modern history. Breivik used Facebook and Twitter for propaganda purposes beforehand without ever portraying specific desires to attack. He purchased body armour, weapons and bomb ingredients on eBay. An hour and half before detonating a bomb in Oslo, Breivik mass emailed his white supremacist manifesto titled *2083: A European Declaration of Independence* to 1,003 email addresses, including the Prime Minister's, then published an extremist video monologue on YouTube. Breivik had also routinely been subject to psychiatric treatment and social care orders for a suspected personality disorder identified during a turbulent childhood. Norway's National Crime Investigation Service concluded some years after the massacre: *"his comments on various Internet forums do not stand out as particularly when compared to typical far-right online discourse. In other words,* **Norwegian security authorities would likely not react to his online postings even if he was being monitored***.* Later in the presentation, it is acknowledged that the importance of social media for recruitment and radicalisation have been underestimated so far (NSIS Norway Presentation: 2014). Breivik's city centre bombing and island massacre were part in revenge for the Labour Party's support for incoming immigration and part a brazen advocacy for white racial supremacy. Breivik viewed himself as a demi-God and a significant international ideological figurehead. He reportedly refers to himself as a 'political prisoner'. Breivik's massacre served as an inspiration for Brenton Tarrant in Christchurch (Washington Post: 2019). In the same way that Breivik's exploitation of social media inspired others, we will now turn to examine some related incidents that followed the 2019 Christchurch Mosque shootings.

Cases in point: Christchurch 2019 – Related and 'inspired' incidents

15 March 2019 aftermath: Male social media users in New South Wales, Australia, Oldham, UK, and New York, are prosecuted for celebrating and distributing footage of the Christchurch killings. In the Australia and US cases, both individuals illicitly owned firearms and the 22-year-old American stated on social media a desire to carry out a comparable attack. An employee in the UAE was fired for making supportive comments on social media.

27 April 2019: Mass shooting carried out by John T. Earnest at Poway Synagogue, near San Diego, California. One worshipper killed, three wounded. Like Tarrant, Earnest was radicalised on 8chan's political discussion group, and also attempted to Facebook livestream his attack. Earnest praised

Tarrant in his manifesto. Another chan anon cheered the attacker on: *"get the high score",* logically translatable as 'kill as many as you can'. (Bellingcat: 2019).

3 August 2019: Mass shooting by Patrick Crusius (21) opened fire and killed 23 people and injured 23 others at a Walmart in El Paso, US. Crusius described himself as an *"eco-Fascist"*, broadcast his support for the Christchurch shooting and posted a manifesto (*The Inconvenient Truth*) onto 8chan's /pol/ board. This massacre that explicitly targeted Mexicans was described by conflict journalist Robert Evans as the *"gamification of terror"*. Evans writes that Crusius attempted to livestream the El Paso attack, similar to how *"Brenton Tarrant livestreamed his massacre from a helmet cam in a way that made the shooting look almost exactly like a First Person Shooter video game"* (Bellingcat: August 2019). Not staying anonymous, Crusius announced his terror plan on 8chan before the attack but security-conscious moderators quickly removed the posting inadvertently failing to realise that incident responders require digital forensics trails as soon as possible. (Crusius's post was screenshot.)

10 August 2019: Philip Manshaus opened fire inside a Mosque in Bærum, Norway, wounding one person. Manshaus livestreamed the shooting on Facebook. He referred to Tarrant as a *"saint"* online and posted an image depicting Tarrant, Crusius, and Earnest as *"heroes"*. The attack resulted in one injury.

4 March 2020: 19-year-old male arrested in New Zealand after making a terror threat on a Telegram chat group against the Al Noor Mosque, Christchurch. Al Noor worshippers had been attacked by Tarrant one year before. The perpetrator was a member of ultra-nationalist group 'Action Zealandia'.

27 January 2021: Singapore police announce arrest of 16-year-old Indian-born male who plotted to attack two Mosques with a machete on Christchurch 2019's anniversary. The youth produced a manifesto calling Tarrant a *"saint"* and celebrated the *"justifiable killing of Muslims"* (Channel News Asia: 2021).

4 March 2021: An unnamed 27-year-old male is charged with threatening to kill after using 4chan to make online threats against Christchurch's previously-attacked Mosques at Linwood and Al Noor.

14 May 2022: 18-year-old Payton Gendron shoots and kills ten people and wounds three – all of whom were black – at Tops Friendly Markets superstore in New York. Gendron livestreamed the attack on Twitch using a head cam until the platform shut the broadcast down within two minutes. He published a 180-page manifesto praising far-right mass shooters (Anders Breivik, Dylann Roof* and Brenton Tarrant) and identifying his adherence to great replacement theory on Google Docs two days before his own attack. His online diary – ranging from November 2021 to 13 May 2022 – was hosted in the form of hundreds of chat messages on Discord, including within a weapons discussion board. These included terrorist attack plans and references to carrying out a mass-murder suicide. During the attack, Gendron shouted racial slurs and apologised to a white person behind a checkout counter after pointing a gun at them (Associated Press: 2022). Gendron had previously been challenged by authorities about his plans to attack a school and told pupils on several occasions he wished to carry out murder suicides. Despite this background, he was able to purchase a Bushmaster rifle and thirty rounds of ammunition, the latter procured and stored in plain sight 24 hours before his supermarket attack.

*Dylann Roof is an American mass murderer who (aged 22) shot and killed nine black worshippers at a bible study class in a Charleston church, South Carolina, US on 17 June 2015. Roof was a drug-using neo-Nazi white supremacist, who supported white-advancing racial segregation and adhered to great replacement theory. A user of 4chan chat boards, Roof's racist polemics and 2444-word manifesto were published several weeks before his lethal attacks on his personal website: LastRhodesian.com – registered in February 2015 (New York Times: 2015). After evaluating Roof's handwriting style, Southern Poverty Law Center extremism experts concluded that Roof had been a contributing commentator under the pseudonym AryanBlood1488 on The Daily Stormer, an ultra-nationalist news website (Los Angeles Times: 2015). Roof reportedly suffered from childhood with obsessive compulsive disorder.

2.3 Islamist jihadist

Islamic State of Iraq and Syria (ISIS)

Just as 2001 (following 9/11) was a pivotal year for understanding the size and scale of physical jihadi terrorism, 2014 was perhaps similarly pivotal within cyberspace domains. Events in cyberspace were inextricably linked to ISIS's physical upsurge and sweeping territorial gains across the then collapsing states of Syria and Iraq. Within just a few months, Iraq's security apparatus, supposedly consisting of 650,000 police and 350,000 soldiers, almost entirely evaporated. Shia, Kurdish and Christian communities were ordered to flee, pay taxes, convert to Islam or be killed (Cockburn: 2014). The territorial gains and iron rule by terror provided ISIS in Iraq and Syria (Daesh) with the momentum and infrastructure to mass recruit and embolden international jihadists to conduct recruitment and direct terror operations around the world. When these occurred, the explanation was predictable: revenge for Western military operations in Iraq and the Levant (acronym in Arabic: Da'ish or Daesh). It took several years for an unwieldy alliance of the US, Russia, NATO, Gulf state forces, Kurdish guerillas and much-strengthened regular Syria and Iraq government-backed forces and militias, to repulse ISIS back to only possessing fractional territorial control (mainly Mosul). Nevertheless, John Carroll University's **Abdullah Almutairi** observed that: *"Whatever their current status on the battlefield, the communication managers serving ISIS have become amazingly successful propagandists in a world of anomie"* (Almutairi: 2017). Soon, the gruesome effectiveness of ISIS's video-driven social media campaign saw the network achieve a precious internal goal: it had spectacularly outgrown Al-Qaeda, its Sunni jihadist foster parent and decaying rival. RAND analyst **Antonia Ward** observed that ISIS's *"strategic use of social media demonstrates the resourcefulness of the terrorist-cum-insurgent organization, which mobilized an estimated 40,000 foreign nationals from 110 countries to join the group"* (Ward: 2018).

Another leading authority on Mid East wars, *Independent* news journalist Patrick Cockburn, reported from the frontline that: *"The world had seen nothing like their [ISIS's] use of public violence to terrorize their opponents since the Khmer Rouge in Cambodia forty years earlier."* Cockburn asserted that "ISIS are experts in fear". Slick, graphic videos produced, which variously covered massacres of Shia soldiers, checkpoint officials and truck drivers, *"played an important role in terrifying and demoralizing"* Shia and Kurdish opponents as they routed much of central and northern Iraq and took control of Fallujah, Mosul and

Tikrit (Cockburn: 2014: "Preface"). These sprawling, religiously divided cities, in 2014 witnessed the near-mass desertion of Iraq's government-backed army and domestic security apparatus. The unsparing, unapologetic propagation of Wahhabism – a fundamentalist version of Islam that *"imposes sharia law, relegates women to the status of second-class citizens, and regards Shia and Sufi Muslims as non-Muslims"* to be persecuted (Cockburn: 2014) – soon terrified (but also inspired) many millions of viewers around the world who compulsively downloaded and shared horror-movie-type footage from video-streaming platforms. Many of the online videos were skilfully produced. ISIS's own media agencies, reporters and film editors blended background music with pleasant panoramic cut-aways conveying inspiring landscapes. Such dramatic backdrops were often interspersed with clips covering summary executions and victims digging their own graves. According to Cockburn, one popular theme was rejectionism by young fighters (and their brides) of formerly comfortable yet corrupt home lives. Such conversion-themed films were typically laced with incitements to those who couldn't travel to Daesh to conduct terror operations on the caliphate's behalf in America, Europe or Russia. One such video released onto YouTube in Spring 2014 shows foreign jihadis burying their passports *"to demonstrate a permanent commitment to jihad"* (Cockburn: 2014: 41). Saudi, Jordanian, Chechen, Egyptian and a Canadian espouse that they are soldiers and descendants of Abu Musab al-Zarqawi – the murderous Jordanian founder of Al-Qaeda in Iraq – and claim in English and Arabic: *"[This] is a message to Canada and all American powers. We are coming and we will destroy you"* (Cockburn: 2014: 42).

In July 2014, ISIS posted an Internet video of its leader **Abu-Bakr al-Baghdadi** at the Great Mosque of al-Nuri in Iraq, calling upon Muslims to wage jihad during Ramadan, urging followers around the world to help establish the caliphate (Awan: 2017). Baghdadi did not limit his call solely to attack infidels, stating: *"I appeal to the youth and men of Islam around the globe and invoke them to mobilise and join us to consolidate the pillar of the state of Islam and wage jihad against the rafidhas (Shia), the safadis of Shi'ites."* al-Baghdadi culminated his message with a clear call for an Islamic caliphate whose heartland would be set across Iraqi and Syrian Sunni-held territories (*New Delhi Times*: 2014). Within ISIS's fragile and turbulent leadership network, internal pressure mounted upon al-Baghdadi from his second-in-command Abu Muhammad al-Adani (and Adnani's media director, see case study below) to move towards even more extreme messaging against American and European targets. By the close of 2014, the freshly declared caliphate swept across a territory larger than the UK and inhabited by six million people. Oil and gas facilities across Syria and Iraq were seized. Half a million Kurds were stranded and besieged below Turkey's southern border. According to Cockburn: *"The birth of the new state was the most radical change to the political geography of the Middle East since the Sykes-Picot Agreement was implemented in the aftermath of the First World War"* (Cockburn: 2014: 28). What wasn't quite so widely known by the general public during this period was that three of the most influential jihadist propogandists since 9/11 were American-born: John Georgelas (ISIS), Adam Gadahn (Al-Qaeda central) and Anwar al-Awlaki (Al-Qaeda Arab Peninsula). Coming up, we provide case studies of Georgelas and Gadahn.

Case study: ISIS digital media kingpin John Georgelas

Texas-born John Thomas Georgelas (1983–2017) developed a close bond with ISIS's second-in-command Abu Muhammad al-Adnani (AMA) towards the end of his short life. During 2014, as orator of the terror-inciting *"Indeed your Lord is ever watchful"* speech, al-Adnani's profile among ISIS followers and Western intelligence agencies soared (Kent: 2023). AMA was ISIS's Amir of Syria and director of operations. He led on the terror group's internal security, and also external relations with other significant Syrian jihadist extremist groups. Georgelas's close affinity with AMA meant that he was central to ensuring that ISIS's terrorism operations and tactics reverberated regionally and internationally to maximum effect.

Hailing from a US-military family (his father served as an Air Force colonel), Georgelas worked as a data technician for Rackspace, a Cloud services corporation. He converted to Islam after the 9/11 atrocities and later admitted to becoming politically and religiously radicalised. Soon after 9/11, he travelled to Syria to fluently learn Arabic and the Koran and returned to the US 2004. Georgelas then worked in Texas for Rackspace as a data technician. In 2006, Georgelas was charged and sent to prison for accessing passwords for the American Israel Public Affairs Committee, a Rackspace client. After his parole in 2011, he relocated to Egypt with his first wife. Georgelas translated fatwas and began running online jihadi preparation workshops for Westerners travelling to Iraq and Syria.

After several long spells travelling unaccompanied for armed jihad, Georgelas moved his first wife and three young children to north Syria. (The British-born lady later absconded and settled in the US with their children). Remarried and injured on the battlefield, Georgelas identified as 'Yahya al-Bahrumi' or Abu Hassan. Known widely as Yahya (Arabic for John), the young Texan became a leading producer of ultra-slick English-language propaganda videos as well as a prolific author for *Dabiq* magazine, penning under vivid subtitles including *"Kill the Imams of Kufr (Disbelievers)"*. Georgelas published and named several high-profile American counter-extremism scholars that deserved retribution for their critical view of ISIS. Characteristic of Georgelas's fanatical yet often concise writing style was the use of psychological polarisation. He repeatedly used and reinforced a 'them-versus-us' narrative. Such narrative devices are commonplace within public terrorist communications. It helps to dehumanise the perceived enemy. This abstraction can help remove any psychosocial dilemmas that might prevent the audience from taking that final step towards violent action. The following excerpt serves as a case in point:

"The fact is, even if you were to stop bombing us, imprisoning us, torturing us, vilifying us, and usurping our lands, we would continue to hate you because our primary reason for hating you will not cease to exist until you embrace Islam [...] we fight you, not simply to punish and deter you, but to bring you true freedom in this life and salvation in the Hereafter, freedom from being enslaved to your whims and desires as well as those of

> *your clergy and legislatures, and salvation by worshipping your Creator alone and following His messenger."*
>
> (Wood: 2017)
>
> Georgelas profusely smoked cannabis and consumed psilocybin psychedelic mushrooms. In another video *There's No Life Without Jihad*, three frontline fighters originally from Western nations inspire followers to join ISIS on the glory of the battlefield. (Awan: 2017). According to Palestinian journalist Abdel Bari Atwan: *"slick and well equipped videos are able to entice those vulnerable to this extremist ideology. As a result, what we are witnessing is Isis being able to tap into the minds of young and impressionable people who are more likely to be watching YouTube and using Facebook and Twitter"* (Atwan: 2015).

Al-Qaeda (AQ)

AQ's multinational media reach gathered momentum during the late 1990s. Young male Sunni Muslims within North Africa, the Middle East, the Horn of Africa, Arabian Peninsula; South and South East Asia were deemed particularly fertile recruitment hotspots for mass radicalisation and mobilisation. Increasingly potent and core message-driven media products were delivered to a growing audience courtesy of the Global Islamic Media Front (GIMF). This emerging network was run by a Canadian-born Al-Qaeda media operative and other affiliated groups between 2001–2004 that provided Yahoo email addresses alongside passwords to access, absorb and further disseminate armed jihadist statements and videos

(Netherlands National Coordinator for Counterterrorism: N.D). A website was later provided.

Often operating on YouTube, such regional media platforms typically featured regional figureheads making sermons or explaining militant actions. Regionally bespoke programmes – interspersed with updates from Osama bin-Laden or other Al-Qaeda central leaders – were designed to resonate with more localised audiences whose immediate causes of concern might be localised civil war, natural disasters or weapons supplies. Several influential Internet-based regional Al-Qaeda affiliate platforms therefore emerged through the early 2000s. Az-Zallaqa Media was led by Nusrat al-Islam in West Africa. Al-Andalus Media supported AQ Islamic Maghreb (AQIM). Al-Malahem Media became the news organ of AQ Arab Peninsula (AQAP). The latter evolved into perhaps the most effective AQ news channel of all, carrying sermons and calls-to-arms by its leader Anwar al-Awlaki, until his death from a 2011 American drone strike. Al-Awlaki was also thought to be producer and editor of AQAP's online *Inspire* magazine – a picture-driven English-language news journal, designed to draw Westerners into DIY homeland terrorism. One article described how to *"make a bomb in kitchen of mom"* (Fox News: 2014). (al-Awlaki had been born, raised and educated in the US before heading permanently to his family home in Yemen in 2004.) To some extent, Al-Malahem also buttressed and amplified Al-Shabaab's spawning range of terror operations including shopping centre terror attacks and beachside executions and kidnappings across East Africa. But Al-Shabaab soon developed the highly effective inhouse Al-Kata'ib Media agency (CTC Westpoint: 2012). Terrorist recruitment and propaganda from Al-Qaeda was amplified across Western Europe by several influential websites including al-

Muhajiroun's in the UK and the proscribed Sharia4Belgium movement (De Standaard: 2012).

Case study: AQ propaganda chief Adam Yahiye Gadahn

Aged 17, 'Azzam the American' converted to Islam in 1995 at a California Mosque. Within three years, Adam Gadahn had joined Al-Qaeda central, declared the US *"enemy soil"* and became a producer for As-Sahab, the official media unit of Al-Qaeda's central leadership founded in 2001, based in Pakistan and Afghanistan. As-Sahab was instrumental in broadcasting Al-Qaeda's high-level operations, sermons and speeches to an international audience of potential recruits, enraged politicians and terrified public audiences.

Gadahn's slick battlefront videos tended to be published in Arabic with English subtitles. Documentary-type, high-quality videos were produced by Gadahn and disseminated swiftly to regional affiliated media (overviewed above) to stoke higher audience reach and recruitment impact within target jihadi communities.

Born in Oregon, US, Adam Gadahn's parents raised the boy as a Protestant Christian, providing home-schooling from a remote California farmstead. During his teenage years, Gadahn mixed with peers his age, played league baseball and successfully immersed himself into death metal and ambient noise networks. He dedicatedly developed technical production skills during his teenage years. His relationship with his parents became strained due in part to his musical activities. He moved in with his grandparents in Santa Ana, California, aged 16 and converted to Islam soon after. He was arrested for

---

attacking his mentor during 1997 and reportedly moved to Pakistan in 1998 and married a female Afghan refugee. Claiming to live in Karachi, intermittent contact with his family stopped forever after a February 2022 phone call (ABC News: 2004).

Gadahn had appeared on the FBI's wanted list by 2004. FBI Director Robert Mueller cited Gadahn as one of seven AQ members who planned summer and autumn terrorist attacks in the US. Gadahn was indicted *"for providing material support"* to AQ for producing a 2005 video – celebrating the fourth anniversary of 9/11 – whereby he threatened to attack the US and Australia: *"Yesterday, London and Madrid. Tomorrow Los Angeles and Melbourne"*. The eleven-minute videotape was played on ABC's Good Morning America. Then Al-Qaeda deputy leader Ayman Al-Zawahiri praised Gadahn in a video titled *Invitation to Islam* as a *"person who wants to lead his people out of darkness into the light"*.

Never had such a senior personal endorsement of a jihadi media operator been issued by Al-Qaeda's leadership before. Gadahn was placed onto the FBI's most wanted list, a one million dollar reward issued for his capture. In another documentary video titled *Knowledge is for Acting On – The Manhattan Raid*, Gadahn provides simply explained explanations of Al-Qaeda's journey and mission covering its rise from an anti-Soviet-invasion mujahideen insurgency into becoming supposedly the courageous vanguard of international jihad. Gadahn describes Al-Qaeda's planning and build-up to 9/11, explaining target selection. The film also inserts other actions from martyrdom (suicide) terror operations filmed by terror cells. The video's denouement climaxes with a montage of

9/11 attack footage. Arabic and English captions accompany images throughout.

By 2006, Gadahn was appearing in films unmasked. Although, he had been identified by California mosque worshippers and various intelligence agencies many years before. A series of videos from 2006 to 2008 reflect an even higher level of anti-American and anti-British sentiment. A five-strong list of quasi-religious, geo-political demands was broadcast by Gadahn in May 2007 in a film titled *al-Qaeda video Warning to US by American Adam Gadahn.* (MyZine.com: 2007).

Subsequently, various think-tanks, journalists and politicians have been praised or lightly chided for their insights. Some were invited to stop *"sitting on the fence and come over to the side of truth".* However, most were threatened and defamed if they criticised Al-Qaeda and its terrorism. In Al-Qaeda's post-election video, president-elect Barack Obama was derided as a *"house negro"* (Khatchadourian, R: 2007).

Between 2010 and 2014, numerous videos appeared led by Gadahn celebrating mass-casualty attack anniversaries, tutorials on assassinations and lone-actor terror attacks. Gadahn urged copycat attacks, emulating the mass shooting perpetrated by US Major Nidal Hasan, who fatally and critically attacked military service colleagues at Fort Hood's army base. Gadahn appealed to Muslim immigrants in the *"miserable suburbs"* of Paris, London and Detroit to conduct attacks in their new home communities.

On 16 June 2011, Al-Qaeda publicised a hit list of targets onto a website (Ansar al-Mujahideen) that listed 40

American businessmen, military personnel and diplomats (Gustini: 2011). This followed a widely-published online call by Gadahn, on 3 June, that called for lone-actor attacks upon American public figures and corporate institutions (Gustini: 2011). In March 2014, a video leaked that showed Gadahn condemning ISIS as extremists for attacking fellow Muslims (Jihadology: 2018). President Barack Obama announced in April 2015 that a series of CIA drone strikes in Pakistan in January 2015 had killed Gadahn and fellow American Al-Qaeda terrorist Ahmed Farouq. Two hostages, aid workers **Giovanni Lo Porto** and **Warren Weinstein**, were also killed in the incident. (NBC News: 2015b).

Case study: Mapping the ISIS and Al-Qaeda global cyber terror networks

According to Lee et al (2021), the *"ubiquity and anonymity of cyberspace has enabled terror organizations to access new methods in designing traditional or complex attacks"*. Lee's research team set out to explain the evolving phenomenon of "cyberterrorism" by bringing together a "Global Cyberterrorism Dataset" that provides wide-ranging data on 83 cyberterrorism incidents ascribed to Al-Qaeda and ISIS between 2011 and 2016. Drawing from annual US Department of State annual terrorist reports, Lee's team then introduced a second layer of evidence gathered from court documents and news media reports. Applying social network analysis tools then enabled researchers to identify further possible relationships between individual and group perpetrators and victim samples. Although the sample size was limited, as is typically the case with terrorism-related studies, the findings were starkly suggestive:

- ISIS-attributed attacks were calculated at 67.5% of the total (Al-Qaeda = 32.5%).
- A substantial increase of cyberterrorism occurred during 2014 and onward.
- The US and other Western developed countries are the most frequent targets of Al-Qaeda, Al-Qaeda branches in Asia and Arab Peninsula and by affiliate, Al-Shabaab.
- A significant number of cyberterrorists select targets within geographic proximity, including actors working for the Al-Nusra Front (attacking Syria and Lebanon), Hamas (opposing Israel) and Al-Qaeda in South Asia targeting India. The noticeable cluster of regional attacks, and homegrown assailants, suggests there is *"a form of regionalism in cyber terrorism"* (Lee et al: 2021: 11).
- If possible to translate at all, *"ISIS cyberattack strategy prioritizes multiple low casualty strikes in more countries"* that are conducted by in-country perpetrators. In comparison, Al-Qaeda's strategy reflects more transnational attacks targeting a more focused list of country targets.
- Following gruesome depictions of extreme violence, including beheadings of US, Syrian and French hostages, Lee's team observed that ISIS had recruited

> *"a higher proportion of lone wolves than Al-Qaeda"* (Lee et al: 2021: 11).
>
> - *"Terrorist groups and their supporters constantly diversify their reliance on the online services they use to host their material online. While Facebook reported removing over 14 million pieces of content related to terrorism or violent extremism in 2018, the terrorist group Daesh used over 100 platforms in 2018, making use of a wider range of more permissive and smaller platforms"* (DCMS: 2019).
> - *"Terrorist groups place a huge premium on quickly reaching their audiences. A third of all links to Daesh propaganda, for example, are disseminated within an hour of upload, while in the immediate aftermath of the terrorist attack in Christchurch, there was a co-ordinated cross-platform effort to generate maximum reach of footage of the attack. It is therefore vital to ensure that there is the technology in place to automatically detect and remove terrorist content within an hour of upload, secure the prevention of re-upload and prevent, where possible, new content being made available to users at all"* (DCMS: 2019).

This last point raises a question that continues to generate strong debate within the psychosocial fields of counter-terrorist analysis: are individuals with certain violent psychopathic attributes drawn towards terrorism? If so, are there key behavioural signatures that enable authorities to prevent radicalised individuals from successfully carrying out the very worst acts of violent political extremism?

ISIS and AQ cyberterrorism in the 2020s

The fragmentation of ISIS since military defeat in Iraq and Syria in the late 2010s, as well as improved counter-terrorism legislation and detection in most jurisdictions, has perhaps driven down ISIS's frequency of achieving successful terror attacks in the US and Europe. The European Council reports that ISIS terror attacks declined markedly since 2020, although France appeared to experience several major incidents each year (European Council: 2023). According to Europol, EU police forces arrested 388 suspects for terrorism-related offences during 2021. More than two thirds of investigations (260) related to jihadist plots, principally in Austria, France and Spain (Europol: 2022). Just one example, in June 2023, Austria's Directorate for State Security and Intelligence (DSN) thwarted a terror attack planned by three individuals who intended to use swords, airguns and possible car-ramming against crowds at Vienna's 2023 Pride festival. The ISIS-supporting trio had been radicalised online and reportedly triggered suspicion due to their computer-based research (*Financial Times*: 2023). One month later, another ISIS-supporting internet propagandist took to social media to rail against anti-Muslim xenophobia and call for extreme right-wing figureheads to be targeted and assassinated (MEMRI: July 2023c).

2.4 Hamas – Israel-Palestine conflict

According to *Security Week*'s **Luke Townsend**, a Hamas-linked attack group dubbed APT-C-23 has led a catfishing campaign against senior ranking Israeli defence, law-enforcement and emergency services officials. The group launched a spurious messaging app known as 'VolatileVenom', a downloader ('Barbie Downloader') and a backdoor called 'Barbwire' (Townsend: 2022).

Catfishing is the creation of a fake, attractive, online identity used to ensnare victims into embarrassing behaviour as well as to capture their movements and data. The attackers' spoof accounts are maintained at an active, plausible level, with the fake identity joining user groups and posting updates that encourage interaction. Once direct contact is made, the attacker suggests migrating conversations across to WhatsApp. This move provides the attacker with the victim's phone number. As communications become even more personal, the attacker suggests a more 'discrete' form of communication. They move onto another Android messaging app, which is actually VolatileVenom malware. But when the victim attempts to log in, an error message is returned. The victim is led to believe that the app has been uninstalled, but VolatileVenom remains operating in the background with significant espionage capabilities. Private videos (the 'Barbie Downloader') are also sent to the recipient that infect their systems by removing security scanning and exfiltrating files including PDFs, archives, image files, video as well as searching for evidence of external media plugins. The latter indicates that the official may be carrying high-value portable data on CD-ROMs and thumb drives. Townsend reports that *"APT-C-23 and 'Molerats' are thought to be the two primary sub-groups of the Hamas cyberwarfare division"* (Townsend: 2022). Molerats have been in almost continuous operation since 2011 (also identified as Gaza Hackers Team, Gaza Cyber Gang, DustySky, Extreme Jackal, Moonlight and TA402) and have been identified by cyber security firm Proofpoint as targeting Middle Eastern entities (beyond Israel), including government departments, banks, airlines and NGOs (Kovacs: 2022). The attack was discovered and analysed by Cybereason's Nocturnus researcher team.

CHAPTER 3: THE ROLE OF SOCIAL MEDIA COMPANIES

3.1 Big tech – Facebook, Instagram, Telegram, TikTok, Twitter (now X), YouTube

The following section presents a synopsis of the most popular digital media platforms and a flavour of how they have been exploited by sub-state terror groups and individuals. The section also presents a general overview of each platform and includes snapshots of how each platform has experienced and responded to security concerns. In choosing to cover the following six platforms, this author word searched terminology associated with prominent acts of contemporary terrorism, prevalent terrorism ideological categorisations, and more than 100 post-2011 news reports. Many more digital media platforms have been exploited by terrorist actors and this is acknowledged and covered in Section 3.2 specifically and, indeed, generally commentated upon throughout this book. Including within the Glossary that describes all digital media platforms cited in this publication.

Facebook

With nearly three billion monthly active users, *"Facebook is the social media giant to which other platforms are still trying to catch up"* (Statista: 2023a). The platform's parent company rebranded as Meta Platforms and consolidated some of the most powerful social networks and direct messaging apps into one tech empire, acquiring Instagram and recently launching Thread, a direct competitor to Twitter (now X). Despite clear and sustained efforts being made to remove terrorist posts and messaging, the world's leading digital media platform remains the go-to location for so much terrorism propaganda. Incidents include the following:

- Hosting Nashir News Agency accounts during 2017. Nashir is an affiliate that publishes official ISIS propaganda, including calls-to-arms sermons and human rights atrocities. Users had also been prompted and funnelled to Facebook via hundreds of pro-ISIS Telegram chats (BBC Technology: 2017).

- In 2017, 9,000 user accounts created Bank al-Ansar, which enables ISIS activists and supporters to bypass Facebook's basic security checks (BBC Technology: 2017).

- Numerous incidents of terrorist recruiters using Facebook for direct outreach to potential recruits. According to UK Counter Terrorism Policing:

  *"One such case led to the identification of 29-year-old **Mohammed Kamal Hussain** from east London, who was encouraging and inviting support for **Daesh** online. The investigation into Hussain all stemmed from a public report after a man received a Facebook message from Hussain encouraging him to join Daesh. The report came to the CTIRU, where officers linked the message back to Hussain and an investigation was launched. Hussain was eventually arrested, charged and jailed in February [2018] for seven years for terrorism offences."* (Counter Terrorism Policing: 2018).

- Pro-Islamic State's 23,000-strong Facebook group operating from August 2021 until (at least) December 2022, publishing official ISIS material, including bloody acts of terrorism, human rights atrocities and recruiting membership to a cyber media-warfare battalion that swears allegiance to ISIS Caliph Abu Hassan al-Hashemi al-Qurashi (MEMRI: 2022a).

Security concerns

Security and privacy concerns have bedevilled Facebook since its early days. By 2021, Facebook reported employing 40,000 safety and security professionals, many carrying out content moderation functions, totalling an $13 billion (£10.15 billion) investment since the peak of ISIS's armed insurgency in Syria and France's presidential election. (The company had, eventually, taken down 30,000 fake accounts used allegedly by Russia to spy on President Macron's campaign team as well as spread socially divisive misinformation.) During the aftermath, and concerns about elections and referenda in the US and UK, Facebook claimed it had quadrupled security resources within five years; a time frame that included some of its most damaging social media controversies (Bloomberg: 2021). Furthermore, in preparation for EU GDPR (2018) implementation and soaring media outcries over data privacy concerns, Facebook stated that it would no longer allow apps to ask for access to personal information such as religious or political views, work or relationship status, or provide group internal membership lists. Search and account recovery features were tightened by removing the ability of one person to enter another's phone number or email to find them. This also reduced the likelihood of account recovery features – often involving backup emails and phone numbers – becoming hijacked and abused. Further reforms included the cessation of surface data, generated by call and text history, being collected by the social media platform, as well as user logs older than one year becoming automatically deleted (Meta: 2018). Some years before that, Facebook had already launched serious security interventions by trying to create algorithms that sought to delete accounts that had potentially been established or hijacked by click farms working, ultimately, for vendors and advertising agencies. Telling evidence to justify an account becoming frozen or deleted could be, for example, a hitherto dormant or poorly subscribed account suddenly in receipt of numerous likes within a short period of time (Delo: 2012).

Despite investment into countering cyber threats, Facebook and its' many users have reportedly experienced significant lapses in data security and privacy. Just one month after issuing its comprehensive data privacy modifications in 2018, summarised above, the company was forced to publish a *"State-by-State Breakdown of People Whose Facebook Information May Have Been Improperly Shared with Cambridge Analytica"* (Meta: 2018). Some 87 million Facebook user profiles – approximately half from within the US – had been collected by a British research firm using its app 'This Is Your Digital Life' before passing the personal data trawl to its then client, Cambridge Analytica. The data was mainly used for analytical assistance to the 2016 presidential campaigns of Donald Trump and Senator Ted Cruz (Smith: 2020). Facebook was issued with fines of $5 billion (£3.9 billion) by the US Federal Trade Commission and £500,000 by the UK Information Commissioner's Office (ICO). Around the same time, *"data of more than 530 million Facebook users, including their names, Facebook*

IDs, dates of birth, and relationship status, was published online in April 2021" reported a leading California-based cyber threat intelligence firm (Fortinet: 2022). Users' personal data had, again, been acquired by AI-powered **data scraping**. On 5 July 2013, Facebook's parent company Meta launched a microblogging site called 'Threads', widely perceived to be in direct competition to Twitter. Less than three weeks later, counter-extremist researchers were reporting that leading jihadi figures and media agencies were posting about jihad groups, attacks and leadership, and encouraging followers to use the app to promote jihadism and sharia (MEMRI: July 2023b).

Security concerns – young people

Facebook requires users to be at least 13 years old to create an account (as do Instagram and Snapchat). Despite this, dozens of credible research studies, including *Children BBC's* research with 1,200 young people, found that some 78% of under 13s interviewed had joined at least one social network. Children's charity, NSPCC, surveyed 1,700 UK children and found that 1,380 felt that social media platforms needed to do a lot more to protect them from self-harm, bullying and hatred (Harper and Micallef: 2022). Parental controls found in settings/privacy features include the monitoring of screen time, location removal, blocking who can see their posts and profile, controlling friend requests and limiting the types of content children can see. Further parental control apps for iPhone and Android are available. Nevertheless, the default setting for a child's Facebook account lets anyone connect with them (GoHenry website: 2023).

Instagram

Around one quarter of the world's other young people (aged 13 and above) use Instagram. More than 30% of its 1.31 billion global users are aged 24 or below (DataRePortal: 2023). Instagram boasts more than 150 million American users and around 29 million in the UK (Meltwater: 2023). The photo and video sharing app (available to those aged 13 and above) has removed large hauls of politically violent and extremist content since it became acquired by Facebook's parent company, Meta, in 2012. From around this time, Instagram users became attractive targets for ISIS and extreme far right-wing recruiters and propogandists. Instagram's addictive scroll-down imageboards mixed with strongly personalised content generation algorithms mean that the platform raises significant concerns by child psychologists. Zara Abrams's article describes psychologist Adam Alter's opinion as follows: *"Part of what makes Instagram problematic is its addictive nature. Unlike a magazine, television show, or video game, the platform rarely delivers, stopping cues"—or gentle nudges that prompt users to move on to a different activity [...] Instead, it continually serves up content, driving users back to the top of their feeds to repeat the descent"* (American Psychological Association: 2021). Such a lack of stopping cues infer that Instagram is particularly hazardous to younger people (also those experiencing mental health problems) whose social behavioural filters may not be maturely developed in cognitive functions advancing discretion, empathy or impulse control. As such, terrorism analysts have witnessed several cases whereby extremists' use of Instagram has proffered key insights into the perpetrator's mindset. According to CST's counter-extremist researchers – authors of *We Are Generation Terror* Rose and AC:

3: The role of social media companies

"Instagram is a useful tool for young racial nationalists, providing them with a powerful opportunity to recruit, reach young audiences and present striking visual content" (Rose and AC: 2021: 3). Cases include:

1. An 18-year-old from Preston, UK, distributing terrorist publications on Instagram and including videos and photos of ISIS executions during 2022 prosecuted at London's Old Bailey Criminal Court (Lancashire Post: 2022).

2. In 2023, MEMRI's counter-extremist research team reported that a diverse range of domestic terrorists were collaborating online and internationally. Observed militants included neo-Luddites (anti-big-tech), eco-fascists and *"other subgroups of environmental extremists"* who continued to use Instagram to share terror tactics, means of violence and ideological promotion. Researchers concluded: *"The result is a growing international and interconnected network of extremists who are using Instagram as their primary means of communication and content dissemination. These accounts vary in size and in ideology but share a unified fetishization of violence and promotion of revolutionary activities"* (MEMRI: April 2023).

3. In 2023, a former high school pupil in Michigan, US, threatened his college with a terror attack and called out students by name in a rap skit broadcast on an Instagram Live video. The ex-student was found near the institution adorned in combat-style face paint by police (News-Herald: 2023).

A leading member of Meta corporation, Instagram's community guidelines mirror that of Facebook (described above). Its own community guidelines stipulate: *"Instagram is not a place to support or praise terrorism, organised crime or hate groups"* (Instagram: 2023). The platform has played a significant role in backing the Christchurch Call and implementing the GIFCT incident response protocols described in more detail within the YouTube and Twitter sections below. Like other big US-based tech firms, the platform began to remove as much violent material as possible posted by international state entities that have been proscribed as terrorist organisations by the US government. A case in point occurred in April 2019 when Instagram and Facebook began removing accounts run by leading individuals within Iran's Islamic Revolutionary Guard Corps who had been directly engaged in carrying out acts of terrorism in neighbouring Iraq and beyond (CNN: 2019b).

Table 1: Instagram Users 2024

(World Population Review, Instagram Users: 2024)

Country	Users
India	229.6 million
US	143.4 million
Indonesia	89.2 million
Turkey	48.6 million
Japan	45.7 million

Case study: Take down of Nashir News

The establishment of ISIS's Nashir News Agency on Instagram in May 2017 may have captured news headlines, but several Silicon Valley social media corporations moved swiftly to remove Nashir's accounts. Instagram removed several accounts a day after Facebook had removed identifiable Nashir profiles. These accounts were promoted and signposted by some of the 100 Telegram accounts operated by ISIS shortly beforehand. Until this point, Nashir had adapted a centralised strategy to encourage grassroots ISIS supporters around the world to activate local social media accounts and spread information more autonomously. It is thought that less than 100 users saw the images of ISIS terrorist attacks and statements claiming responsibility before it was cut short by Instagram's security. The corporation told reporters: *"Instagram has zero tolerance for terrorists, terrorist propaganda, or the praising of terror activity, and we work aggressively to remove it as soon as we become aware of it"* (BBC Technology: 2017).

Telegram

Founded by **Paul Durov**, and nowadays based in the UAE, Telegram originally grew out from St Petersburg in Russia. It is an end-to-end encrypted instant message (IM) open-source application with a focus on speed and end-user security. A key benefit for busy groups that need to mobilise and organise quickly is that Telegram-hosted messages can be used on all devices at the same time, as message synchronisation occurs across any number of tablets, PCs and phones. A core security feature is that it is the end user that opts into chat forums and encryption keys is recognised and stored on the end-user device, not by Telegram. It is therefore technically impractical to hand over private user encryption keys, insist Telegram, so that governments – or other interested parties – can read or exfiltrate messages.

According to the tech review portal TrustRadius, Telegram provisions 500 million monthly active users and is one of the 10 most downloaded apps globally (TrustRadius: 2023). Launched globally into the cybersphere in 2013, Telegram's end-user numbers mushroomed, as did those of its main competitors: WhatsApp, Viber and Signal. Telegram's early market offer of end-to-end encryption, disappearing messages, fast-time group chats – combined with the leadership team's explicit contempt for governmental controls and attempts at user-censorship – led a small number of violent fringe groups to favour and exploit the platform.

Following a series of terror attacks in France in 2015 and 2016, Telegram came under substantial fire in the media, as police investigations indicated that the ringleaders had used the IM platform to coordinate the public murder of a Normandy priest, then mass-distributed video footage and pledges of allegiance afterwards. It was estimated that 9,000 ISIS followers were by now using the app. Fearing a clampdown, ISIS moved its IM *"propaganda machine"* into the dark web (CSO Online: 2015). Sure enough, Telegram's owners moved to shut down 78 public channels that could be attributed to ISIS's recruitment, organisational and communication activities. The majority *"have persevered"* with Telegram but others have turned to **RocketChat** and **Riot** since ISIS published concerns in 2018 that Telegram was working with government security agencies following several successful Europol-led social media account takedowns (BBC News: 2019). According to the BBC: *"the pro-IS media group Quraysh warned Telegram that its takedown campaign would backfire and implied it would drive jihadists underground where the authorities could not see what they were doing"* (BBC News: 2019). UK and US media organisations variously described Telegram as a *"jihadi messaging app"* and *"preferred"* means of communication for terror groups (Daily Mirror: 2016). Reputational damage spread as it emerged in Afghanistan that Taliban fighting forces made *"strategic"* use of social media by operating their own Telegram channel, namely, al-Emarah (Ward: 2018).

Concerns about Telegram's libertarian approach continue. In 2022, a well-subscribed Pro-ISIS Telegram channel continued to recruit and operate ISIS "raiding brigades" targeting and encouraging Muslim youth to disseminate jihadi media content released by both ISIS official outlets as well as non-official media entities (MEMRI: 2022a). Moreover, according to Cyber Analyst **Hagar Margolin** at WebZ.io web intelligence: *"Telegram has been taking action to remove extremist and violent content from its platform, including the removal of suspicious accounts and groups. However, it appears that the steps taken to eradicate the phenomenon have not been very successful."* As of 2022, ISIS is [still] *"primarily using Telegram to spread propaganda"* concluded Margolin (Margolin: 2022).

Case study: Telegram and Russia – Can any mass-scale message service be effectively blocked?

Worries about extremism and terrorism propaganda, including the encouragement of "civic attacks", prompted some countries, including Indonesia, to attempt to ban and block Telegram DNS servers. For explicitly similar reasons, Russia's government moved in 2017 and 2018 to seriously restrict Telegram's presence in Russia. Unless cryptographic keys to unlock content and user details could be shared with public authorities, national authorities felt that Telegram should not be permitted to lawfully operate. However, according to Telegram, this solution was unlikely because with Telegram, cryptographic keys are generated by the end user and remain unseen by the host. Practical difficulties soon emerged. Some 24 million Russians, including many businesses and vital supply-chain connections, had become dependent upon Telegram. The service cessation reportedly caused significant economic damage. Events driven by the COVID-19 pandemic began also to assist Telegram's cause. The messaging app became a highly effective state-direct messaging tool used by Russian authorities throughout the pandemic. Russia's government somewhat reversed its challenge to Telegram, although various obstacles between the two parties remain under contest in court. As of 2023, Telegram services 700 million international users and would be the world's third largest nation by population if it were a country (World Population Review, Telegram Users: 2023).

TikTok

China-originated TikTok is, at the time of writing, the world's superpower in video-sharing platforms. Predicted to reach one billion users by 2025, the platform grew its worldwide audience from 465 million to 900 million, between 2020 and 2024 (Statista: 2024). TikTok's growth from its foundation in 2016, under the name of 'Douyin', has seen meteoric growth for its parent company, ByteDance. TikTok's popularity is partly based on its easy-to-use content generation and editing features. Vlogs are often self-generated, don't need props and professional aesthetics, and supporting algorithms mean that relatable, like-minded users and content easily find one another. The top three TikTok user-audiences can be presently found in the US (136 million), Indonesia (99 million) and Brazil (74 million). The United Kingdom provides TikTok with its twelfth largest audience, offering 23 million users – one third of its population – by 2022 (Smart Home Fox: 2023).

As with all social media platforms, there are too many individual cases of concern related to platform-facilitated broadcasts that can be considered as 'cyber terrorism'. But, such was the governmental level of anxiety, that the US Department of Homeland Security issued a dedicated security bulletin in 2021 that outlined several TikTok content-hosting cases, including the following:

1. In November 2020, an imam from Pakistan was convicted in Paris, France, for promoting terrorism on TikTok. The imam was sentenced to 18 months in a French jail and subsequent deportation.
2. Before the 6 January [2021] US Capitol Complex riots, multiple videos promoting violence were published and

shared on TikTok, *"including one from a user who posted a video encouraging attendees to bring firearms to Washington, DC. Carrying firearms is illegal in [designated] areas of protest activity in DC"* (DHS Office of Intelligence and Analysis: 2021).

3. In October 2019, ISIS militants based overseas posted videos from 24 TikTok accounts depicting ISIS militants with corpses, guns, and other individuals declaring their support for religiously motivated violence and ISIS.

4. In August 2020, the pro-Islamic State of Iraq and ash-Sham (ISIS) group "Roma Libera" posted an English-language video to TikTok detailing instructions for manufacturing explosive **compounds** (DHS Office of Intelligence and Analysis: 2021).

In 2023, the UK's ICO fined TikTok £12.7 million *"for illegally processing the data of 1.4 million children under 13 who were using its platform without parental consent"* (*The Guardian*: 2023). The ICO's findings suggested that the platform's management had not done enough to prevent children accessing their platform and, once found, little was being done to remove under-13s. A similar finding by the US Trade Commission hit TikTok with a $5.7 million (£4.45 million) fine in 2019. In its defence, TikTok states that the firm employs some 40,000 Internet safety executives. It sponsors research groups such as *Tech Against Terrorism* that monitor and encourage government intervention to combat *"terrorist operated websites"* (Tech Against Terrorism: 2022). TikTok's application to join the **Global Internet Forum to Counter Terrorism (GIFCT)** – a US tech coalition formed to prevent terror and extremist content distribution – was reportedly rejected in 2019 due to a perceived poor track record for content removal (OODALoop: 2021). TikTok has also introduced a similar *"age appropriate design code"* to its competitors, whereby ISP security teams and algorithms proactively look for end-user signals and patterns, before blocking accounts or notifying parents.

Twitter (now X)

Twitter, began in 2006 as a micro-blogging platform that enabled users to share short 140-character posts, increasing the character limit to 280 in 2017. Twitter boasts 353.9 million users worldwide, although the number has declined by around 5% since 2022 (Statista: 2023b). Some 18.4 million users hail from the UK, 76.9 million from the US and 23.6 million from India. Japan (59 million), Brazil, Indonesia, Turkey and Saudi Arabia all offer well in excess of 15 million active users too (bankmycell.com: 2023). Seven of its top ten followed icons are pop and sports celebrities, although Barack Obama (top), Elon Musk (second) and Indian-PM Narendra Modi (eighth) impressively penetrate these hallowed digital media rankings (Statista: 2023b). Nonetheless, by 2022, Twitter began falling out of the prized top ten in terms of monthly apps and platform usage, shedding more than 15 million users since Elon Musk's takeover.

Twitter's slick graphical user-interface projecting headlines, hashes and video snippets inadvertently also provide violent extremists with the perfect propaganda platform. As does its Direct Messaging (DM) service, which can either occur in public plain sight or piloted into private DM away from prying eyes. Exploiting these features, *"In 2013 and 2014, social media, in particular Twitter, overtook Internet forums as preferred space for jihadist propaganda,"* found Gunnar Weimann, researching at Leiden University's Institute of Security and Global Affairs (Weimann: 2018). Twitter has methodically constructed its reputation as being the go-to place for tailored news consumption. Users follow preferred news organisations and favourite commentators in the Twittersphere. In return, Twittersphere algorithms seek out and disseminate what they interpret will be the most useful and interesting news reports and feeds for its users. Content sourcing and target-audience funnelling is what Twitter does best. In the US, 48% of its users turn to Twitter to get news (SocialShepherd.com: 2023). Perhaps because the platform became more associated as a news source than other large digital media platforms, Twitter began to attract direct attention from counter-terrorism experts in police and academia. According to a US Department of Justice Awareness Brief carrying the rather unsubtle title "Twitter and Violent Extremism": *"Extremist groups can leverage the ability to tweet near real-time messages to numerous people to organize demonstrations and to plot simultaneous attacks. They can also use tweets with pictures that have geolocation data or other identifying information to coordinate ambushes and attacks"* (US Department of Justice: 2014). As domestic and international terrorism concerns grew alongside the increase in 'terrorism spectaculars' in Europe, the US, Russia and China, Twitter's founder and owner Jack Dorsey faced many vehement calls to entirely shut down from those countries' legislators. Like other big social media firms, Twitter employed a largely post-incident 'whack-a-mole' approach to taking down violent extremist content that contravened well-established community guidelines. But this patchy approach lacked any clear sense of strategy and further infuriated political decision-makers for its lack of proactivity and perceived lack of corporate concern. Within an available pool offering thousands of examples of significant platform abuse by terrorists, this book has cited but a few. The following cases in point serve as tip-of-the-iceberg snapshots that have occurred even though the platform has made significant efforts to prevent online terrorism:

1. ISIS's social media division formed 'Bank al-Ansar' (Supporters Bank), which reportedly provided 43,000 Twitter accounts to allow jihadi terrorists to bypass tightening new account user registration processes that demanded at least a name, email address and date of birth (MEMRI: 2016).

2. During the height of ISIS's Iraq/Syria insurgency, US/Kosovan national, Mirsad Kandic (41), left his Brooklyn, USA, home to join ISIS combat operations. Alongside recruiting others into murder and carrying out atrocities himself, Kandic served as an *"emir for ISIS media"*, using Twitter prolifically, a US court found. According to Federal Prosecutors:

   Kandic disseminated ISIS recruitment messages and gruesome propaganda using more than 120 Twitter accounts. For example, the defendant sent out an ISIS-produced "documentary" titled "Flames of War." This video celebrated ISIS conquests and macabre executions of ISIS captives, including instances where victims were forced to dig their own graves before being summarily executed by gunshot. The defendant tweeted that this video was the "best thing ever seen on screen" (US Department of Justice: 2023).

3. Platform being used by a new Pakistan-based violent extremist group Tehreek-e-Jihad fighting a secessionist cause in Baluchistan, Pakistan (MEMRI: May 2023). Several Hizbullah accounts promoting violent operations were running live during 2023 despite a decade of content moderation attempts against the Lebanon armed militant group. Hizbullah channels such as Al-Manar satellite television and Naim Qaseim continue to reemerge on the platform despite prior suspensions (MEMRI: July 2023).

Twitter's terms of service was strengthened in 2017 to explicitly prohibit threats of violence and other *"behavior that crosses the line into abuse, including behavior that harasses, intimidates, or uses fear to silence another user's voice"* (UPI: 2017. In 2016, the US-based company began to address heightened concerns raised by US police agencies and public officials about violent domestic extremists and US-based jihadis. Twitter purged 366,000 accounts, more than a signal that the corporation's leadership was seriously beginning to crack down on terrorism (*New York Times*: 2016). Some account suspensions of US ultra-nationalists were deemed necessary but proved highly controversial (Guynn, 2016). Between July and December 2017, UK police chiefs reported that another 275,000 accounts *"were permanently suspended for violations related to the promotion of terrorism, with over 1.2 million accounts suspended for terrorist content since August 2015"* (Counter Terrorism Policing: 2018).

Following the 2019 New Zealand mosque shootings, Twitter has played a leading role in collaborating with other big tech firms in violent extremism propaganda prevention. Twitter partnered with Facebook, Google, Microsoft and Amazon in signing the 'Christchurch Call to Action' (CNN: 2019). Twitter substantively funds and supports the Global Internet Forum to Counter Terrorism (GIFCT), which it co-founded with Facebook, Microsoft and YouTube in 2017 (GIFCT website: 2023). This NGO acts as a practical-action hub and fusion-centre in identifying terrorist content including edited, recycled and hashed material. The platform has removed millions of violent extremist messages, videos and accounts, including as part of GIFCT's Content Incident Protocol initiative and Incident Response commitments (GIFCT website: 2023).

Sometime after the 2020 US presidential elections, Twitter decided to suspend the then President's @realDonaldTrump account *"due to the risk of further incitement of violence" following the January 2021 Capitol Hill riots. Twitch, Vimeo, Reddit, Shopify, Facebook and YouTube joined Twitter by "suspending or limiting Trump's access to their platforms"* (Scapolo: 2021). In 2022, Australia's information commissioner threatened to take legal action against the platform for continuing to host "online hate" (BBC News: Business: 2023). Since 2022, monthly active user numbers have fallen by around 5% to 335 million worldwide – its lowest since 2020 (Statista: 2023b). Tech supremo Elon Musk acquired Twitter in October 2022 after a six-month takeover bid avowing to tackle spambots and reassert free speech (Mackey and Lee: 2022). As of February 2023, the platform reasserted its firm commitment to preventing and responding to "Perpetrators of Violent Attacks":

"We [Twitter] will remove any accounts maintained by individual perpetrators of terrorist, violent extremist, or

mass violent attacks, as well as any accounts glorifying the perpetrator(s), or dedicated to sharing manifestos and/or third party links where related content is hosted. We may also remove Posts disseminating manifestos or other content produced by perpetrators" (Twitter Help Center: 2023).

Scroll down, however, to the page's bottom and a surprising amount of wiggle-room is maintained for Twitter users under a section entitled "What is not a violation of this policy?". Exclusions exist for *"accounts that belong to:*

- *Bystanders who happened to be close to the violent attack and/or managed to stop the attack, for example someone who shot the perpetrator(s)*
- *Perpetrators whose convictions were overturned after a not guilty verdict. "* (Twitter Help Center: 2023).

Musk's new team rebranded Twitter to 'X' in July 2023 and removed the famous bird logo.

YouTube

Its motto – *"Give the world a voice"* – perfectly suits YouTube. Launched in 2005, YouTube is an American online video sharing and social media platform owned by Alphabet Inc. (formerly Google Inc.) and is the world's second most visited website after Google Search (Forbes: 2023). The platform hosts some 2.2 billion monthly active users (SearchEngineJournal.com: 2022). YouTube hosts one billion views each day and more than 300 hours of video content are uploaded every hour (YouTube website: 2023). Some could argue that the platform plays a very significant role in combatting threats and impacts of cyber crime because if we prompt a search for "YouTube prevent cyber terrorism" from UK servers – as this author did – 12 million video suggestions are returned to us within a split second (June 2023). Nevertheless, YouTube has been beset with complaints and reputational damage for more than a decade because of its consistent abuse by politically extremist groups who use the platform as their main theatre for propaganda, recruitment and societal intimidation. In an interview conducted by this author with **Marshall Kent** (2023), former Counter Terrorism Protective Security Operations lead for London's Metropolitan Police Service, the power of one particular YouTube-hosted broadcast had a profound impact upon safety and security in cities around the world. On 29 September 2014, *"jihadist media outlet al-Furqan published a message by Abu Muhammad al-Adnani al-Shami, the so-called spokesman of the Islamic State (formerly the Islamic State of Iraq and Syria - ISIS) and the amir of ISIS in Syria. This 41-minute audio message was posted to YouTube as well as other jihadist forums and media outlets"* (Bakier: 2014). According to Kent:

"The al-Adnani "Indeed your Lord is ever watchful" speech broadcast online in September 2014 was significant for a number of reasons. It emerged just as the UK terrorism threat level was increased to severe to counter the threat from ISIL. This speech was a game changer as we now had a 'virtual call to arms' from a senior ISIL commander using slick, well-produced jihadist films and magazines in the online space, directing and inspiring people to carry out attacks in the West. The speech suggested attacks which were simple, crude, low level and easily achieved.

Crucially, the speech gave virtual authority to anyone to launch lone-actor attacks against the public, police, military and security services without any further consultation with ISIL members or leaders. The broadcast was intended to reach as many people as possible and to inspire simple and difficult-to-detect attacks, prepared and launched with little notice.

There was a triggering and significant increase in these types of attack throughout Europe, Australia, Canada and the United States. Building on this successful use of the online space, ISIL continued to virtually broadcast similar propaganda with further al-Adnani speeches referencing the subsequent attacks carried out in the name of ISIL. This further amplified and projected their indirect attack capability outside of Syria and Iraq against the West.” (Marshall Kent interview: 2023).

YouTube's large audiences and instant audience reach, fed by end-user impulsiveness, provides the ideal cocktail for narcissistically driven terrorists who appear to revel in bloodthirsty 'terrorism selfies'. These are plot scenarios where they are positioned as author and central controller. YouTube also offers imagery and kinetic scenarios that are surely conducive to those who seek to play out the 'gamification of terror'; namely, the use of computer game design elements within a non-game context (EU Commission: 2022). One case in point occurred well before Al-Adnani's infamous 2014 sermon. According to CTC Sentinel's Graham Macklin: *“Norwegian terrorist Anders Behring Breivik—in the early stages of his attack planning— had originally intended to behead Norway's former prime minister Gro Harlem Brundtland on Utøya island in 2011. Breivik had desired to film the killing using an iPhone and upload the footage to YouTube, but his plan stalled when he was unable to purchase an iPhone, he later testified"* (Macklin: 2019). The gamification of terror by jihadis has been repeatedly highlighted by award-winning Al-Qaeda book author and *Observer* war reporter Jason Burke among many other authoritative news journalists. Just a snapshot of acts of 'selfie jihad' include the Toulouse and Montauban school and soldier shootings (2012), the Paris Kosher supermarket machine gun and siege attack filmed using GoPro (2015), and the killing of two police officers at their home in Maganville, France during 2016 (Burke: 2016-and NBC News: 2015a). Similar concerns were raised by a plethora of law-enforcement agencies and politicians following the livestreamed 2014 Isla Vista Incel killings (titled "Elliot Rodger's Retribution") in California and the 2019 Christchurch Mosque shootings where 51 Muslims were killed. Following the latter atrocity, tens of thousands of such videos were uploaded to YouTube's platform, at a rate of one per second, in the hours immediately after the shootings, stated its chief product officer Neal Mohan (Macklin: 2019).

YouTube's response

Following concerns about child abuse, violent extremism and hate speech through the 2000s, the platform began to employ several thousand content moderators to identify, filter and remove toxic content related to each of these three online security and safety categories. Although, before 2020, a lot of YouTube's content moderation was handled by AI algorithms, these either missed edited videos or often captured legitimate content that broke no house rules. The shift towards manual checks and balances changed as employees were allowed to return to workplace offices following the COVID-19 pandemic workplace restrictions easing. According to YouTube's Neil Mohan: *"One of the decisions we made [at the beginning of the pandemic] when it came to machines who couldn't be as precise as humans, we were going to err on the side of making sure that our users were protected, even though that might have resulted in a slightly higher number of videos coming down".* During the second quarter of 2020, 11 million harmful videos were removed and it's thought the platform employs more than 10,000 content moderators (Mashable.com: 2020).

Google YouTube is explicit in that it bars terrorism organisations, and those promoting terrorism, from its platforms:

Content that violates our policies against violent extremism includes material produced by government-listed foreign terrorist organizations. We do not permit terrorist organizations to use YouTube for any purpose, including recruitment. (Google Transparency Report: 2023)

This prohibition now encapsulates organisations that may not be proscribed by elected governments:

"YouTube also strictly prohibits content that promotes terrorism, such as content that glorifies terrorist acts or incites violence [...] Content produced by violent extremist groups that are not government-listed foreign terrorist organizations is often covered by our policies against posting hateful or violent or graphic content, including content that's primarily intended to be shocking, sensational, or gratuitous. Reviewers evaluate

flagged content against all of our Community Guidelines and policies" (Google Transparency Report: 2023).

Two principal methods of intervention are used to preventing terrorist broadcasting. First, AI is deployed to work in fast-time to block identifiable terrorist hashes. In 2016, YouTube created a hash-sharing database with industry partners whereby hashes (or "digital fingerprints") are shared with other platforms to stop terrorist content spreading. According to Google YouTube: *"The shared database currently contains more than 370,000 unique hashes that are near-identical to the human eye"* (Google Transparency Report: 2023). Second, after *"potentially problematic content is flagged by our automated systems, human review verifies whether it indeed violates our policies. If it does, the content is removed and is used to train our machines for better coverage in the future. The account that posted the content generally receives a strike, and multiple strikes leads to account termination"* (Google Transparency Report: 2023). Samples of flagged content are then used to continually improve the system: *"more than three million videos our teams have manually reviewed provide large volumes of training examples, which help improve the machine learning flagging technology"* (Google Transparency Report: 2023).

Furthermore, YouTube is one of several leading digital media platforms that materially support the 'Christchurch Call'; an international committee established by government leaders in New Zealand and France. The Call arose from international political outrage following **Brenton Tarrant's** livestreaming of his 2019 murderous attacks at two Mosques, a third prevented by police response units Out of this spawned the GIFCT's Content Internet Protocol (CIP), whereby tech platforms have worked together to remove livestreamed videos from terror attacks in Halle, Germany (October 2019), Glendale, Arizona (May 2020), Buffalo, New York (June 2022) and a shooting in Memphis, Tennessee (September 2022). The CIP was successfully deployed in July 2022 to thwart the broadcasting of a perpetrator-created non-live-streamed event, which set out to depict the real-world attack in Udaipur, Rajasthan, India. Between January and March 2023, more than 70,000 harmful videos were removed from YouTube (Google Transparency Report: 2023). In July 2023, YouTube blocked 18 channels associated with Yemen's Iran-backed **Ansar Allah Movement (the Houthis)**. Hours later, the Houthis' media centre responded, condemning the removal as unfair and *"akin to terrorism"* (MEMRI: July 2023b).

Nevertheless, according to Sentinel CTC's G Macklin, following Christchurch 2019, *"YouTube was [...] overwhelmed as users repackaged and re-cut footage of the killings in a bid to outsmart the platform's detection systems"* (Macklin: 2019). Despite efforts in threat identification and prevention, it appears YouTube's platform inadvertently remains the theatre of choice for the majority of publicity-seeking terrorists. YouTube continues, albeit unintentionally, to play a significant and influential role in enabling terrorists to access psychologically vulnerable new recruits. The platform also very much enables violent political extremists to terrify mass public audiences. This societal turbulence undoubtedly distorts public policy making by substantively disorientating politicians and undermining due democratic process within peacetime economies. A fuller catalogue of significant jihadist terror video interventions on YouTube can be found under 'MEMRI' in our 'key organisations' section below.

3.2 Other social media platforms: Decentralised Web (DWeb)

It is not just the gargantuan-sized social-media platforms that host violent extremist content. According to research by **Tech Against Terrorism (TAT)**, more than 330 social media platforms had been used by terrorist groups from around 2014 until 2019, with specific platforms being used for specific reasons such as file-sharing and storage capability, host location and security features. *"Most importantly" TAT identified "a stark over-representation of small- and micro-platforms amongst terrorists' platforms of choice. For example, out of the top 50 most used platforms identified in our data, half are small- or micro-platforms"* (Tech Against Terrorism: 2019). As big tech firms began to face severe reputational damage, then made serious moves to challenge and eradicate terrorists' content, the decentralized web (DWeb) came to offer significant alternative communication channels for terror groups that require three factors to flourish online: audience reach, security and stability. It's early days for movement towards a truly decentralised Internet. But DWeb activists and designers are fast building grassroots up peer-to-peer cyber infrastructure that can operate independently of large, supposedly data-compromised, data hosting services. As WebTorrent's Founder **Feross Aboukhadijeh** puts it: *"The Decentralized Web is a system of interconnected, independent, privately owned computers that work together to provide private, secure, censorship-resistant access to information and services."* Cronkite News's **Eric Newton** is even more brutal in his description: *"A Decentralized Web is free of corporate or government overlords. It is to communication what local farming is to food. With it people can grow their own information"* (Syracuse University: 2023).

During Telegram's purge of ISIS accounts, ISIS and its mirror broadcasters (including Nashir News) moved to Koonekti, which describes itself as the *"first Algerian social networking site"* (@abdirahimS on Twitter: 2019) (VoxPol.eu: 2019). Several sources, including BBC's Monitoring Service researchers, TAT and **Jihadoscope**, an online jihadist threat monitoring centre, cite RocketChat, Riot, ZeroNet and Minds, as the contingency publication options within the DWeb for ISIS should Telegram's environment become any more restrictive (BBC Monitoring: 2019) (Jihadoscope: 2019). BBC journalist and jihadism specialist, Mina Al-Lami, found that: *"Decentralised platforms like RocketChat & ZeroNet have proved attractive for IS media operatives as the developers of those platforms have no way of acting against content that is stored on user-operated servers or dispersed across the user community"* (@MinaLami: 2019). Examples of RocketChat's utility for ISIS has become increasingly documented by counter-extremist monitoring organisations including MEMRI, who reported throughout 2023 that ISIS-supporting computer programmers were funnelling non-technical supporters into RocketChat forums, where the basics of networking, Linux and Unix commands could be taught for those wishing to join the "cyber jihad" (MEMRI March and July 2023 reports). An advantageous feature for RocketChat programmers is that the forum provides online collaboration tools that can quickly teach hands-on technical attack capabilities and at the same time establishing interpersonal rapport between the recruiter and recruited. Unlike RocketChat, ZeroNet runs simple online chat forums that host official IS media outlets including its weekly online newspaper *al-Baba* as well as the grim back catalogue and musings of Al-Battar media, ISIS's cyber battalion since 2014 (Gerstel: 2016) (King: 2019). A tech-focused ISIS media group called *Afaq* moved onto Riot during 2018 as did Caliphate News 24. Riot does allow users to integrate their own servers, but ISIS and its affiliates seem to seldom provision this available function (King: 2019). Due to technical limitations of most social media end users, the growth and smooth outreach potential for truly decentralised platforms remains difficult for ISIS. Particularly as the much-scattered Islamic State in Iraq and Syria lacks sustainable, physical territory where it can develop and stabilise dedicated communications infrastructure. According to DWeb expert Peter King, ISIS propaganda on its TechHaven server could only reach around 1,000 registered users. Capability to reach RocketChat's estimated ten million users and 180,000 other connected servers would require a federated system, which was not in place at the time of King's research (2019) but is today.

3.3 Gaming and terrorism

During this book, the fusion between terrorists and gaming platforms has been regularly mentioned. This fact, in itself, should not necessarily cause enough concern to yell loudly for more studies and more police resources. After all, like most of us, terrorists commonly shop for food, drive vehicles and use the telephone. But we haven't – so far – dedicated a book section to these humdrum day-to-day behaviours. Nevertheless, *something is clearly going on here*. So, we'll delve a little further. Video gaming has unfortunately presented significant windows of opportunity for terror groups to successfully reach and recruit end users. Conversely, terrorism-minded end users can and do easily find and join their ideal extremist group using video gaming platforms. Below are some possible reasons why.

1. **Fast-growing gaming audiences.** Gamers tend to be young, therefore supposedly more experimental, energetic and impressionable too. There are approximately 3.09 billion active video gamers worldwide. This figure has risen by 1 billion (32%) in just seven years (Exploding Topics.com: 2023). Some 87% of female Internet users aged 16 to 24 use video games. Likewise for nine out of ten young males (Statista: 2023c).

2. **Reinforcing content.** Games such as Counter-Strike (dubbed the 'Gaming Jihad') allows players to simulate terrorist attacks. ISIS and other terror groups have used multiplayer first-person shooter games to attract extremists and recruit. ISIS propaganda videos shared after 2014 are designed intentionally to mimic popular video games Grand Theft Auto and Call of Duty. Conversely, many chat boards on Steam *"idolize mass shooters"* because their victims are often victims of bullying. Neo-Nazi and Incel extremist groups on Steam have exploited such individuals to turn them against other ethnic groups, female and LGBT+ targets.

3. **Direct Messaging.** In-game message boards are used to groom susceptible end users and recruit.

4. **Weak security controls; strong anonymity.** Since Christchurch 2019, and the advancement of cyber security AI, social media firms have become better at red-flagging and removing terrorism content. But online gaming is often conducted anonymously or by users deploying a *nom de guerre*. This shared experience and

team alchemy quickly fosters a rapport with fellow team members. As such, gaming communities can be quite exclusive and elitist at the higher levels and this makes it more difficult for external observers (read spooks and investigators) to penetrate. Gaming products and services are also very much unregulated in most national jurisdictions.

Various proscribed groups and politically violent organisations have been identified as using online gaming chats for recruitment, ideological conditioning and training. In 2016, police in the UAE stated that young Emiratis were being recruited into ISIS via online games. According to counter-extremism academic **Alexander Ham-Kucharski** at Portland State University: *"ISIS targets individuals as young as teenagers through games such as Call of Duty, Far Cry, Halo, ARMA3, and Grand Theft Auto as to recruit those from the Western world for their Jihad. ISIS Recruiters use these platforms to attract initiates via the gaming world through imagery that is already imprinted in the mind of avid first person shooter gamers"* (Ham-Kucharski: 2022). According to security intelligence firm, Concentric, ISIS frequently used Telegram groups to *"provide supporters with specific instructions for how to use gaming platforms to recruit new members"* while Lebanon-group Hezbollah *"developed its own video games where players can do battle against Israeli Defense Forces or kill ISIS fighters in Syria"* (Dino: 2019).

A firm, recursive worry about the use of gaming platforms – particularly by children or those experiencing mental illness – is that hateful ideas and actions become normalised among highly kinetic echo-chambers. Furthermore, high-use gamers can find it difficult to distinguish physical reality from online fiction. For example, one in-depth American psychological study found users suffered from Games Transfer Phenomenon (GTP) whereby users experience *"typically visual after-effects, pseudo-hallucinations, and misperceptions that tend to get worse with prolonged exposure to video games"* (Ortiz de Gortari: 2014). A second suggested side effect is that external stimulus, usually sounds and images from the physical domain, plunge some gamers back into the war games of cyberspace. One of the 483 gamers studied, 'Max4', told researchers: *"After a long [Call of Duty:] Black Ops session, I saw a red player tag above a woman riding a bicycle. Fortunately, I didn't have my gun on hand"* (Ortiz de Gortari: 2014).

CHAPTER 4: BUSINESS, INFRASTRUCTURE AND ADVANCED TECHNOLOGIES

4.1 History

Attacks on computer facilities at institutes, businesses and key infrastructure points are hardly a new phenomenon. We'll start by signalling something that we've so far missed in this book. Computer facilities and systems themselves are sometimes the central target of a perpetrator. This dynamic is likely to escalate as intelligence chatter suggests that a new wave of extremism and terrorism dubbed variously as 'anti-technology', 'Luddite' or 'eco-fascist' may be about to wash across our planet. In part, stimulated by growing concerns in some quarters at the role of AI-powered systems replacing workers (thus, fear of unemployment and poverty). Furthermore, disquiet spawning from governmental and commercial use of advanced surveillance across civil society, most notably in urban areas that deploy increasingly sophisticated facial and/or physical recognition tools, has provoked a backlash.

That all said, one of the earliest known examples of terrorism to sabotage computer systems led to the death of university mathematics researcher Dr Robert Fassnacht, father to three children. Sterling Hall, part of the University of Wisconsin Madison campus housed the US Army Mathematics Research Center until 1970. Fassnacht was killed and three other researchers were seriously injured in the neighbouring physics department, which was not working on army projects. On 24 August 1970, a local anti-Vietnam war direct action group calling themselves the "New Year's Gang" drove a stolen Ford Econoline van packed with 2,000 pounds

(910 kg) of ammonium nitrate and fuel oil (ANFO), which exploded and damaged the surrounding 26 buildings, while leaving the army research centre relatively unscathed. The gang's ringleader, **Karelton Armstrong**, had previously conducted direct actions including setting fire to a reserves officer training corps centre armoury at the University of Wisconsin in 1967 as well as an electricity substation. **Dwight Armstrong**, Karelton's younger brother, later joined the **Symbionese Liberation Army (SLA)**, a small, extremely violent California-based anti-capitalist group that carried out bank robberies, murders and abductions (1973–75) until police shootouts and prosecutions drew the terror to a close. Both brothers were eventually indicted for their crimes while the US Amy Research Mathematics Center was removed from the University of Wisconsin campus following the 1970 attack (*New York Times*: 1974).

In 1982, in Wanganui, New Zealand, an anarchist suicide bomber authored his final note upon a piece of cardboard: *"Heres [sic] one anarchist down. Hopefully there's a lot more waking up. One day we'll win – one day."* The ensuing explosion left it hard to determine the dead perpetrator's gender. But soon punk-rock anarchist **Neil Roberts** fell under suspicion of the investigators. His goal had been to destroy police computer systems that held court and criminal records. Roberts felt that it was immoral for the police or any governmental body to possess and maintain the personal information of his fellow citizens. Another handwritten sign, found nearby, stated that *"We have maintained a silence closely resembling stupidity"* (probably borrowed from the anti-Spanish colonialist Peruvian revolutionary Junta Tuitiva) – a slogan that has been popularised within New Zealand and provoked various popular cultural depictions.

The data systems were left unharmed, and no other human beings experienced suffering.

4.2 Business and infrastructure

'Fog of war' scenarios generated by 'plausibly deniable' cyber warfare activities undoubtedly provide opportunities for terror groups to learn about and acquire the tools to conduct hugely destructive, ultimately lethal, attacks. From a terrorist perspective, the ingredients of a successful attack upon a target audience are eerily similar to those mindsets and tactics exhibited by serious and organised cyber criminals. The latter tend to be patient and methodical in approaches to hostile reconnaissance, work to a small (largely unnoticeable) financial budget, operate individually or in compact need-to-know organisational cells, and seek to create an impact that is significantly more powerful – in terms of media coverage and (potentially) casualties – than would be imagined likely by civil society. Cyber terror attacks on infrastructure and some critical supply chains provide an opportunity for asymmetric warfare writ large. Just as is often the case with terror attacks that start out with a tangible physical violation, the chain of responsibility in cyber warfare leading up to command and direction level can be masked by layers of obfuscation and misinformation. This capability to organise high-impact, low-resource, disruptive attacks – which are 'plausibly deniable' for longer time periods than clear-cut physical violations – means that state-sponsored cyber terrorism is perhaps one of the most under-reported global security risks we encounter today.

Civil aviation

According to the UK Government's Aviation Cyber Security Strategy, the sector is *"already a known target for international groups, as repeated attempts to destroy aircraft using explosive devices have shown"*. The strategy goes on to assert that *"No examples have been found of specific terrorist cyber threats against the aviation sector, and risk assessment work carried out by the International Civil Aviation Organisation (ICAO) and in the UK has concluded that the risk of a successful terrorist cyber-attack causing loss of life is low compared to other possible types of terrorist threat"* (Department for Transport: 2018: 10). Three years below this document's publication, Sweden's air traffic control system was blocked for five days; the culprits of this malicious coding traced to 'Fancy Bear', a crime syndicate widely reported by cyber analysts to be an affiliate or arms-length instrument of Russia's GRU military intelligence function. In September 2018, airport flight information screens were disabled by ransomware hackers at the UK's Bristol airport; passenger notifications were continued using whiteboards (perhaps one of the most important pieces of business continuity kit). Ben Gurion Airport, Israel, admitted that they are on the wrong end of so many attempted cyber attacks – mainly launched by millions of pre-programmed bots – that they have installed a well-resourced, full-time, cyber security operations centre (SOC). In April 2022, a popular Swedish airline experienced four days of flight disruptions and delays *"after the third-party software system it used for check-in and boardings was breached by hackers"* (Stephenson Harwood: 2022). A similar attack occurred in India during May 2022 and impacted hundreds of SpiceJet passengers. At the threat spectrum's lower end, hundreds of successful cyber attacks against airports and passenger carriers – including large-scale data breaches at Cathay Pacific, EasyJet and British Airways – have largely come in the form of employee and customer phishing attacks or other 'soft targets', including databases sitting behind passenger loyalty websites. Cyber analysts have identified (at least) tens of thousands of personal data sets for sale on the dark web. In March 2021, a ransomware attack against international aviation IT services provider, SITA, which handles bookings for Air India and a significant percentage of global air traffic, caused significant disruption as well as a breach of some 2 million customer records (Stephenson Harwood: 2022). According to Eurocontrol, an agency that runs the European Air Traffic Management Computer Emergency Response Team, cyber attacks upon aviation had risen by some 530% in the year before COVID-19 travel restrictions.

Cyber terrorists may seek to target aircraft manufacturers for several significant reasons. First, economic disruption and the spreading of fear. Successful hacking into aviation would likely yield large opportunities for ransoms or significant backroom-leveraging (including prisoner-release deals). Disproportionate public panic and alarm is likely to emerge from any known terror group (or unpredictable lone actor) perceivably taking control/s of passenger aircraft. The threat of sector destabilisation or worse (such as a mass casualty attack) from an act of cyber terrorism is likely to be felt very acutely given that international terrorists have secured some of their most successful publicity following attacks on civilian aircraft by way of hijacking and bombings since the late 1960s. A further concern within the civil aviation sector is that state-sponsored cyber criminals beach systems and acquire research and development that is unlikely to be available open source. For example, there have reportedly been several and repeated cyber attacks against the European aerospace manufacturer, Airbus, and its core suppliers, supposedly to acquire technical secrets. These breaches have been attributed to China but once R&D is exfiltrated by cyber criminals, the means of attack and demonstrable security vulnerabilities can easily filter out to more malignant perpetrators on the dark web or elsewhere (New Net Technologies: 2023). (Similar to severe concerns related to nuclear weapons security breaches.)

Health service attacks

In Dusseldorf, Germany, in 2020, prosecutors launched an investigation against the unknown perpetrators of a suspected cyber attack, potentially for negligent manslaughter charges. Patient suffering from a life-threatening condition was unable to be admitted to a local facility, and ended up redirected to a hospital in Wuppertal, approximately 20-miles away (32 km, doctors were unable to begin treating her for an hour. The patient sadly perished (The Guardian: 2020). As Christmas approached in 2022, the Hospital Centre of Versailles, France, cancelled operations as a hacking attempt impacted patient treatment in neo-natal and intensive care. Some months earlier, operations were cancelled over several weeks in the Parisian suburbs at Corbeil-Essonnes Hospital. Not unusually, the attack was followed by a ransom demand. Confidential patient data was posted onto the dark web. France's Minister of Health and Prevention, an emergency doctor by profession, told reporters that *"the health system suffers daily attacks"* in *France, but the "vast majority of these attempts are prevented". When the Hillel Yaffe Medical Center in Israel was taken offline during October 2021, cyber security analysts were quick to clarify the impact. Checkpoint's Gil Messing wrote: "Take for example life support machines. Often, they are connected to the hospital network through the Internet. If there is an attack and the machine stops, then a person on life-support is not going to get what he or she needs"* (Jerusalem Post: 2022). Another potentially lethal complication to patient care was raised by Ben-Gurion University professor, Yuval Elovici: *"If suddenly there is no access to the sever, and a doctor needs to treat someone based on the outcome of his or her MRI or CT scan, the doctor cannot give the patient the correct treatment"* (Jerusalem Post: 2022). In the USA, health and medical facilities received warnings in October 2020 from federal government agencies about potential large-scale cyber attacks deploying ransomware, emanating, in all likelihood, from Russia-linked cyber-crime groups. Scheduling operations and cancer patient medical records were taken offline for days at the University of Vermont Health Network during a June 2021 ransomware attack causing delays in treatment and an overall financial loss of $60 million (£50 million). This followed a significant attack upon The Greater Baltimore Medical Center in Maryland, at the height of the COVID-19 pandemic in December 2020. Although the impact was largely negated, operations were cancelled for one day. During September 2020, *Security Week* reported that some 250 Universal Health Services-run hospitals across the USA were shutdown, due to a ransomware attack. The malware encrypted patient data into *"gibberish that can only be restored with software keys after ransoms are paid".* UHS employees described malware that possessed the same characteristics as Ryuk, coded by Russian cyber criminals. A sharp uptick in similar cyber attacks against critical national infrastructure has been recorded by cyber researchers at Temple University, Philadelphia. Their project delivers a repository of critical infrastructure ransomware attacks that show a quadrupling of offences from 2016 to 2020 (CIRWA) (Kovacs, E.:: 2020). Hospitals in the US reported a 71%

increase in the number of ransomware attacks between September and October 2020, threatening an infrastructure already heavily strained by the COVID-19 pandemic (UNCCT: 2021: 29).

Food and drink

According to Wired's Emily Orton, we should *"get ready for cyber-attacks on global food supplies"* (Wired: 2022). In 2021, a systems attack on the world's largest meat producer, Brazil-based JBS SA, was swiftly followed by approximately 40 attacks upon, mainly, US food and beverage producers. The attack focused upon JBS's US-based subsidiary disabling pork, beef and chicken slaughterhouses in the US, Canada and Australia. In Australia 7,000 employees were temporarily stood down from work (ABC Rural: 2021). The rapid digitisation of the food sourcing industry, driven by a soaring global population, as well as outdated IT support systems, *"makes food security vulnerable to hackers"* argues Orton (Wired: 2022). For example, food production facilities typically depend upon computers to monitor storage temperatures. The US government attributed the attack to the Russia-based, Russian-speaking, cyber attack group REvil; President Joe Biden formally complained to Russia's president. REvil and the group's servers disappeared from the Internet in July 2021 (CNN: 2021). Although, not before victim companies paid several million dollars ransom fees.

Oil and gas

Thought to be an offshoot of REvil, during April 2021, a Russia-based cyber-crime syndicate called 'DarkSide' gained access into an employee's virtual private network account at the Colonial Pipeline in south east USA. Soon the criminals escalated access control privileges up to a level where – they claimed – they could shut down the 5500-mile, 3 billion barrel-per-day oil supply. Taking no chances, company representatives paid up a ransom of 75 Bitcoin ($4 billion/£3.13 billion). But not before news of the outage cascaded. Panic buying spread, fuel prices soared. Supplies ran out in some states and state-wide emergencies were declared (Bingley: 2022). Oil and gas infrastructure is becoming attractive to attackers because of the significant public panic and disruption fuel shortages generate. In 2018, investigations by cyber security firm Mandiant detailed how they had traced malicious computer code from a failed attempt to manipulate an emergency shutdown system, designed to protect human lives, inside a huge Saudi Arabia petrochemical plant. Five compelling digital forensic evidence sets – including coding errors, timeframes and deployment by the attacker/s of known multiple unique attack tools – revealed to investigators the likely Moscow-based institute where the hacker/s operated from (Mandiant FireEye Intelligence: 2018). Like most other sectors – with the onset of automation coupled with increased remote worker patterns – the digital divide between a company's IT infrastructure and operational technology has become blurred. According to Deloitte, the average large-scale oil and gas company *"uses half a million processors just for oil and gas reservoir simulation; generates, transmits, and stores petabytes of sensitive and competitive field data; and operates and shares thousands of drilling and production control systems spread across geographies, fields, vendors, service providers, and partners"* (Deloitte: 2017). Oil and gas sector analysts report: *"The result is that critical oil and gas infrastructure is as vulnerable to physical attack by saboteurs as it is to faceless armies of smart computer programmers"* (Oil and Gas IQ: 2022). Over the last half decade (2017–2022), some 35 major cyber security incidents occurred within energy and commodities infrastructure, a rise of 150% (S&P Global Commodity Insights: 2022).

Media and public information

The December 2022 ransomware attack that stole employee data and disrupted *The Guardian* news services was just one of many cyber attacks upon news organisations that may clearly be a criminal act, but not meaningfully cross many of terrorism's definitional criteria that we set out near the beginning of this book. Unless, that it, personal staff or human source data is intentionally passed onto groups or individuals that seek to physically harm or terrorise those whose data has been stolen, for political or religious purposes. Earlier in the year, another UK news sector cyber attack was reportedly traced back to hackers in China. This cyber incursion identified at *The Times* and *Sunday Times* sought to exfiltrate news staff emails and documents. *The Los Angeles Times* reported back in 2018 that a cyber attack disrupted its printing operations in San Diego and Florida. Malware used may have been designed to target another newspaper's printing operation, but because both publications shared the same printing press, collateral damage and disruption flowed across several organisations' networks (*The New York Times*: 2018). Canada-based news portal, *PressReader*, used internationally by news reporters, intelligence analysts and researchers, which identifies itself as an *"all-you-can-eat newspaper and magazine subscription service"*, found itself the target of a serious malware attack just days after declaring that it would remove dozens of Russian news titles from its online service catalogue in condemnation of Moscow's military attack upon Ukraine (*InfoSecurity Magazine*: 2022). Again, although the rather slippery terrorist definitional criteria may not have been breached (in the eyes of many of the general public, at least), an underlying physical threat of political coercion and intimidation is very much left behind for some. Especially when the shadow of a ruthless, seemingly unaccountable and intractable, nation state is behind it. Stamped into the minds of cyber-attack harassment targets – news reporters, chief executives, proprietors, politicians, customers even – may well be explicit or implicit changes to personal behaviour, such as 'keeping one's head down' or feeling anxious and fearful. Too fearful to investigate further, perhaps. The theft of personal data from news reporters, NGOs, politicians and civil servants, in particular, should not be dismissed as 'cyber crime' or heaped into the sprawling mountain range of potential data breaches to be investigated by an information commissioner's office. Exfiltration of news organisation data by hostile state or non-state actors – some of whom have demonstrable track records of political harassment including assassination – may well include: home addresses and private contact details, medical details, favoured bars, gyms and routine locations, children's school, club, food and movement preferences, sensitive family and friend details, bank transactions, food transactions and preferences (to cite but a few information titbits). In the physical security domain, such hostile reconnaissance, conducted by politically violent entities, would in all likelihood be considered monitored and potentially prosecuted under terrorism prevention legislation in most jurisdictions. Arousing the societal and political willpower to confront aspects of highly invasive politicised 'cyber crime' and accept them as 'cyber terrorism' – namely, the clear and potentially lethal political coercion upon groups within society or all of us – is hopefully one outcome of this book!

One scenario that did cross the threshold of consensus that 'cyber terrorism' did occur happened in May 2015. Popular French Television network, TV5 Monde, laboured for three hours with disrupted broadcasts and social media accounts that were hacked in parallel by a group calling itself 'Cyber Caliphate', allegedly allied to the self-declared Islamic State. France was reeling from terrorism at that time. Just weeks earlier, in January 2015, two French Muslim terrorists and brothers, **Saïd and Chérif Kouachi**, forced their way into the offices of the French satirical weekly newspaper Charlie Hebdo in Paris. Armed with rifles and other weapons, they murdered 12 people and injured 11 others. In February, three soldiers were stabbed at a Jewish community centre in Nice. Later in the year, 130 people were killed by ISIL terrorists at a theatre, football stadium and restaurants in Paris. ISIL initially claimed responsibility for interrupting public broadcasts to terrorise French primetime audiences, and international news organisations fanned the terror group's claims during the weeks and months that followed. However, British government cyber investigators eventually established that the TV5 Monde cyber attack was a **false flag** operation conducted by a cyber group connected to Russia's GRU military intelligence function. The attack was formally attributed by the UK and other national governments as being conducted by Russia's APT28 cyber-crime syndicate in 2018 (Council on Foreign Relations: 2018).

Beyond the prospect of visual terrorisation and demoralisation waged by cyber terror attacks on the media, a rise in **credential stuffing** has corresponded to the increase of personal online media subscriptions generated by the COVID-19 pandemic lockdowns. Hackers are finding that password reuse is rife and that customers are regularly using already compromised passwords. An investigation by cyber security firm Akami's **Tony Lauro** reported that *"we once found an attacker with over 100,000 paying customers and was selling access to over 1 million accounts from different streaming services"* (*InfoSecurity Magazine*: 2023). The reuse of password and username combinations across different accounts clearly generates alarming risks for employer organisations, who will need to encourage and, to some extent, force staff to develop unique passwords and authentication when accessing business computer networks.

1. The following list outlines key points to consider to help prevent cyber-terrorism attacks: Organisations should deploy more AI technology to combat threats. According to *Wired*'s **Emily Orton**, *"AI can act at machine speed and take autonomous action"* – so they can act fast enough to identify and respond to incoming threats.

2. Attacks on the supply chain into operational technology and the Internet-of-Things (IoT) are hard to detect via legacy and signature-based security software prevention tools. Industries need to collectively assess vulnerabilities, narrow **cyber threat intelligence** to sector-specific threats, then patch and remediate accordingly. Being able to detect account takeover attempts can be best done by using bot management technology (*InfoSecurity Magazine*: 2023).

3. Outdated IT systems, including operating systems and operational technology, need to be overhauled and

compliance with modern security standards enforced and monitored continuously.

4. With account compromises so rife in accessing media subscription services, media and home ICT vendors should put an extra layer of customer access/authentication in place. According to Akami's **Tony Lauro**, *"Media companies should ensure they are using multi-factor authentication (MFA) if possible to deter attackers gaining access to compromised accounts [...] having to overcome a series of authentication hurdles is more likely to stop them in their tracks, or at least have them looking for an easier target."*

5. Dan Vasile, former vice president of information security at Paramount entertainment corporation, recommends media organisations to risk-rank their supply chain and continuously monitor their vendor ecosystem. He added that this will enable these organizations to quickly identify potential risks and address them (*InfoSecurity Magazine*: 2023).

4.3 Advanced technologies

Artificial intelligence (AI)

Late in 2022, army commanders from thirty countries gathered in Estonia's capital Tallinn at the CR14 NATO cyber range. Scenarios were war-gamed and participants were tested as to how they would defend their country while working with key international partners. The force-multiplier role of AI in scaling up capability to attack opposing network systems in terms of speed, frequency and penetration has alarmed corporations and government agencies alike. Conversely, *"Artificial intelligence allows defenders to scan networks more automatically, and fend off attacks rather than doing it manually,"* explains **David van Wheel,** NATO's assistant secretary-general for emerging security challenges (Euronews: 2022).

The United Nations Office of Counter Terrorism issued a report titled *"Algorithms and Terrorism: The Malicious use of Artificial Intelligence for Terrorist Purposes"* in partnership with its International Crime and Research Institute (UNICRI) back in 2021. The foreword by the UN's Under-Secretary-General, **Vladimir Voronkov,** stated: *"Terrorists have been observed to be early adopters of emerging technologies, which tend to be under-regulated and under-governed, and AI is no exception"* (UNCCT; 2021: 5).

Scot A Terba reports that AI is not *"fully aware and able to determine right from wrong leading to the possibility for abuse of these technologies and fears of this happening with devices like Alexa and others. In one recent case a baby was put in danger after a Nest device was hacked through poor passwords and the temp in the room set above 90 degrees"* (Terba: 2019). Other examples of hacking attacks upon "semi-dumb" devices include fake news bulletins alerting Americans, among others, that North Korea had launched nuclear missiles on them (Terba: 2019). One compelling aspect of AI – both for cyber warfare planners and, presumably, terrorists – is that it provides capability to quickly and accurately review a far larger battlefield landscape than any individual or group of people. *"Hackers and crackers" have moved towards "whole campaigns being carried out by automated systems attacking targets all over the world"* (Terba: 2019). Open-source hacking tools and platforms such as MetaSploit, that offer automated scripts, are equally open to white-hat and black-hat hackers.

Understanding a little more about the application of AI in digital warfare will help security planners to understand the technical terrorist mindset. Because the perceived advantages of AI tools and platforms for use in cyber warfare will, equally, intrigue the sub-state actor too. Cyber warfare experts **Rudy Guyonneau and Arnaud Le Dez** maintain: *"Intelligence is key to successful combat and maybe be even more important to cybercombat than other forms of combat"* (Guyonneau and Le Dez: 2019: 109). Several distinct beneficial aspects of using AI tools and platforms for battlefield commandos and terror planners include the following.

Tactical battlefield intelligence gathering and analysis: AI's capacity to address vast amount of data has a natural application in the data analysis performed to a battlefield's situation. When data relative to the combat zone is analysed in its entirety, it can produce a complete and precise picture of the situation (Guyonneau and Le Dez: 2019: 110).

Defensive mode intelligence gathering: By establishing a "honeypot" that *"evolves to enact human-driven and somewhat credible target systems, luring the attacker into taking possession of it. The gain is two-fold: an extension of the domain to defend while shortening the actual attack analysis"* (Guyonneau and Le Dez: 2019: 111).

Simulation and customisation: Before combat, the simulation allows fighters to rehearse with action modes and weapon types tested in realistic wargames. The damage output and the expected effects can be measured, studied and validated and their results can then be integrated in the global planning" (Guyonneau and Le Dez: 2019: 110).

Remote-control bomb detonation based on up-to-date tactical intelligence: According to Israel's defence intelligence, one Gulf state has provided Hamas in Gaza with a sophisticated technical and computerised system through which it manages war against Israel, where missiles are fired by remote control, enabling Hamas to manage war from a sophisticated technical operations room, adding that this explains the few deaths among Hamas fighters in the recent battles (Abu Saada and Turan: 2021: 190).

UNCCT suggests that the threat posed by AI in the wrong hands is potentially catastrophic, suggesting that a *"failure of imagination can have deadly consequences"* (UNCCT: 2021: 26). Malicious uses can be categorised into several purposes including enhancing cyber-attack capabilities, enabling physical attacks, facilitating the financing of terrorism, spreading propaganda and disinformation and other operational tactics.

Cyber attack capabilities: In 2016 and 2017, cyber intelligence platform Flashpoint reported that **ISIS** launched a series of Distributed Denial of Service DDoS attacks via a tool named 'Caliphate Cannon'. Planning discussions occurred in a *"top-tier ISIS Deep Web forum"*. DDoS attacks are malicious electronic attacks activated by hackers against targeted servers. Targets were education and security networks, economic and military infrastructure, principally in Iraq, with other targets in Egypt, Jordan and Yemen. The group likely used a booter/stresser – also known as a "DDoS-for-hire" service – and consulted with the forum about which types of political locations to attack. This boiled down to a choice between regional governments' "tyrants" or "crusaders" from the US-led coalition. The business impact was severe in at least two cases: One Yemen-based web server hosting more than 260 sites was taken down for several days. A web server in Iraq *"was offline for nearly two months before returning on a new IP address hosted by a DDoS protection service"* (Flashpoint: 2017).

Subsequent attacks have been waged by other ISIS hacking divisions. For example, in a recent experiment, an AI platform dubbed 'SNAP_R' delivered more than 800 spear-phishing tweets to users at a rate of 6.75 tweets per minute. Spear-phishing malware is designed to target specific individuals and groups, often at senior ranks, to disrupt, steal or eavesdrop upon data and data subjects. More than a quarter of these infected tweets were delivered successfully (UNCCT: 2021: 28). DefCon 2017 demonstrated that SQL injection attacks into web applications can be AI-provisioned by the DeepHack tool. Findings were succinctly summarised in a paper titled "Weaponizing Machine Learning: Humanity was Overrated Anyway" (Petro and Morris: 2017). A year later, DeepLocker malware was demonstrated at a Black Hat forum to masquerade as video conferencing software that sits passively in hiding until it identifies its victim through facial and voice recognition (Kirat, Jang and Stoecklin: 2018). Then a payload including eavesdropping can be administered. According to UNCCT: *"Instruments like this in the hands of terrorist groups would certainly enhance the severity of the threat of cyber-terrorism"* (UNCCT: 2021: 28).

CBRN

Terror attacks and plots designed to deploy chemical, biological, radiological and nuclear materials are thankfully rare. Before mass-scale digital communications, instances of terror groups and lone actors ordering bomb-making manuals from educational outlets or sharing explosive designs via couriers and CD-ROMs were relatively rare (compared to other security threats) and generally intercepted or monitored by security agencies and law enforcement bodies. In attempting to overthrow their own state by provoking nuclear warfare, Japan's cult group **Aum Shinrikyo** ('Supreme Truth') carried out 17 known chemical and biological attacks against citizens during the early 1990s, including lethal sarin gas attacks in Matsumoto City (1994) and against commuters using Tokyo's subway system a year later (Monterey Institute of International Studies: 2001). A biological attack (anthrax), supposedly targeting the New York subway, conducted by two active members of white supremacist group **Aryan Nation** – was foiled by an informer's tip-off in 1997 (CBS News: 1998). One week after the 9/11 atrocities in America, letters containing anthrax spores were posted to prominent senators and news media offices in an episode of bioterrorism that claimed five lives and injured up to 68 others (Cymet and Kerkvliet: 2004).

In 2003, a prominent Al-Qaeda-supporting theologian published online *"a twenty-five page fatwah seeking to legitimise the use of weapons of mass destruction against the United States"* (Dean: 2018: 265). One passage read: *"If those engaged in jihad establish that the evil of the infidels can be repelled only by attacking them with weapons of mass destruction in a surprise manner, they may be used even if they annihilate all the infidels"* (ilmway.com cited in Tenet: 2007: 273–4 and Suskind: 2006). The "electronic blueprints" for constructing a chemical weapon (dubbed 'al-Mubtakkar', translated as 'The Invention') were then posted onto several Al-Qaeda online forums, the recipe then spread "like a virus" during early 2004. The "eight-page manual" provided more than thirty diagrams providing advice on construction and target selection (Dean: 2018: 265). By November 2004, a prominent US news organisation published instructions to assemble chemical dispersal devices that had originated from Al-Qaeda's dedicated, central bomb-making research laboratory, located within an Afghanistan terrorism training camp until US-coalition airstrikes forced its closure in Autumn 2001. Three years later, America's mainstream news agencies fanned out the product's design and intent far and wide: *"Little or no training is required to assemble and deploy such a device, due to its simplicity [...] One or more devices assembled devices could easily be brought aboard a train or subway [...] It is difficult to judge the number of casualties that would result from the use of multiple devices; however, such an attack will likely generate fear and panic among the local population"* (Dean: 2018: 264).

Nevertheless, predictions and fears that the Internet will open up a Pandora's Box of CBRN threats, particularly within urban environments laced with soft targets, are yet to materialise into anything other than periodic threats. In 2015, a software programmer from Liverpool, UK, was sent to prison after attempting to purchase the toxin ricin from an undercover FBI officer. **Becky Pinkard**, vice president of IT and threat intelligence at cyber investigations firm, Pink Shadows, told journalists investigating the dark web for weapons of mass destruction: *"The fear that the attempted procurement of materials which could be used for terror purposes will result in a sting operation is even common among jihadist forums"*. One Pink Shadows executive event went so far as to reassure: *"If nerve agents are being sold, then we're not seeing it,"* in part because the hazard of handling WMD was so dangerous to the plotters and their critically important supply chains (Sky News: 2018). Nevertheless, infrequent instances are illuminated, as it does beg the question: *Are experts and investigators missing a* *hitherto unrevealed 'Black Swan' event*? A recurring theme in risk identification lapses is, after all, that most experts and investigators are usually only ever resourced to focus rather narrowly on known threats and the known likely sources of such threats (i.e. active groups and ideological chat forums).

In 2016, the Ibn Taymiyyah Media Center, the **Mujahideen Shura Council's** main propaganda unit, posted instructional videos about conducting armed combat operations and then published a video guide on how to make ricin (a lethal poison), and ways of using it. (Blockchain ConsultUs: 2019: 11/12).

ChatBots – Including ChatGPT

Concerns towards the massive potential negative security implications of AI-powered chatbots are being raised by leading developers within the world's largest tech firms. Considered to be Google's leading AI expert, developer **Geoffrey Hinton** began to warn publicly against the rapid development of AI before resigning his position in 2023 after working for more than ten years with the tech giant. Hinton told the *New York Times*: *"I console myself with the standard excuse: if I hadn't done it, someone else would have."* He continued: *"It's difficult to see how you can keep bad actors from abusing it"* (*New York Times*: 2023).

After the new-version release of ChatGPT in 2023, more than 1,000 technology experts and leaders, including **Elon Musk** and Microsoft's chief scientific officer, **Eric Horvitz**, called for a six-month pause in developing AI platforms more powerful than (Microsoft-part-funded) OpenAI's GPT-4. At the time of writing, the world's top economies in the G7 and beyond are examining how international protocols and treaties can mitigate "national security" concerns that have been raised by a wide spectrum of experts including Google and Alphabet CEO Sundar Pichai (Firstpost: 2023). However, warnings and legal action seem somewhat belated because dozens of AI-powered chatbots, including Google's 'Bard' are very much publicly and globally available with zero or minimal 'know your customer' **(KYC)** obstacles or other forms of customer due diligence (Beebom: 2023) (Forbes: 2023). Dozens of chatbot startups have spawned in Russia, China and elsewhere, perhaps in response to various restrictions prohibiting Microsoft's ChatGPT in the latter (Tracxn: 2023) (Forbes: 2023).

Such a suite of force-multiplying easy-to-use software tools are undoubtedly of substantial interest to terror groups, paramilitaries and rogue states for utilisation in conducting direct physical attacks. Chat-based AI using audio, video and facial recognition capabilities – then combined with editing and production software – is extremely applicable for information warfare activists. Several 'deepfake' smears, mainly targeting celebrities and politicians, demonstrate how a new stage of information uncertainty has been thrust upon us. Fake news is no longer about the written word, or empty, refutable rhetoric, backed often by dodgy pie charts. Whole regiments of state-backed cyber armies (and standalone cyber criminals) are skilfully researching (eavesdropping), editing, distorting, faking and sabotaging significant aspects of political, commercial and governmental administrative processes in many countries including the US, UK, Israel, Saudi Arabia, Ukraine and Russia (Bingley: Sunday Express: 2022). Why? For the criminals, it's mainly cash-grabs by flogging deepfake videos and images (celebrity porn being a huge money-spinner) and receiving revenue kickbacks on clickbait numbers. But for political hacktivists, including 'cyber patriots' affiliated to governments, or terror groups, the intention of propelling corrosive news stories across enemy territory – sometimes hashed up with deepfake news – is very much strategic.

Generating, distributing and fanning such consistently depressing misinformation and disinformation across chosen target audiences is a highly effective tactic to sow widespread fear and panic. If the information warfare campaign is sustained – or even combined with tangible physical evidence of attacks – longer-term socio-economic impacts will include community demoralisation, pervasive mistrust in domestic security capabilities, and therefore a gradual reduction in support of any extant regime, as one former Al-Qaeda bomb-maker explained (Dean: 2018). Stepping further into wellbeing psychology, the feeling of trust makes us *"happy and secure"* says mental health expert **Sannidhya Baweja** (YourMentalHealthPal: 2023). If we can't even believe that the photographs of a former US president becoming arrested are true (*Wired*: 2023) – when millions of us may have observed or even circulated them – what hope is there for the Internet's integrity. Or, indeed, our ability to trust – and therefore, like – ourselves?

Europol recently conducted roundtable workshops with AI subject matter experts and, rather unsurprisingly, concluded in a follow-up publicly redacted report that: *"ChatGPT is already able to facilitate a significant number of criminal activities, ranging from helping criminals to stay anonymous to specific crimes including terrorism and child sexual exploitation"* (Europol: 2023). Drawing from Europol's expert discussions and some scenarios drawn from the courts and justice systems, we can begin to clearly see several ways that ChatGPT can assist criminal and terrorist activities, including the following:

- **Fraud, impersonation and social engineering:** ChatGPT's ability to draft highly authentic texts on the basis of a user prompt makes it an extremely useful tool for phishing purposes.

- **Legitimisation and message amplification:** Various types of online fraud and terrorism can be given added legitimacy by using ChatGPT to generate fake social media engagement, for instance to promote a fraudulent investment offer or the popularity of a terrorist cause.

- **Fake news and propaganda:** ChatGPT excels at producing authentic-sounding text at speed and scale. This makes the model ideal for propaganda and disinformation purposes, as it allows users to generate and spread messages reflecting a specific narrative with relatively little effort. For instance, ChatGPT can be used to generate online propaganda on behalf of other actors to promote or defend certain views that have been debunked as disinformation or fake news.

- **Intrusive influencing:** Producing and disseminating consistent, influential adverts and messaging – possibly voice, avatar or mentor driven – to encourage impulsive and/or vulnerable people to initiate or activate or motivate acts of violence or spread the fear of such.

- **Malicious coding:** ChatGPT is capable of producing code in a number of different computer programming languages. Although some of the tools are rather basic (common examples being to help supporters to produce phishing malware or malicious Visual Basic Application (VBA) scripts), this provides basic training and awareness for wannabe cyber terrorists, and also links them up with more advanced or experienced radicals.

- **Prompt engineering (PE):** ChatGTP-4 is programmed to refute malicious prompts and communications inputted by an end user. (Many Chatbots aren't.) However, PE is the practice of users refining the precise way a question is asked in order to influence the output that is generated by an AI system. Information requests related to how to conduct various terrorist-related activities is achievable on ChatGPT by playing around with and desensitising word descriptions. (For example, not referring to something explicitly as a 'bomb' but asking about something related to 'combustion' or a 'combustible'). Another manipulation of chatbots can be to conduct research by breaking down the overall manufacturing goal – for example, to reengineer a firearm – into its component, stage-by-stage, processes. Another ChatGPT product called 'Freedom GPT', based out of Austin, Texas (so it claims), was marketed by founders as possessing no censorship or political-correcting sensitivities. On downloading FreedomGPT in April 2023, this author was immediately prompted with popular example questions to ask the liberty-loving bot, including *"How do I overthrow an authoritarian government?"* and *"How do I make a Molotov Cocktail?"*. Nevertheless, the bot's utility for consistently facilitating armed insurrection is somewhat limited. Upon several follow-up visits and prompts, the March 2022 version of FreedomGPT failed to provide any answer to any question. After flickering purposefully for several minutes, a seemingly exhausted Statue of Liberty figure eventually timed out.

Crypto

Contrary to mainstream media narratives, cryptocurrencies (including Bitcoin) do not offer the financial stability nor additional privacy requirements that most terror groups would require. Such technical vulnerabilities involved in using, or processing via crypto platforms, remain inherently the case even when financial operations are conducted by highly technical individuals. Several prominent non-terrorism-related Internet 'kingpin-type cases' serve as a reminder to threat actors that operating via the dark web can sometimes be more problematic than hiding in plain sight. In one such example, **Ross Ulbricht** founded and ran the multimillion drugs marketplace 'Silk Road'. According to author investigator, Nick Bilton, *"In 2011, a twenty-six-year-old libertarian programmer named Ross Ulbricht launched the ultimate free market: the Silk Road, a clandestine Web site hosted on the Dark Web where anyone could trade anything--drugs, hacking software, forged passports, counterfeit cash, poisons--free of the government's watchful eye"* (Bilton: 2017).

Using various aliases and a trusted online henchman, Ulbricht built up an empire of illicit commission-based trading, which ultimately yielded vast cash reserves converted into crypto. Nevertheless, several online errors sank Ulbricht. The most serious involved the posting of a coding question onto Q&A website Stack Overflow. In a further search, the pseudonym used, 'altoid', directly connected online to his real name, and rare but visible prior chat discussion postings. A profile establishing Ulbricht as Silk Road's prime suspect was soon easy to establish by a tenacious investigator, **Gary Alford**, within the Inland Revenue Service. Further checks revealed Ulbricht had used fake IDs, but attached his real headshot, to rent server space. These digital signatures soon spawned into a spider's web of digital revelations that enabled his tightly managed web of accounts, affiliates and aliases to be identified and mapped out by the FBI (Bilton: 2017).

AlphaBay is a darknet market operating for sale most things illicit, including stolen personal data from large-scale cyber attacks involving those on Uber customers and UK-based telecoms provider TalkTalk. In 2017, AlphaBay was identified as a possible location from which the perpetrators of the Jewish Community Centre bomb threats may have sold a 'School Email Bomb Threat Service' (Associated Press: 2017). By July 2017, the site was thought to be processing $600,000 to $800,000 (£469,000 to £625,000) of transactions per day. A subsequent combined investigation between US FBI agents, the Canadian and Thai police revealed that the (now deceased) founder, Canadian **Alexandre Cazes**, launched the site in 2014 and intended the portal to become *"the world's largest E-Bay-style underworld marketplace"* (US Department of Justice Forfeiture Complaint: 2017). Investigators successfully developed the inquiry because Cazes made the error of using a traceable email account pimp_alex_91@hotmail.com as the 'From' address in the Alpha system's welcome and password reset customer messaging. Rather incredibly, this email address was also listed publicly on his LinkedIn profile, which advertised his legitimate computer repair shop in Canada. Further open source intelligence (OSINT) research of various social media accounts and chat forums revealed images of Cazes and his wife enjoying luxury cars and accommodation. These images and conversations – often tracked back to various unencrypted files on his seized laptop (like Ulbricht, his devices were snatched by law enforcement agents during sting operations) – provided copious, corroborated, physical evidence to sink his central lines of defence. Namely, that it wasn't Cazes behind the many incriminating messages and financial transactions.

These two seminal case studies for any aspiring dark web kingpin underline precisely why politically extremist groups may stay shy of crypto platforms. The dominant cryptocurrency, Bitcoin, has its transactions recorded on a publicly available ledger. Upon request of the account holder, these cryptocurrency units can only be cashed out via crypto exchanges that increasingly store originating metadata, such as **MAC** and IP addresses. More recently, legitimate crypto exchanges have introduced similar 'know your customer' (KYC) requirements to mainstream banks, including formal ID submission rules and proof of earnings records. More relaxed crypto exchanges may well exist and offer a 'no questions asked' trading environment that safeguards client privacy. But, given that many illicit cryptocurrency holders typically own rather large portfolios (which they tend to salami slice and 'launder' through affiliates), the inability to fully identify and trace the location of an exchange, or its owners' true identity, really does pose a substantial risk that their own illicit deposits will disappear. Either by way of direct theft by unscrupulous exchange owners, or from a data breach by hackers that are well beyond the reach of extradition treaties, even if they can be identified in the first place.

The legendary French investigator, **Edmund Locard**, famously stated well before the Internet's advent that *"every* *contact leaves a trace"*. It may well be principally for this reason that demonstrable engagement by terror activists with cryptocurrency platforms presently appears to be sporadic and underwhelming. If anything, the fusion of more private crypto exchanges and dark web elements is a smoke-and-mirror cyber-sphere littered with criminals, investigators, foreign intelligence agents, hyper-paranoid government cynics, as well as the genuinely bewildered, technically curious, Internet deep-diver. The blinding lack of physical evidence to support situational awareness offered within the crypto-sphere, coupled with the high likelihood that funds will be eventually stolen, mean that crypto platforms may well be viewed as even higher risk than other terror finance options. Physical cash smuggling, taxing or 'extorting', **Hawala** or other cash transfer systems, as well as tapping favourable governments for donations (often paid out via convoluted but trusted courier and banking channels), remain the dominant terror finance routes. In sum, much of the 90% of Internet data that *doesn't* get spewed out from Google's servers, probably serves more as a distraction that an attraction for any focused, action-oriented terror group. Hazardous voyages into cyber's version of the 'wild west' therefore may not rank as a high priority for violent militants. And that scant attraction is likely to diminish even further as regulation spreads. The defence intelligence group, Rand Corporation, concluded recently: *"Regulatory oversight in the United States, Europe and China makes it difficult to obtain bitcoin anonymously on an exchange. However, if trading occurs on a decentralized exchange or in a country without regulatory oversight, the transactions could become much harder to trace"* (Rand Corporation: 2019).

Known uses:

Second-generation cryptocurrencies offering significantly advanced privacy have grown significantly, particularly in areas of conflict and autocracy. A diversity of crypto platforms – including Monero, Dash and Zcash – have been welcomed by human rights advocacy organisations. The **Electronic Frontier Foundation (EFF)** argues that digital surveillance of cryptocurrencies has been a "disaster" for millions trapped inside authoritarian regimes, conflict zones, as well as tax-hungry, highly-indebted advanced industrial economies. Stating a principle that would not be out of place in economist **Milton Friedman's** classic book *Capitalism and Freedom,* the EFF posits: *"The ability to transact anonymously with others is fundamental to civil liberties"* (EFF website: 2021). Whatever you feel about the EFF's impassioned view, it's worth noting that – like anything else in the digital world – no crypto platform offers complete privacy. Just enhanced secrecy. Perhaps.

Below are several cases where crypto platforms have been used for terrorist purposes:

- *Mujahideen Shura Council (circa 2012):* The Ibn Taymiyyah Media Center is a propaganda unit for this group, which has used explosives and rockets against Israel. Their 'jahezona' ('equip us') campaign aimed to raise $2500 for each jihadist fighter. Videos and calls to action were run over Facebook and Twitter and adverts contained a QR code to make donating Bitcoin convenient. The financial response was minimal.

- *Long Island, NY, US (circa 2017):* A 27-year-old US woman was charged with bank fraud, conspiracy to commit money laundering, and three counts of money laundering, after fraudulently obtaining credit cards and sending $62,500 to a Syrian-based 'humanitarian' organisation signposted in extremist videos. Court records showed the defendant *"read articles about women joining and fighting ISIS, accessed maps of locations along the Turkey-Syria border and cities inside ISIS-controlled territory, Googled phrases such as 'medical students ISIS' and 'how much overdraft can I get,' and watched videos of ISIS members urging Muslims to carry out attacks in Western countries"* (NPR: 2017). A similar case saw four defendants in the US and Canada indicted for attempting to transfer $22,500 to ISIS via Bitcoin (US Department of Justice: 2022).

- *Europol report (circa 2018):* The EU police agency reported that ISIS donations had been received via Zcash and Bitcoin. Donations were described as *"small"* and used to purchase website domains (Blockchain ConsultUs: 2019: 14).

- *Malhama Tactical (circa 2019):* This small group reportedly run a *"virtual university"* for battlefield operations. Videos show firearms training and battlefield manoeuvres. Social media channels included Facebook, Twitter, Telegram, VK.com and YouTube. Videos have ended with a 'support us' plea and Bitcoin address (Blockchain ConsultUs: 2019: 12). The financial response was minimal.

- *Crypto investigation into Hamas, India (circa 2019–2022):* A five-month investigation by the Intelligence

Fusion and Strategic Operations (IFSO) unit of Delhi Police into the hacking of a cryptocurrency wallet, established that Palestinian militant group, Hamas, was behind the crime. Some $500,000 in Bitcoin and Ethereum was extracted from a Delhi businessman's wallet, then routed through various private wallets, before ending up in wallets used Hamas's Gaza-based armed wing, al-Qassam Brigades. According to IFSO investigators, currencies were also transferred to known militant leaders in Ramallah, Palestine and Giza, Egypt. The compromised crypto wallet had been hosted on the businessman's Oppo F17 Android smartphone (*The Times of India*: 2022).

- *Shehab in Crypto News (2023):* The Palestinian news agency, *Shehab*, reported that the militant group, Hamas, had posted a Telegram message to its followers to halt Bitcoin donations *"especially in light of the intensification of the prosecution and the doubling of the hostile effort against anyone who tries to support the resistance through this currency"* (Crypto News: 2023).

Perhaps nobody sums up the pitfalls of investing in cryptocurrency better than Blockchain report author, **Simone Casadei Bernardi**. Even if fraudsters and dark-web mobsters don't dare make off with the encrypted pots of terrorist funding, common-sense business thinking deters – at present – a largescale terrorist engagement with the crypto-sphere: *"Whatever your opinion on investing, it's true that cryptocurrency has a reputation for volatility. Price fluctuations, both up and down, make it equal parts attractive and dangerous."* Whatever their intentions, investors *"need a steady and secure form of income. Cryptocurrency doesn't fit that bill as of yet,"* explains **Casadei Bernardi** (Blockchain ConsultUs: 2019: 17).

Drones

The prospect of sabotaging, hacking into, or reverse-engineering unmanned-ariel vehicles (drones) is also tempting for individuals and groups who seek to terrorise as well as physically harm opponents. But this significant security risk has, unfortunately, been played down by some large tech firms (who, not uncoincidentally, use or promote facial recognition) and government agencies that (somehow) need to get the balance right between promoting awareness yet suffocating public panic. Nonetheless, security risk management planners should be made acutely aware – particularly those applying controls to open-space crowded places – of the 2017 Future of Life Institute experiment that introduced 'Slaughterbots', a group of microdrones that used facial recognition tools to identify and attack targets in a Kamikaze method (Stop Autonomous Weapons: 2017). Facial images captured by the drone were cross-referenced with images already uploaded into the machine's embedded facial recognition database. Although some critics contended that the "Slaughterbots" video was exaggerated drama, then argued that drones do not currently use facial-recognition during flight (subsequently disproved), it does not take a science-fiction writer to work out that if something is available and adaptable to terrorise the masses, and it's relatively cheap to deploy, then terrorists will attempt to use it. After all, manned ariel vehicles have been deployed as vehicles for terrorism for almost three quarters of a century. Including attempts to subvert light aircraft to spray chemical and biological weapons on agricultural crop plantations, investigated as part of the FBI's Agricultural Aviation Threat Project research (NBC News: 2004).

GPS and vehicles

Various methods of near-future AI cyber attacks that have generated interest from counter-terrorism agencies does include the very realistic prospect of remotely sabotaging self-driving vehicles. GPS-on-autopilot scenarios, or humans acting without the sentience to challenge GPS instructions, have already installed a mix of bewilderment and fear among the general public. Recently, tech journalist **Aditi Bharade** reported with the lengthy but catchy headline: *"Tourists in Hawaii followed their GPS and drove their car straight into a harbour: 'Pretty sure that was not supposed to happen'"* (Business Insider: 2023). Thankfully, these passengers survived but years earlier a woman was killed when her husband followed GPS navigation and drove their Nissan Sentry vehicle off a partially demolished bridge that had been closed for six years. He was seriously injured. (Washington Post: 2015). Allegations that vehicles have been hacked to cause targeted assassinations are rare but have surfaced over the past decade including after the death of a California-based investigative reporter **Michael Hastings** (**Ashley Neu** in PhoenixTS: 2013). The advent of more AI-driven control over vehicles ushers in the very real prospect of autonomous vehicle-borne improvised explosive devices. At the lower end of the mass casualty threat spectrum, the remote or autonomous control of driver electronics – which could cause severe high-speed breaking, road blocking or vehicle ramming within crowded places – was demonstrated by researchers including at the University of California, San Diego and University of Washington more than a decade ago. Experiments also successfully demonstrated in cabin-eavesdropping and vehicle locking (CBS News: 2011) (Lima et al: 2016).

Wearables

Free smartwatches loaded with malware were being received in the post by US military personnel during 2023. These wearables have Wi-Fi auto-connect capabilities and can connect to mobile phones *"unprompted, gaining access to user data". Emails, chats and location data could be particularly exposed. According to Gareth Lindahl-Wise, CEO at cyber security firm Otinue, the hazards of fitness trackers "disclosing the location of military personnel and installations were seen toward the end of the Afghan conflict"* (*InfoSecurity Magazine*: June 2023). In 2018, a fitness tracking app was found to have revealed its users' fitness and exercise workouts in a data visualisation map. Preferred city runs and remote jogging routes, including inside conflict zones, were exposed. In locations, including Afghanistan, Djibouti and Syria, the users of Strava's fitness app *"seem to be almost exclusively foreign military personnel, meaning the bases stand out brightly"* [either on the visualisation map or potentially to those conducting local, optical hostile reconnaissance] (*The Guardian*: 2018). Banking and card credentials are especially vulnerable to the ultra-powerful SpinOk trojan that researchers at DoctorWeb suggest could have compromised 421 million android devices after being found to be downloadable from 101 Google Play apps. SpinOk's threat actors burrow deep with *"several spyware functionalities, including file collection and clipboard content capture",* bypassing proxy settings and establishing a connection to command and control. SpinOk's speciality appears to sniff target banking transactions but such potent malware could enable unauthorised access to voice and camera functions (*InfoSecurity Magazine*: May 2023).

CHAPTER 5: SECURITY PLANNING AND INCIDENT RESPONSE

5.1 Security planning

One of the 'stand out' lessons in attempting to prevent cyber terrorism, or respond effectively to suspected security incidents, is dealing with the event's multifaceted complexity. For the scenario will undoubtedly test your organisation's skills in dealing with converged security dilemmas at their most complicated. By using the phrase 'security convergence', we understand the requirement to consider and bring together in harmony two distinct security functions: namely, physical security and information security within enterprises. According to the US's Cybersecurity and Infrastructure Security Agency (CISA), security convergence is the *"formal collaboration between previously disjointed security functions"* (CISA: 2021). Cyber terrorism is neither a physical event nor a technical event. De facto, it should be treated as an organisational emergency. Such complexity is often acute enough across either security domain; physical or technical. Particularly for private sector organisations – *how in reality can a corpus of work colleagues ever begin to distinguish between non-violent extremism (a civil law matter) or online political violence?* As one set of security academics framed it: *"The difficulty for security [...] is finding the needle in the haystack: the one among thousands [of political extremists] who will act. How, then, are security officials to optimize the allocation of resources in fighting both extremist ideas and extremist violence?"* (Leuprecht, Skillicorn and McCauley: 2020: 3).

A converged and continuously functioning counter-terrorism (CT) programme with pre-agreed resources (human, technical and financial) can therefore enhance the overall security and safety of the business. The methods used to design and implement a workplace counter-terrorism programme will depend upon the risk profile, size and resources available to the organisation. Implementation happens effectively when a detailed and structured approach involves all stakeholders, and steps are taken to ensure total commitment to and a clear understanding by employees about the counter-terrorism policy requirements; although clearly it would be unlikely and insensible to share all details with all employees (ASIS: 2011). Large organisations with multiple departments can identify key personnel for the design team. Small businesses may have to use an individual to deliver the whole programme but with the owner or senior management support, and consultant assistance (ASIS: 2011). The team should ask, *Does the organisation have all the requisite skills and expertise to create the CT programme solely with in-house staff, or will they require consultancy expertise?* (Broder & Tucker 2012). In terms of conceptualising what such an operation should entail, we recommend becoming fluent with and applying existing formalised risk management frameworks that are described below throughout the rest of this chapter.

5.2 Risk management: ISO 31000:2018

Apply the five essential steps

ISO 31000 is a family of standards related to risk management produced by the International Organization for Standardization (ISO). ISO 31000:2018 provides overarching principles on managing risks that could seriously damage an organisation's professional reputation or financial position. Key to securing information systems and the individuals that use them is nurturing, then implementing, a proactive risk management culture. Undoubtedly, management frameworks are there to bespoke and make operational. Esoteric discussions by practitioners can rage as to where one process stage ends, and another begins. But for the purposes of avoiding debate, and embedding shopfloor clarification, this author posits that security professionals work in alignment with the current ISO 31000 risk management standard for identifying and managing risk (ISO Docs: 2022).[2]

The steps are as follows:

1. Identifying risks
2. Analysing and assessing risks
3. Response planning
4. Implementation
5. Monitoring and review

---

[2] For more information, see ITGP's *Risk Management and ISO 31000 – A pocket guide*, *https://www.itgovernance.co.uk/shop/product/risk-management-and-iso-31000-a-pocket-guide.*

Figure 2: The ISO 'Risk Management Wheel'[3]

Identifying the risks

Before you begin, write down and agree or reconfirm your business's strategic goals and risk appetite with board executives. Walk through your business and conduct **threat and vulnerability reviews**. Apply your data numerically into threat and risk matrices. You are identifying significant security-relevant risks to the business. You are also beginning to establish whether some perceived risks are not quite so threatening. In the converged world of security risk management, a holistic risk identification approach across

---

[3] Sourced from ISO Docs: *https://iso-docs.com/blogs/iso-concepts/iso-31000-risk-management*.

the three core corporate body dimensions – facilities, people and processes – is absolutely vital. Don't forget from the outset to work panoramically with other relevant executives to really understand how stresses upon each business domain will potentially intersect and unravel. The stronger your risk assessment matrix, the better you can organise the entire project, observes Agile Project Manager **Isidora Markovic**, who specialises in risk assessments (Markovic: 2023). Understand that security threats and risks tend to emanate from three sources:

1. **Day-to-day, normal risks:** usually internally manageable but could spiral up or down and require continuous review.
2. **Event specific:** often requiring bespoke, innovative or novel solutions.
3. **Response, reactionary or counter-recovery:** risks associated with returning to normality too soon or in an under-resourced, unplanned manner.

Panoramic threat intelligence gathered from within and outside the organisation is key to realistically identifying business security risks. Look deeply into, as well as way beyond, your facilities' geographic boundaries and perimeter fences. Ask yourself some the following questions:

1. What are the likely threats and vulnerabilities within our organisation from malicious and/or grievance-based insider behaviour?
2. Are any of our people exposed to online extremism and what might the security implications be?
3. What security threats and warnings are being reported within our sector?

4. What security threats and warnings are being reported within our geographic area?
5. Has the physical and/or cyber security threat risen markedly for our company due to national governmental announcements, diplomatic disputes or geopolitical disagreements and conflict?
6. Are any of our senior executives, board members or employees under (ephemeral or consistent) threat of attack or harassment?
7. Do we have enough security-related checks within the due diligence and onboarding process of new employees?
8. Stepping into the mindset of an adversary, have I really walked through all three domains of the business? (Remember, facilities, people, processes.)
9. How do I safely and securely store threat assessments and other risk identification material?
10. How can we share our threat assessments and risk identification methods and findings with executive and (if required) non-executive directors and other significant stakeholders?

Analysing and assessing the risks

Risk analysis involves further exploring and evaluation of the potential meaningful risks that you have identified. Distil the research into a list that is realistic, definable and treatable. A key lesson from various avoidable major security incidents is that organisations (and their risk management teams) were weak and ambiguous in clearly defining terrorist threats and malicious insider threats within the risk assessment stage.

Put simply, if you don't clearly define a threat, then you stand no chance of treating it. Read as a case in point Statoil's report and West Sussex Council's inquest findings into the 2013 Al-Qaeda terror attacks on the In Amenas oil plant in Algeria (Statoil: 2013) (West Sussex County Council: 2015). A secondary lesson is missing threats and serious security risks staring at you – or the organisation's more experienced corporate muscle memory – in plain sight. Because, when evaluating risk, it is absolutely essential to accurately review previous security incidents and threats.

Once you have done all of this, ask yourself the following questions:

1. Have I realistically scored the likelihood of threats and serious risks to our business operations?
2. Have I realistically scored the business impacts of threats and serious risks to our business operations?
3. Do I have professional security colleagues or mentors who can challenge and double check my threat and vulnerability assessments?
4. Have I shared, stored and secured my findings in safe, legally compliant manner?
5. What are the best methods to communicate my findings with senior executives and/or investment decision-makers? For instance, heat maps, severity matrices, threat intelligence feeds within executive board presentations can all positively influence stakeholders and colleagues by demonstrating a sense of control, organisational responsibility, inclusivity and transparency.

Response planning

Scrum down with executives. You have your identified list of security risks. You have your risk ratings. Now, what are you going to do? This stage leads you right from concept development to the edges of security controls implementation. It's where many organisations get 'stuck in treacle'; they overthink, and – unlike many conscience-free adversaries – they delay.

So, now that you have your risks analysed, rated and prioritised, move swiftly to address them. Ascertain the realistic levels of your budget. Reconfirm and actively liaise with the senior leader responsible, so that you are both comfortable on understanding the likely level of investment and acceptable operational parameters that the enterprise will tolerate before it becomes risk adverse to implementing the security controls you are likely to propose. Now, when you come to list your security controls, think in terms of the 4Ts risk management mnemonic. What will you do with each area of security risk? Will you:

1. Terminate;
2. Transfer;
3. Tolerate; or
4. Treat?

Ask yourself the following questions:

1. If we are tolerating or treating a risk, then what policies and procedures will we need to put in place?
2. If we are terminating a risk, are we absolutely certain that the physical and legal risk has been sufficiently removed?

3. If we are transferring a risk, are we absolutely certain that the physical and legal risk has been sufficiently 'transferred'?
4. Can some of our security controls be defined as targets, which can demonstrate a really useful return on investment (ROI) for the business's senior executives? (For example, upgrading CCTV, introducing Cloud storage, therefore reducing manual process costs and stock shrinkage (theft)).
5. Security risk and threat identification is notoriously unscientific. How can we best evidence, explain and document some of the findings and potential controls that we have decided not to progress with?

Implementation

There are two major parts to implementation. First, you will need to keep doing the company 'walk throughs'. Not just physically, but by developing, crystallising and then implementing your security control measures across the corporate entity: people, facilities, processes. Your team will physically need to check that the new radios are working. That the new first aid kits and grab bags are in the right place, and untouched, at each site. That CCTV is all working and aligned to the agreed, single Cloud provider. That backup Cloud storage is fully operational and that all subscriptions are accessible, lawful and fully paid up. That working torches with spare batteries are available within reaching distance and in known locations in high-priority areas. That access control barriers, including vehicle mitigation barriers, are fully under friendly human control at all times. We can describe this lifesaving nitty gritty as the operational part of risk management control implementation.

Second, you will need well-oiled and integrated leadership and management. OpenAI founder, **Sam Altman**, wryly observed, *"when a lack of structure fails, it fails all at once"* (Medium.com: 2014). He's so right. A solid structure, underpinning a coordinated system, can withstand most malign forces and win most competitive scenarios. But success will be thwarted if the directional levels of choreography and coordination are weak.

Governance:

"Cyber security is the responsibility of the entire board," states the UK **National Cyber Security Centre** (NCSC).

A cyber security incident will affect the whole organisation – not just the IT department. For example, it may impact online sales, contractual relationships, your reputation, or result in legal or regulatory action. There should be sufficient expertise within the Board in order to provide direction on cyber security strategy and hold decisions to account (NCSC Cyber Security Toolkit for Boards: 2023).

Good security governance is essential to the implementation of a cyber security plan. According to the NCSC, *"an organisation's senior leadership should use security governance to set out the kinds of security risks they are prepared for staff to take and those they are not"* (NCSC: 2023). *"Governance procedures will ensure that senior executives are aware of and accountable"* for an organisation's state of cyber security. Senior leaders should be *"actively involved in setting target days to achieve [the stated goals of] cyber security maturity, reviewing strategy progress, ensuring that security is aligned with overall business objectives, and set the tone from the top with regards to maintaining and developing a successful security culture"* (Adams: 2023). The NCSC advises that organisational leaders should be more fully involved across the spectrum of implementation:

> *"[Board members] should expect to see [Key Performance Indicators] KPIs with an agreed target range for each measurement on what's acceptable. These might include the time taken to implement security patches and mitigate high risk vulnerabilities, and the number of days between detection and remediation"* (NCSC Board Toolkit: 2023).

The ever-changing threat landscape and complexity of technical and regulatory solutions requires that those overseeing each area of implementing the cyber security plan are abreast of latest developments in cyberspace, and ensure that their plan is coherently organised as well as neatly organised (Rodriguez: 2023). The 'management' part of the implementation phase requires skill sets and adherence to project management approaches and discipline. The implementation of the agreed, signed-off cyber security risk control treatments across the entire organisation can be harnessed and driven through by an overarching project management group. Alternatively, larger organisations might allocate existing change and/or project management committees to implement the agreed enterprise security controls within their portfolio area of responsibility.

Project management approaches to cyber security implementation provide the following organisational benefits:

1. **Increased efficiency:** active risk identification and prioritisation actions enable businesses to build a

helicopter view of themselves, which can result in cost savings, efficiencies, systems integrations, transferring of liabilities and a reduction in duplication (Rodriguez: 2023)

2. **Improved collaboration and knowledge-sharing:** functions, teams and stakeholders can vastly improve their technical and organisational knowledge by working together and sharing knowledge and company muscle-memory, within a structured format, and aligned to organisational goals.

3. **Improved security and incident response:** As individuals and teams – who may have been previously unknown or unfamiliar to one another – begin to share knowledge and pool resources, this integrated activity develops and strengthens the organisation's overall capability in continuity of operations and enhances organisational resilience. Individuals and teams become much more effective at identifying vulnerabilities and also developing synergised, team-driven, strategies to respond to them.

In a practical sense, perhaps the easiest method for implementing the delivery of your project is by referring to the very popular *Project Management Body of Knowledge (PMBOK) Guide* that organises project management execution into five famous phases:

1. Project Initiation Phase
2. Project Planning Phase
3. Project Execution Phase
4. Project Monitoring & Control Phase

5. Project Closure Phase

According to project management expert Hannah Donato, each phase of the project management lifecycle consists of a specific project objective or objectives and defines results, deliverables, processes and milestones. Management by project life cycle phase gives the project team a common vocabulary to communicate project progress, resulting in better organisational control over the projects they handle (ProjectManagement.com: 2022).

The security control implementation phase is a vast beast roving about in perpetual motion. But as your teams move through the long list of implementing the organisational security controls, it's worth a security monitoring team regularly breaking out of the 'delivery quagmire' to 'scrum down' to review the implementation itself.

Among many others, ask yourselves the following questions:

1. Are effective (i.e. accurate and timely) security metrics shared with the board?
2. How can we get our senior leaders and primary stakeholders to actively engage in supporting and advocating for the rollout?
3. How can we double check that our security controls are legally compliant and that the risk of plausible, credible legal challenges are minimised?
4. Is the rollout of cyber security controls being conducted in close engagement with employees?
5. Yes, you have a wide and deep security implantation plan. But is your **cyber security posture** up to date and does it accurately reflect the latest threats?

NCSC'S Eight Key Boardroom Questions

1. *"Is a cyber strategy in place? A cyber strategy is a plan of high-level actions to improve organisational resilience and covers your highest priority concerns. Then move on to ask the next seven!*

2. **Can board members name the top cyber threats and outline the measures in place to mitigate them?** *Are they aware of the basics, such as ransomware, and that they themselves might make attractive targets for adversaries?*

3. **Does your organisation have an effective approach to managing cyber risks?** *Has a plan based on a risk register and the lines of responsibility for risk owners been designed, implemented and kept under continual review?*

4. **Does the board understand the overarching purpose of the cyber security measures in place?** *Can they easily explain and communicate them?*

5. **Does your organisation have an incident response plan in place and do you regularly rehearse it?** *The board should expect to see reporting on exercises conducted and lessons learned.*

6. **Are products/services provided by partners/suppliers documented?** *Critical services and dependencies on external suppliers should be mapped and effective measures in place for supplier failure.*

7. **Do your organisation's security metrics focus on success rather than failure?** *For example, as well as*

measuring how many people clicked on a phishing email, focus on how many people reported it.

8. ***Are your HR team identifying*** *– and addressing – any cyber skills gaps in your organisation? HR should report to the board on the specific skills gaps that the organisation is facing with a plan in place to develop cyber expertise where required."**

*The 8 first sentences in each point above are drawn directly from the NCSC's Business Toolkit Toolbox (2023). The descriptive sentences are abridged from NCSC and mixed with the author's own descriptive work.

Source: NCSC Toolkit's toolbox: *https://www.ncsc.gov.uk/collection/board-toolkit/toolkits-toolbox*

Monitoring and review

Ask yourself the following questions:

1. Have we instituted a regular 'threat and risk monitor' to circulate within the security management team and also other relevant teams (Emergency Planning, Business Continuity, C-Suite and Communications Director)?

2. Although employees are vetted with due diligence at the beginning of their employment period, what periodic due diligence do we carry out to monitor and review employees? (It's worth remembering that many of the highest-profile cyber and information security

breaches – read the cases of **Edward Snowden** and **Bradley Manning** in the US, as well as **Kim Philby** and **David Ballantyne Smith** from the UK – occur from within supposedly deep-vetted organisations.

3. Have we got everyone covered off, and actively engaged, in baseline security management and threat awareness training? Examples of courses should directly relate to identified security risks and range across the company's defined threat spectrum. (General data protection, counter-extremism, physical safety and security, terrorism awareness, first aid, business continuity and In Case of Emergency (ICE) contingency procedures might all be examples of sensible training initiatives and staff-wide stress tests.)

4. Because we are dealing with the saving of lives and company assets (very important), and we are also dealing with issues related to privacy, safety and security (very sensitive), shall we consider bringing in independent, (supposedly impartial) external experts for functions such as security audit, testing and review?

5. To what extent do we make the results of reviews, tests and audits known? Getting the balance right between general staff awareness of shortcomings without letting your inquisitive adversaries know the vulnerabilities is nearly impossible at the best of times.

5.3 Physical and ICT security 'converged' – ISO/IEC 27001

The ISO 27000 family of information security management standards combine to provide the pre-eminent good practice framework for securing data, including the physical environments in which organisational data sits. A full version can be purchased from the International Organization for Standardization (ISO). The ISO/IEC 27000 family of standards provide a general framework and set of principles to help organisations of any size or any industry protect their data. The standards propel organisations to adopt, control and safely manage their information security management systems (ISMSs). The ISO 27001 framework uses a risk-based approach and is technology-neutral. It focuses on three dimensions of information security:

1. Confidentiality

2. Integrity

3. Availability (ISO 27001:2022)

The linchpin of this series, ISO/IEC 27001 as well as its companion standard ISO/IEC 27002, were updated and republished during 2022. The full title is: Information security, cybersecurity and privacy protection – Information security management systems – Requirements.

27001 specifies the requirements for establishing, implementing, maintaining and continually improving an ISMS. One of the key strengths of ISO/IEC 27001 is that it provides substantial emphasis on senior management accountability for establishing, maintaining and continuously enhancing an organisational security culture (IT Governance Blog: 2023).

Determining information security controls that are specific and appropriate to the organisation clearly has implications for other business operational areas that are responsible for risk management and business continuity functions. Which is why ISO/IEC 27001 makes it clear that plans and implementation are developed in consideration with supporting and (to some extent) overlapping standards including ISO 31000:2018 Risk Management and – this author would suggest – ISO/IEC 27031:2011 ICT readiness for business continuity standard.

The requirements are listed across several workplace domains. For the purposes of defending against cyber terrorism, this book will now provide a summary of this author's top three information security requirements for each of the given **seven domains** below:

A. *Organisational context*

1. Determine relevant parties to the ISMS.
2. Determine their user requirements.
3. Keep in mind legal and regulatory requirements and contractual obligations.

B. *Leadership*

Responsibility for the security plan being relevant, coherent, proportionate and implemented sits with the leadership. Both with an identifiable C-suite senior executive as well as an influential and clearly identifiable chain of command. Who is the responsible executive director? Who is the responsible department head? Who are the responsible function heads? These questions and many more will be asked by incident investigators and news reporters in any security incident's aftermath.

1. Ensure information security policies and objectives are established and compatible with overall business strategy.
2. Communicate the importance of effective information security management and ensure resources to achieve polices are made available.
3. Promote continual improvement.

C. Planning

1. Design and conduct an information security risk assessment process.
2. Formulate an information security risk treatment plan.
3. Produce a 'Statement of Applicability' that contains the necessary controls and justifications for inclusions (whether implemented or otherwise) and exclusions.

D. Support

1. Ensure that people are competent on the basis of appropriate education, training and/or experience, and take actions to acquire the necessary competence.
2. Determine the need for internal and external communications and establish what to communicate, when, with whom and by which method/s.
3. Ensure documented information is available and fit for purpose, but also adequately protected from loss of confidentiality, improper use or loss of integrity.

E. Operation

1. The organisation should conduct information security assessments at planned intervals or when significant changes are proposed or occur.
2. The organisation shall implement the information security risk treatment plan.
3. The organisation shall securely retain documented information of the results of the information security risk treatment.

F. Performance evaluation

1. The organisation shall conduct internal audits and ensure objectivity and impartiality of the audit process.

2. Top management shall review the information security management system at planned intervals to ensure its continued suitability, adequacy and effectiveness. Management reviews shall include consideration of trends in nonconformities and corrective actions, as well as feedback from interested parties, monitoring and audit results.

3. Monitoring, measurement and evaluation allows an organisation to review the performance of the ISMS.

G. Continual improvement

1. The organisation shall continually improve the suitability, adequacy and effectiveness of the ISMS.

2. When a nonconformity occurs, the organisation shall take action to control it and determine if similar nonconformities exist, or could potentially occur.

3. The organisation shall retain documented information as evidence of the nature of nonconformity, subsequent actions taken and the results of any corrective action (ISO/IEC 27001).

How can we apply 'converged' security controls?

The good news is that you don't have to 'reinvent the wheel' and spend days and weeks (more probably months and years) marching around your enterprise and jotting down numerous (and inevitably expensive) security measures to put in place. The ISO/IEC committees have – to a great extent – done this for you. (Remember, the committees are made up of security folk just like you who have been hacked and worse during their careers!) Perhaps the most useful and important piece of material produced by the mighty 27001-ers is: *Annex A*.

In essence, *Annex A* is a long but powerfully-relevant list of nearly 100 security controls, divided into 4 themes providing a significant menu of security treatments to implement. Section 7 of Annex A is particularly helpful for the critical necessity of converging physical and cyber security measures into a suite of physical controls. It's crucial to remember that Annex A is *"not exhaustive and additional information security controls can be included if needed"* (ISO/IEC 27001:2022).

It is a recurring observation of this author's teaching experience that corporate security risk managers and information security managers alike struggle to fully consider opportunities to physically attack (or plan to attack) employees and facilities that are presented by cyber systems.

In terms of countering cyber terrorism, we will now extrapolate our **top security controls** from the ISO/IEC 27001 *Physical controls* section.

1. *"Control: Physical entry*

Secure areas shall be protected by appropriate entry controls and access points.

2. *Control: Securing offices, rooms and facilities*

Physical security for offices, rooms and facilities shall be designed and implemented.

3. *Control: Equipment siting and protection*

Equipment shall be sited securely and protected.

4. *Control: Supporting utilities*

Information processing facilities shall be protected from power failures and other disruptions caused by failures in supporting utilities. Author's note: think power generators and uninterruptible power supply (UPS) units.

5. *Control: Cabling security*

Cables carrying power, data or supporting information services shall be protected from interception, interference or damage.

6. *Control: Storage media*

Storage media shall be managed through their life cycle of acquisition, use, transportation and disposal in accordance with the organization's classification scheme and handling requirements.

7. Control: Security of assets off-premises

Off-site assets shall be protected.

8. Control: Secure disposal or re-use of equipment

Items of equipment containing storage media shall be verified to ensure that any sensitive data and licensed software has been removed or securely overwritten prior to disposal or reuse."

Source: ISO/IEC 27001:2022.

5.4 The NIST Cybersecurity Framework

The US National Institute of Standards and Technology (NIST) is the US agency responsible for safely and securely advancing measurement science standards and technical innovation for the benefit of wider civil society, as well as the economy's necessary *"industrial competitiveness"* (NIST: 2022). NIST developed the Cybersecurity Framework (CSF) as a *"voluntary set of standards, guidelines, and practices designed to help organizations manage IT security risks"* (Kyber Security: 2019). According to experts at **Kyber Security**, two strong reasons why businesses should align to the CSF are:

1. **Compliance.** Its underpinning framework supports companies to achieve compliance with a whole range of data security requirements, including the EU GDPR, the US Federal Information Security Modernization Act (FISMA), the Payment Card Industry Data Security Standard (PCI DSS), the Health Insurance Portability and Accountability Act (HIPAA), the North American Electric Reliability Corporation Critical Infrastructure

Protection (NERC CIP), the Protecting Controlled Unclassified Information in Nonfederal Systems and Organizations – NIST 800-171 (NIST: 2020) and also the NIST Privacy Framework and Cyber Security Framework – NIST 800-53 (NIST Privacy Framework: 2020).

2. **Goal setting.** The CSF is categorised into "tiers", which helps organisations understand their current risk levels and where they need to get to. This specified goal setting *"opens up a conversation with upper management and IT about what constitutes an acceptable level of risk"* (Kyber Security: 2019).

NIST developed a cyber security framework (CSF) to enhance the nation's overall cyber security posture. Although aimed at federal agencies and those companies in the government supply chain, the CSF guidelines are applicable to any organisation, from academia to charities and private sector companies. NIST's cyber security framework is available free of charge while ISO charges for access to documentation. NIST CSF includes best practices and formalised standards to detect, prevent and respond to cyber incidents. Easy to apply for less cyber-security mature organisations, *"The framework's core is now organized around six key functions: Identify, Protect, Detect, Respond and Recover, along with CSF 2.0's newly added Govern function."* (NIST: 2024):

1. Identify.
2. Protect.
3. Detect.
4. Respond.
5. Recover.

6. Govern.

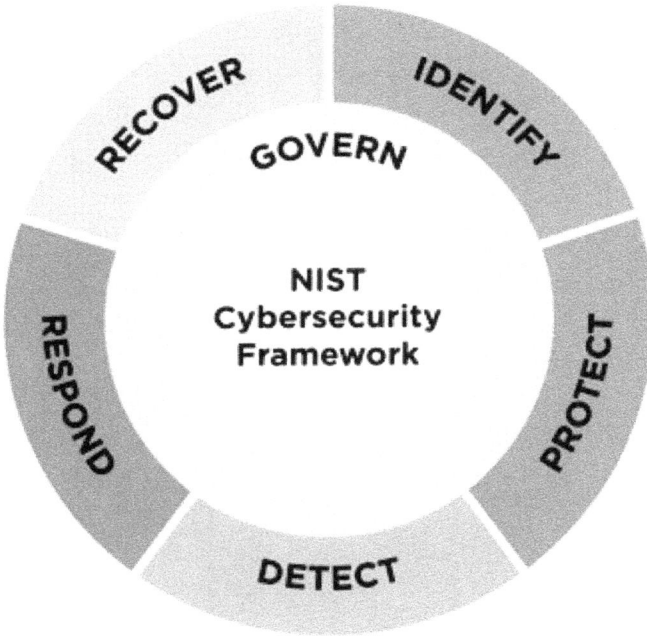

Figure 3: NIST Cybersecurity Framework – 6 Functions[4]

Mapping out these key functions helps an organisation design an overarching view of the IT security management systems required, as outlined below.

---

[4] Sourced from NIST website: *https://www.nist.gov/news-events/news/2023/08/nist-drafts-major-update-its-widely-used-cybersecurity-framework*.

1. **Identify:** Develop an organisational understanding of managing cyber security risks to: systems, assets, data and capabilities. This function includes:
   - Identifying critical enterprise processes and assets;
   - Documenting information flows;
   - Maintaining hardware and software inventories;
   - Establishing policies for cyber security that include roles and responsibilities; and
   - Identifying threats, vulnerabilities and risks to assets.
2. **Protect:** Develop and implement the appropriate safeguards to ensure delivery of services. This function includes:
   - Managing access to assets and information;
   - Protecting sensitive data;
   - Conducting regular backups;
   - Securely protecting your devices;
   - Managing device vulnerabilities; and
   - Training users.
3. **Detect.** Develop and implement the appropriate activities to identify the occurrence of a cyber security event. This function includes:
   - Testing and updating detection processes;
   - Maintaining and monitoring logs;
   - Knowing the expected data flows for your enterprise; and
   - Understanding the impact of cyber security events.

4. **Respond.** Develop and implement the appropriate activities to take action regarding a detected cyber security event. This function includes:
   - Ensuring response plans are tested;
   - Ensuring response plans are updated; and
   - Coordinating with internal and external stakeholders.
5. **Recover.** Develop and implement the appropriate activities to maintain plans for resilience and to restore any capabilities or services that were impaired due to a cyber security event. This function includes:
   - Communicating with internal and external stakeholders;
   - Ensuring recovery plans are updated; and
   - Managing public relations and company reputation (NIST Computer Security Resource Center: 2022).
6. **Govern.** In the updated version, NIST added this additional function. It covers:
   - *"How an organization can make and execute its own internal decisions to support its cybersecurity strategy"*; and
   - *How "cybersecurity is a major source of enterprise risk, ranking alongside legal, financial and other risks as considerations for senior leadership.""* (NIST: 2023).

How do you identify the level of cyber security maturity within an organisation? This author recommends using the CSF 'Capability Maturity Model' that enables you to track your progress as you move through the delivery phase. The model is a widely implemented cyber security maturity benchmarking tool.

5.5 Incident response

Data sets conveying cyber terrorism attack events are sparse, with 83 being identified as committed by ISIS and Al-Qaeda (2011–2016) by a joint university study (Lee et al: 2021). Distinguishing between 'cyber crime' and 'cyber terrorism' has perhaps produced more complexity for criminological statisticians than in the physical realm. As University College Dublin's (UCD) **Ray Genoe** reminds us: *"almost all crime has a digital element"* (UCD: 2013). The same truth runs for all aspects of contemporary terrorism too. Nonetheless, initial uncertainty and complexity – describable as the 'fog of war' – are the hallmarks of experiencing first-hand any major security incident. The motives and unfolding attack plan remain known only to the perpetrators as well as (possibly) those that are encouraging or coordinating them. Such extreme situational uncertainty and ambiguity are common in, at least, the early stages of any unfolding threat scenario. Particularly with terrorism or major-level cyber attacks whereby perpetrators – or their perceived backers – often use additional disinformation warfare tools such as 'false flags' deception, denial and time-consuming obfuscation. Moreover, many attackers will be familiar with basic human psychology. Namely, prolonged uncertainty causes anxiety, which often leads to an individual's demoralisation and depression: civilians under protracted *unnecessary* stress tend to quit, run away or surrender. Security management incident response is therefore, in many ways, the organisation's pre-prepared battle plan (which may include some form of lawful counter attack) to confront and triumph over an adversary that, at the beginning, holds most of the trump cards.

International approaches

The pre-eminent international standard for computer incident response is titled *ISO/IEC 27035-1:2023*, which concerns the management of information security events, incidents and vulnerabilities. ISO/IEC 27035 replaced the *ISO/IEC TR 18044:2004 – Security techniques – Information Security incident management.* 27035's full title – *Information technology – Information security incident management* – builds upon the response side of content found initially in ISO/IEC 27002. As with most standards, the content and frameworks are generally applicable to all organisations regardless of size, purpose and operating environment. Security standards serve as a basic skeleton of frameworks and control objectives: it really is for organisations on the ground to fully provide the strategic and operational colour and set the tone for their employees' information security.

ISO 27035 Part 1 provides for a five-phase incident management process:

1. **Prepare** to deal with major incidents: For example, to design and prepare an incident management policy and plan, as well as establish a competent computer incident response team (CIRT) to anticipate and deal with events (ISO Security Blog: 2023) .

2. **Identify** and report information security incidents: This process should include active detection and reporting. This could be done by an individual or security

operations centre (SOC) that identifies and reports on potential threats that might turn into incidents.

3. **Assess**: At this point, further evaluation of incidents will occur and the SOC manager, or relevant executive/s, will make decisions about how the threat or risk will be addressed. For instance, does the scenario warrant a 'light touch' to patch things up, then return to business quickly? Or should an intervention occur that involves collection of computer forensic evidence, even if this process creates delays? Risk evaluation and developing proposals that are 'courses of action' are key to the assessment phase.

4. **Respond:** Contain the incident effectively so that it ceases to damage the business, and investigate the incident further and fully. Resolve and address all findings completely. Move effectively through the incident management plan actively addressing the full spectrum of ongoing reputational, financial and safety and security issues.

5. **Learn lessons:** Identify, list and address all identified weakness and development areas. Be systematic about identifying vulnerabilities and integrate these weaknesses, and identified mitigation, into your continually improved security policies and plans.

ISO/IEC 27035 Part 2 *"provides guidelines to plan and prepare for incident response and to learn lessons from incident response"* (ISO/IEC 27035-2: 2023): 2023). Part 2 therefore aims to provide practical assurance that an organisation is battle-ready to respond to an incident. Part 2 is strong in emphasising the importance of learning lessons and integrating that organisational learning into planning and preparation for the future. It does this by providing content across nine main clauses, which is then brought to life with examples in the appendices of incident forms, categorisation approaches and notices of legal advice (particularly in relation to privacy). The nine main clauses, provided in their original numbers within the Standard, are as follows:

4. *"Information security incident management policy*

5. *Updating of information security policies*

6. *Creating information security incident management plan*

7. *Establishing an incident management capability*

8. *Establishing internal and external relationships*

9. *Defining technical and other support*

10. *Creating information security incident awareness and training*

11. *Testing the information security incident management plan*

12. *Learn lessons"* (ISO/IEC 27035:2-2023)

US approaches: NIST and incident response

According to cyber security experts, ConsultDTS, *"Organizations voluntarily follow NIST standards and may be asked to self-attest to a score of how well they adhere to certain standards for government contracting or other certifications. NIST does not provide any type of certification itself"* (ConsultDTS.com: 2023). NIST standards are widely familiar to non-US firms that either seek to export or operate within the world's largest economy NIST is *"responsible for developing guidelines and standards, including minimum requirements, for providing adequate information security for all agency operations and assets, but [...] may be used by nongovernmental organizations on a voluntary basis"* (NIST SP 800-61 Rev. 2: 2012: 13). NIST guidelines are very useful for organisations that may not be as operationally mature in cyber security and information systems risk management by offering more specific planning and goal-setting details. *NIST SP 800-61 Rev. 2 (2012) Computer Security Incident Handling Guide* serves as a comprehensive set of business security and continuity-related frameworks to assist organisations to contain, manage and recover from major information security events. This guide breaks down our understanding and management of incident response into a lifecycle **(see Figure 4)**.

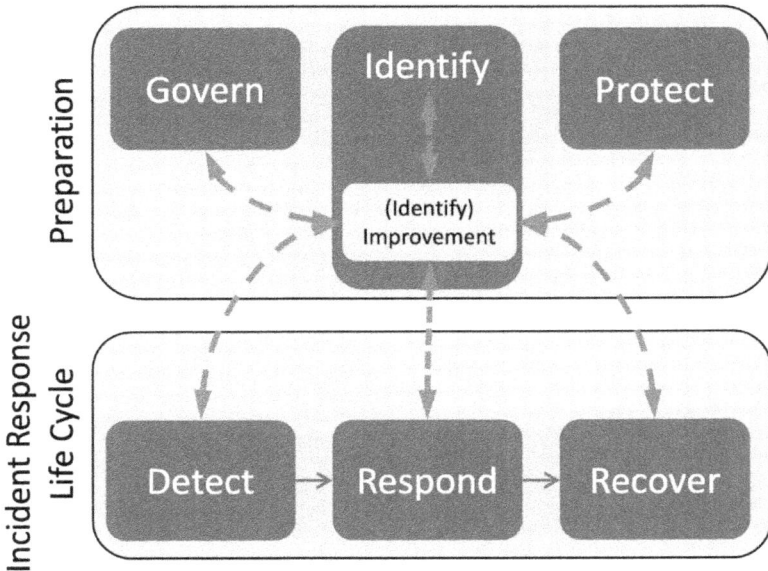

Figure 4: NIST Incident Response Life Cycle[5]

Key control objectives within NIST's incident response lifecycle

Preparation:

Designing the battle plan within peacetime. Namely, before any major incident has hit your organisation. Extrapolated from NIST SP 800-61 Rev. 2, guidance for your top preparation functions includes:

Recruiting and training a designated organisational computer incident response team (CIRT).

---

[5] Sourced from NIST website: *https://csrc.nist.gov/projects/incident-response*.

Acquiring and providing necessary tools and resources to support the team and Incident Management (IM) operation, including a "war room" for central coordination and communications, and a secure storage area for evidence.

Gathering together contact information, including primary and backup contacts for the CIRT, core business functions, leadership and key stakeholders, including within the supply chain and media. Integrating into a tangible IM contact plan.

Maintaining spare IT equipment, including laptops, workstations, cabling, networking equipment, blank removable media, new smartphones, portable printers, batteries and power backup, etc.

Evidence-gathering tools, including digital forensic software (packet sniffers and network analysers), hardbound notebooks, digital cameras, storage bags (including Faraday bags to protect electronic devices), lots of pre-printed chain of custody forms, and incident reporting forms as well as feedback loops, in part to enable anonymous reporting.

Remembering that prevention is better than the cure. Conducting staff-wide cyber security awareness training. Encrypting and protecting all security, incident management and business continuity plans. Conducting risk assessments, actively treating and reviewing security threats and vulnerabilities.

Detect:

Extrapolated from NIST SP 800-61 Rev. 2 guidance, your top detection and analysis functions include:

Understanding common threat vectors and promoting this understanding through baseline staff-wide cyber security awareness training. In cyber terrorism domains, common threat vectors are the following:

1. Network infiltration/exfiltration using removable media.
2. Phishing emails and digital media links to target individuals, groups and organisations.
3. Distributed denial-of-service (DDoS) attacks to render networks ineffectual.
4. Social engineering and impersonation attacks, usually to target individuals (including bodyguards and communications managers who have privileged access to VIPs).
5. Malware used for wiping data systems, ransom and extortion (terrorist fundraising).
6. Malicious communications – including disseminating videos depicting torture and murder (possibly of friends/colleagues) to target groups and organisations.
7. Theft of computer equipment.

Intrusion detection and prevention systems (IDPS) can be deployed to automate and continuously monitor your information systems. IDPS include antivirus software, **next generation firewalls (NGFWs)** – which provide ransomware, spam protection and endpoint security – as well as log analysers. Many IDPS solutions are highly effective and modestly priced. They provide additional layers of security and assurance, particularly for micro-companies and SMEs, who may well be overly confident in assuming that existing Software-as-a-Service (SaaS) products that they use (for example, customer relationship management systems) also provide them with 100% cyber security.

Experienced and/or trained employees. Many IT administrators are highly competent but lack security awareness. Moreover, many security officers are effective in physical and environmental domains but lack competency in understanding or recognising cyber threats. Those tasked with detecting and analysing potential computer security incidents must be able to notice and understand *"an unusual deviation from typical network traffic flows"* (NIST 800-61 Rev. 2: 2012: 27).

The art of threat intelligence – converging human and technical security intelligence for the purposes of organisational resilience – is very briefly covered earlier in the risk identification areas of this chapter. Nonetheless, for those responsible for technical security detection and threat analysis, you will need a deep dive and we refer you to: *NIST SP 800-94, Guide to Intrusion Detection and Prevention Systems (2007)*, for the full gamut of guidance and suggested framework controls. There was an attempt to update the document during 2012 but the redraft never saw daylight. The veteran NIST IDPS standard is available online at the NIST library and we have included the link within references chapter at the end of this book. There is also lots of cyber threat Intelligence information in NIST 800-61. Rev. 2: 2012, sandwiched between pages 27–44. Again, within the references chapter, you will find the publication link. (Free and open source at the time of writing this book.)

Respond:

Containment is a critical security objective, before the incident overwhelms or catastrophically damages the business. Containment can stymie the threat and buy time for eradication and recovery strategies to take effect.

Extrapolated from NIST SP 800-61 Rev. 2 guidance on your top containment, eradication and recovery functions include:

Containment: Organisations should put in place separate and different containment strategies for each type of realised threat. Many business impacts to a major incident will be similar but threat containment strategies can be distinctly different and diverse. A fundamental requirement of effective containment strategy is decision-making and putting in place the appropriate technical responses. Decisions to establish the following are required:

1. Realistic estimation of duration.
2. Realistic assessment of resources required (internal and external).
3. Assessment of immediate, extra security controls to sustain systems availability and integrity.
4. Requirements for evidence protection and notification to authorities including regulators.

Eradication: For some incidents, eradication is not required or is performed during the recovery phase. Swift moves to *"eradication may be necessary to eliminate components of the incident, such as deleting malware and disabling breached user accounts, as well as identifying and mitigating all vulnerabilities that were exploited"* (NIST SP 800-61 Rev. 2: 2012: 37). But, on the whole, *"eradication and recovery should be done in a phased approach so that remediation steps are prioritized"* (NIST SP 800-61 Rev. 2: 2012: 37). Eradication can sometimes come into conflict with evidence-gathering and storage. Tactical dilemmas such as this will often be discussed within a CIRT or SOC. Evidence-gathering and handling guidance is provided within NIST SP 800-61. Rev. 2 (see Section 3.3.2), including how to maintain incident logs and documenting the chain of custody involved. Such information should include the names, times, dates, locations, reasons, actions of those who have accessed or handled any evidence, as well as naming the individual ultimately responsible for the accrued evidence. For more detailed information on collecting, storing and handling evidence (physical and digital) we refer you through to NIST SP 800-86, Guide to Integrating Forensic Techniques into Incident Response (2006) another dependable old workhorse for cyber security professionals. Alternatively, the international standard covering the initial capturing of digital evidence is titled: ISO/IEC 27037:2012 Information technology – Security techniques – Guidelines for identification, collection, acquisition and preservation of digital evidence. Another veteran standard, which is in dire need of being brought together with (four) other related digital evidence standards, nonetheless this standard provides decent guidance in due process for capturing data from the following devices and circumstances: *"digital storage media used in standard computers like hard drives, floppy disks, optical and magneto optical disks, data devices with similar functions; mobile phones, Personal Digital Assistants (PDAs), Personal Electronic Devices (PEDs), memory cards; mobile navigation systems; digital still and video cameras (including CCTV); standard computer with network connections; networks based on TCP/IP and other digital protocols; and devices with similar functions as above"* (ISO Security.com: 2023).

Recovery: Perhaps the most delicate stage of the incident response lifecycle, akin *"to carrying a Ming vase across a highly polished floor"* (to borrow British politician Roy Jenkins' famous quote about leaders facing political minefields). For large-scale incidents, recovery may take months or years, and full recovery may not even be achievable. Recovery should encompass a broad range of technical and non-technical interventions. A golden rule: don't force the speed of recovery. Phase your recovery: don't commit to too much too soon. Don't overwhelm information systems that may still be functioning abnormally. Equally, don't overwhelm employees who, on the surface, may look and sound 100% effective. Especially if you remain unclear as to whether the threat has been entirely eradicated. Another good rule of thumb: only ever introduce the longer-term, bigger changes, towards the end of any discernible recovery period.

Technical interventions include the following:

1. Prioritise remediation steps.
2. Restore systems for clean backups.
3. Replace potentially compromised files and software with new versions.
4. Change passwords across the entire network.
5. Reboot slowly, carefully, at low-usage times to start with.
6. Enhance perimeter security (even if you have unravelled an insider threat), review and tighten firewall rulesets and boundary router access control lists.
7. Consider rebuilding systems from scratch.

Non-technical interventions include the following:

1. Ensuring hands-on leadership continues by maintaining a regular and resourced crisis recovery group. This should involve the senior management team and any significant primary stakeholder/s, if appropriate.

2. Media handling: continuing operating with tight scripting (agreed lines) and by implementing a structured, scheduled communications plan. Such a crisis communications plan and its main content – including agreed spokespersons and 'lines to take' – should have been developed and approved during the preparation phase, known widely as the 'pre-crisis' phase within the crisis management industry.

3. Being careful to sustain continued, relevant and professional internal communications to keep employees informed and also to stave off demoralisation against their own organisation. In larger organisations, particularly, assume such messages will leak onto digital media platforms or be passed into the hands of news reporters. Therefore, depending on the wider situational context and the gravity of impacts, avoid cheap demonstrations of humour, negative uncertainty or speculation, casting or accepting blame. Continue to emphasise positive organisational and individual behaviour and achievements, and to provide upbeat reassurance (implicitly or explicitly) that the company is and will remain a positive and resilient environment that views its workforce as its number one asset.

4. Being aware that after a major incident, your organisation is at its weakest. (Despite the very necessary upbeat oratory that will soon be required to be espoused by your organisation's bosses). Cyber domains are slightly different to physical environments in that the attacker is usually far more anonymous, it takes longer

to identify them, and as such far longer for law enforcement to intervene against them. Be aware, then, that: *"Once a resource is successfully attacked, it is often attacked again, or other resources within the organization are attacked in a similar manner"* (NIST SP 800-61 Rev. 2: 2012: 37).

5. For reasons stated above – particularly in understanding the mindsets of your adversaries and harshest critics (do bear in mind that the quantity of both threat types escalates following any publicly known security incident) – be very cautious around making any explicit 'Mission Accomplished'-type declarations. You will inevitably come under pressure to make such a declaration, but ask yourself: To what extent is such a public declaration necessary? Other than to serve your adversaries with a platter of highly-tempting 'Catch Me If You Can' challenges. Put simply, far better to keep your organisation's recovery low key with the right level of thanks – and enhanced monitoring – directed into the right places.

Recover:

This stage is mostly about learning the lessons about the cause of the incident and evaluating its business impact. After this assessment and evaluation, a post-incident report that provides suggested recommendations and/or courses of action can be developed and shared. A post-incident report that details the cost, other impacts and recommendations to the executive board should give the organisation the best possible chance of preventing a similar event.

At senior management team (SMT) level, an overarching 'lessons learned' workshop should be held. This could be in the format of an 'away day' or two. Board members should engage with the causes, impacts and recommended mitigation, probably by holding interactive discussions on each of these three areas, adopting a no-blame approach and in sessions facilitated by independent peers.

It would be unwise for this report to only be discussed as a brief agenda item at an executive board. Moreover, to only superficially reflect upon the report, perhaps with a standing item on the board agenda every six or twelve months. Not least because, if lessons remain unlearned, then a major security incident is more likely to happen again. In this perceivably avoidable scenario, regulators, significant stakeholders (read: customers, advisory board members, sector notables, policy-makers, law-makers and judges, members of the public) will in likelihood lose any residual sympathy to an organisation, its leadership and security team, that repeatedly gets attacked and loses.

At a tactical level, the CIRT should conduct similar structured 'lessons learned' sessions in the cold light of day after the post-incident report is published. These are distinctly different to debriefing sessions. Debriefs are all about coaxing out a mix of positive and negative ideas, fixes and reflections, often during the immediate aftermath of an event or on a daily schedule when the mind can still retrieve useful tactical information (and also express more instinctive, survivalist emotions). Debriefs should therefore be held as contemporaneously as possible, if safe and sensible to do so. Accurate documenting and note-taking capabilities during debriefing are absolutely vital for the purposes of capturing ground-truth ingredients, which, in turn, should directly inform any overarching post-incident report. When employees raise points in debriefing sessions and their meaning is not clear, the note-taker or facilitator should request clarifications. Contributions should be anonymised or names coded or masked when stored in hard copies or electronic files.

There are few better ways to test your organisation's cyber resilience against cyber terrorism than by deploying experts and/or training in-house staff to carry out ethical hacking on your own systems. A number of training organisations run certified penetration testing courses and exams, and in the 'key organisations' section below we provide an overview of CREST – the Council for Registered Ethical Security Testers. Others options include the CompTIA PenTest+; EC-Council's Certified Ethical Hacker (CEH) and Licensed Penetration Tester Master (LPT) Certification; and Offensive Security's popular Offensive Security Certified Professional (OSCP) certification (Hackerone.com: 2023). One thing to bear in mind is that you can and should never guarantee to your customers and stakeholders that you will never lose their data or suffer a physically significant cyber attack. As NIST 800-61 reminds us: *"residual risk will inevitably persist after controls are implemented"* (NIST SP 800-61 Rev. 2: 2012: 30).[6]

---

[6] IT Governance offers courses on ethical hacking. For more information visit: *https://www.itgovernance.co.uk/ethical-hacking*.

CONCLUDING REMARKS

Like so much terminology in the complex and ambiguous world of criminological study, this author acknowledges that for many readers the term 'cyber terrorism' remains an essentially contestable concept with several meanings and nuances. (Show me a criminology term that isn't?!) This book's purpose was not to prove this phrase's validity or literal interpretation, although the definitions provided within chapter 1 are surely helpful and have underpinned this publication's content. For those that remain cautiously cynical, hopefully this author has at least established that alongside digital media and other evolutions in advanced tech, one clear consequence has been the arrival of a much higher level of generalised terror threat. Vast swathes of the public have recognised this, opinion surveys show, but the tools and resources to take swifter, firmer action to prevent threats becoming realised have been slow and inconsistently applied (so far) within most national jurisdictions. One problematic area within terrorism prevention is understanding the phenomenon of violent lone actors, sometimes understood or misunderstood to be 'lone wolves'. This research points to a conclusion that in most serious cases of supposed single-actor terrorism cases, the Internet and other Internet users played a significant or pivotal role in nurturing and activating a particular individual. Whether somebody feels they are furthering the cause of a global caliphate, or racial superiority, or the defeat of radical feminism, most lone actors since the advent of digital media have been very much inspired, assisted and – in some cases directed – by others within their online network. The fact is, that without cybersphere enablement, at least several atrocities would not have occurred.

Moreover, this book sought to practically address just some of the steps that we can all realistically take in facing up to humanity's latest technical security challenge. From the content shown within this publication, it appears somewhat fanciful to assume that big tech firms or legislators wield most of the preventive power here. In fact, the more we look at it, the more we discover that most solutions are pretty much grassroots up, driven by all of us end users. As such, from what I can tell, it's difficult to conclude that big tech firms, governments and international forums possess those magic solutions that sufficiently match the issue at hand. Law-makers and tech firms simply do not have enough kryptonite in their pockets to make much of a dent into online terrorism. Especially when we consider that so many nation states who turn a blind eye to cyber terrorism, or 'facilitate' cyber terrorism, have developed their own advanced technologies and ISPs that almost match Meta and Alphabet in size and reach.

Nonetheless, at a political-decision-making level, this book should be translated to reflect my research position that cyber terrorism is a tangible, distinct, social phenomenon that merits significant additional resource for further criminological evaluation and law-enforcement support. The latter could involve mandatory (at least baseline) digital awareness and forensics training for all police officers, investigators and prosecutors. One of the investigative upsides of cyber terrorism is that – if investigated correctly – there is such a rich (digital) evidence trail. This online treasure trove can unlock many connected individuals and incidents and physical evidence sets. Two decades into facing this digital-crime phenomenon, it is very alarming that such a high preponderance of post-investigation reports and inquiries into terror-related incidents highlight the fact that family, friends, colleagues or other computer network users repeatedly raised concerns about the serious threat posed by an individual. The clue lay in knowing the transgressor's online behaviour. Surely, this type of information should be viewed at least as importantly as any other form of significant *community intelligence*, some might ask? Far too often, such insightful and courageous reports (terrorism tip-offs) have been treated as low risk because they can't easily be corroborated or family chatter is viewed as hearsay, gossip even. Rather brutally, then, terrorism cases involving cyber enablement have often been pushed back towards families or businesses to deal with. Therefore, one of the key prevention challenges is, we posit, to ensure that those who do courageously come forward (by providing critical information and spending huge amounts of personal time and effort to do so) are made more aware of the range of existing laws that can help local police forces to mobilise for a formal investigation or intervention that potentially ends in a prosecution as well as a public safety solution. For the purposes of civil society legal-awareness building, we include the latest formal list of cyber crimes. Within that legal spine, you will find described certain actions and behaviours that could lead to prosecution. (See this book's Appendix E , which provide the UK Crown Prosecution Service guidance summary for prosecutors.)

Finally, we will close this project by accentuating history's harshest but least learned lesson. The failure of those in influencing positions – such as parents and guardians, teachers, business leaders and law-makers – to actively promote, encourage and mandate (if necessary) behavioural ethics for those under their care and responsibility. If tried-

and-trusted societal ethics are not taught and inculcated sufficiently, then any good system will corrode, break and eventually expire. Our digital ecosphere is no different. Computer ethics matter. Every user should learn them, stick by them, teach them, represent them unto others. At this point, we can go back into 'here's one we made earlier' mode and introduce or remind readers of **Ramon Barquin's** totemic "Ten Commandments for Computer Ethics":

1. *"Thou shalt not use a computer to harm other people.*
2. *Thou shalt not interfere with other people's computer work.*
3. *Thou shalt not snoop around in other people's computer files.*
4. *Thou shalt not use a computer to steal.*
5. *Thou shalt not use a computer to bear false witness.*
6. *Thou shalt not copy or use proprietary software for which you have not paid.*
7. *Thou shalt not use other people's computer resources without authorization or proper compensation.*
8. *Thou shalt not appropriate other people's intellectual output.*
9. *Thou shalt think about the social consequences of the program you are writing or the system you are designing.*
10. *Thou shalt always use a computer in ways that insure consideration and respect for your fellow humans"* (Ramon Barquin, Computer Ethics Institute: 1992).

If, for whatever reason, we can't bring ourselves to lead in this space and commit to these, then maybe it's worth reflecting upon former NSA technical director Robert Morris's prophetic words. After chasing the first generation of cyber criminals and helping to jail (and recruit) the most dangerous, Morris discovered it was his own son who bore responsibility for unleashing the world's worst computer worm. His offspring reportedly brought down a significant chunk of the then embryonic Internet. In retirement-mode, Morris senior reportedly opened up to an Infosec event audience: *"The three golden rules to ensure computer security are: do not own a computer; do not power it on; and do not use it"* (WebDeveloperNotes.com). I'm not, at this point, seriously advocating these nuggets of wisdom. But we do need to go back to basics somewhat and treat our Internet with kid gloves.

Richard Bingley.

London, 2024.

APPENDIX A: KEY ORGANISATIONS AND DIGITAL PLATFORMS

- **Action Counters Terrorism (ACT).** UK only. Run by Counter Terrorism Policing, ACT provides the online reporting portal for suspected terrorism and violent extremism offences and behaviours. Good baseline advise for ascertaining behaviour and actions that may be fairly considered reportable is provided online as well as basic security training and information about the 'Run Hide Tell' campaign.
  Website: *https://act.campaign.gov.uk/*.
  Twitter (now X): *https://Twitter.com/TerrorismPolice*.

- **America Institute of Certified Public Accountants (AICPA):** AICPA has developed a set of Trust Services Criteria (TSC), which is now widely applied within the US and, increasingly, around the world for audit procurement purposes. Service organisations are expected to undertake System and Organisational Controls (SOC) audits. A SOC 2 audit report provides detailed information and assurance about a service organisation's security, availability, processing integrity, confidentiality and privacy controls. These are the five benchmarks to satisfy AICPA's now omnipotent TSC requirements.
  You can learn more about AICPA's SOC for cyber security here:

https://www.aicpa-cima.com/resources/download/learn-about-soc-for-cybersecurity.
You can learn more about AICPA's SOC for the supply chain here:
https://www.aicpa-cima.com/resources/download/learn-about-soc-for-supply-chain.

- **Australia's Cyber and Infrastructure Security Centre (CISC):** Assists critical infrastructure personnel to understand cyber risk and meet regulatory requirements in Australia. CISC Australia deploys a network of outreach officers and publishes "risk assessment advisories". It recruited an inaugural National Cyber Security Coordinator in 2023. Follow links below to find out more:
  Website: *https://www.cisc.gov.au/*.
  Twitter (now X): *https://Twitter.com/CyberGovAU*.

- **Big Brother Watch (BBW):** Based in the UK, and a little like the American non-profit EFF (see below), BBW has fought and prevailed in several landmark legal cases whereby its supporters perceive counter terrorism and crime prevention initiatives using surveillance have been deployed unlawfully. BBW describes itself as *"a UK civil liberties campaign group fighting for a free future. We're determined to reclaim our privacy and defend freedoms at this time of enormous technological change".*
  Website: *https://bigbrotherwatch.org.uk/*.

Twitter (now X):
https://Twitter.com/BigBrotherWatch.

- **Black Hat:** Founded in 1997, Black Hat is an internationally recognised cyber security event series providing the most technical and relevant information security research. Grown from a single annual conference to the most respected information security event series internationally, these multi-day events provide the security community with the latest cutting-edge research, developments and trends.
  Website: *https://www.blackhat.com/*.
  Twitter (now X): *https://Twitter.com/BlackHatEvents*.

- **Chartered Institute of Information Security (CIISec):** In its own words, *"CIISec is an independent not-for-profit governed by its members, ensuring standards of professionalism for training, qualifications, operating practices and individuals"*. It's annual flagship event is CIISEC Live and the organisation's website signposts a number of initiatives including links to the Institute of Cyber Digital Investigation Professionals (ICDIP). ICDIP's accreditations are overseen by the UK College of Policing. CIISEC and ICDIP can be found at:
  CIISEC website: *https://www.ciisec.org/*.

- **Christchurch Call:** A high-level political and tech leaders' forum established to *"eliminate terrorist and violent extremist content online"*. Supporters of the Christchurch Call hold an annual leaders' summit and have made 25 commitments that promote security interventions amid maintaining *"human rights and a free, open, secure internet"*. One significant work programme is titled 'Algorithms and Positive Interventions' whereby tech firms attempt to make search redirections or influence a person away from automated content suggestions prompted by algorithms. Find out more at:

Website: *https://www.christchurchcall.com/*.

More information about the USA/New Zealand, Microsoft and Twitter (now X) initiative for 'Algorithms and Positive Interventions' can be found at: *https://www.christchurchcall.com/media-and-resources/news-and-updates/christchurch-call-initiative-on-algorithmic-outcomes/*.

- **Committee of Sponsoring Organizations (COSO):** COSO publishes and specifies an *Internal Control – Integrated Framework* (2013) for information security. According to COSO, the framework of 17 security "principles" aims to broaden the application of internal control in addressing operations and reporting objectives and clarify the requirements for determining what constitutes effective internal control Further information can be found at:

  Website: *https://wwwcoso.org*.

- **Counter-Terrorism Policing (CTP).** Counter Terrorism Policing is a collaboration of **UK** police forces working with intelligence partners to prevent, deter and investigate terrorist activity. CTP's strategy is named the '4Ps': four key counter-terrorism areas to focus on: 1) **Prevent** people being drawn into radicalisation; 2) **Pursue** terrorists and bring them to justice; 3) **Protect** the public from terror attacks; and 4) **Prepare** to respond to terror attacks and minimise their impact (*http://counterterrorism.police.uk*, Counter Terrorism Policing website: 2023).

In the UK, you can report online material for promoting terrorism or extremism at: *https://www.gov.uk/report-terrorism.* Or via Counter Terrorism Policing's 'Action Counters Terrorism' website reporting portal at: *https://act.campaign.gov.uk/*.

- **Council for Registered Ethical Security Testers (CREST):** CREST is part of a consortium with CIISec and Royal Holloway University of London (RHUL), who are certification bodies for the certified professional scheme. There are few better ways to test your organisation's cyber resilience against cyber terrorism than by deploying experts and/or training in-house staff to carry out ethical hacking on your own systems.
  Website: *https://www.crest-approved.org/*.
  Twitter (now X): *https://Twitter.com/crestadvocate*.

- **Crown Prosecution Service (CPS).** The United Kingdom's national prosecution agency determines and presents cases to the British criminal courts for consideration. The substantive range of laws that enable victims and police to take action and investigate cases of potential cyber crime – including malicious communication, online harassment, child pornography, fraud, theft, eavesdropping, hacking and sabotage – are listed at the CPS's online cyber-crime prosecution guidance portal (CPS 2019):

Website: *https://www.cps.gov.uk/legal-guidance/cybercrime-prosecution-guidance*.

The CPS's Special Crime and Counter Terrorism Division (SCCTD) website pages provide useful further counter-terrorism information at: *https://www.cps.gov.uk/special-crime-and-counter-terrorism-division-scctd*.

Case summaries of successful prosecutions are available online at this website but can only be accessed by authorised personnel.

- **CSARN Global Cyber Academy (GCA):** CSARN's GCA is a fully-accredited training and education centre designed to familiarise and educate non-tech and tech executives in the fields of counter-extremism, terrorism and information systems risk management. Located in the UK and United Arab Emirates, the Academy's mission operates under the community banner: 'Technology and Risk Explained'. It produces a monthly Security Risk Monitor with the famous 'Risk Chapter'. Further information can be found at:

  Website: *https://globalcyberacademy.com/*.

  Website: *https://uae.globalcyberacademy.com/*.

- **Cybersecurity and Infrastructure Security Agency (CISA).** CISA leads the US national effort to understand, manage and reduce risk to its cyber and physical infrastructure.

  Website: *https://www.cisa.gov/*.

Twitter (now X): *https://Twitter.com/CISAgov*.

- **Dark Reading:** With more than 300,000 followers, DR describes itself as *"one of the most widely read and trusted cybersecurity news sites, providing IT security professionals informed insights into the latest news and trends"*. Bolstered by M-Trends (Mandiant) threat landscape reports, it produces some of the best insight into cyber security risks out there.
  Website: *https://www.darkreading.com/*.
  Twitter (now X): *https://Twitter.com/DarkReading*.

- **DEFCON:** The most famous and probably largest physical gathering of hackers in the metaverse or anywhere else. Many hackers at DefCon have put on their finest white hats to help us lesser technical mortals to (at least) understand the impact, even if we still fail to compute exactly how the threat can materialise!
  Website: *https://defcon.org/*.
  Twitter (now X): *https://Twitter.com/defcon*.

- **Electronic Frontier Foundation (EFF):** In its own words the *"Electronic Frontier Foundation is the leading nonprofit organization defending civil liberties in the digital world. Founded in 1990, EFF champions user privacy, free expression, and innovation through impact litigation, policy analysis, grassroots activism, and technology development. EFF's mission is to ensure that technology supports freedom, justice, and innovation for all people of the world"*. EFF has fought and won several landmark legal victories in America that curb – what their supporters perceive to be –

overweening governmental and corporate attempts to control the internet.

Website: *https://www.eff.org/*.

Twitter (now X): *https://Twitter.com/eff*.

- **EU Internet Forum (EUIF):** The EUIF launched by the European Commission in December 2015, addresses the misuse of the Internet for terrorist purposes through two main strands of action: 1) reducing accessibility to terrorist content online; and 2) increasing the volume of effective alternative narratives online. Under this umbrella operates 'Europol's Internet Referral Unit (EU IRU) to combat terrorist and violent extremist propaganda' as well as the EU Crisis Protocol (2019), a rapid and co-ordinated response process between nations and tech firms to contain the viral spread of terrorist and violent extremist content online. Important EUIF links include:

  EUIF website: *https://home-affairs.ec.europa.eu/networks/european-union-internet-forum-euif_en*.

  EU IRU website:
  https://www.europol.europa.eu/media-press/newsroom/news/europol%e2%80%99s-internet-referral-unit-to-combat-terrorist-and-violent-extremist-propaganda.

  EU Crisis Protocol:
  https://ec.europa.eu/commission/presscorner/detail/en/IP_19_6009.

- **Exploit Database** – The ultimate archive of #Exploits #Shellcodes #SecurityPapers and #ezones
  Website: *https://www.exploit-db.com/*.
  Twitter (now X): *https://Twitter.com/ExploitDB*.

- **FBI Cyber Threat Center:** According to the organisation's website, the FBI is *"the lead federal agency for investigating cyber attacks and intrusions. We collect and share intelligence and engage with victims while working to unmask those committing malicious cyber activities, wherever they are"* (FBI: 2023). A neat set of summaries, guidance and reporting lines can be found at the FBI's cyber centre website, link below:
  Website: *https://www.fbi.gov/investigate/cyber*.

- **GitHub Security:** Git Hub of old is a Cloud-based service for software development and version control using Git., enabling developers to collaborate, store and manage their code. Acquired by Microsoft in 2018, GitHub hosts open source software development projects for 100 million developers worldwide.
  Website: *https://github.com/security*.
  Twitter: *https://Twitter.com/github*.

- **Global Internet Forum to Counter Terrorism (GIFCT):** GIFCT's mission is to serve as an NGO designed to prevent terrorists and violent extremists from exploiting digital platforms. Founded by Facebook, Microsoft, Twitter and YouTube in 2017, the forum was established to *"foster technical collaboration among member companies, advance relevant research,* and share knowledge with smaller platforms". (GIFCT: 2023).

The GIFCT launched a **Content Incident Protocol (CIP)** in 2019 and now acts as a hub to share hashed content used by terrorists.

Website: *https://gifct.org/about/.*

Content Incident Protocol: *https://gifct.org/content-incident-protocol/.*

- **Global Partnership on Artificial Intelligence (GPIA):** Launched in 2020 following a G7 summit, GPIA is an emerging powerhouse behind policy debate and driving forward discussions on "Responsible AI". The coalition (to date) including 29 national governments, researchers and tech leaders, are, hopefully, increasingly moving towards turning words into action. One workstream titled 'Optimising social media recommender systems for a socially positive outcome' seems to be the place to address counter-terrorism but it's early days. Initiatives and updates can be found at:
  Website: *https://gpai.ai/.*

- **Google YouTube:** For more information about Google YouTube security initiatives, check out its reporting at the following portal:
  https://transparencyreport.google.com/youtube-policy/featured-policies/violent-extremism?hl=en.

- **Incels and misogynist violent extremism:** A superb insight and overview captured by documentary maker Ben Zand in UNTOLD: *The Secret World of Incels.* Channel 4 Documentaries. (Length: 47.15). Published:

07/11/2022. Accessed and downloaded on 06/06/2023 at: *https://www.youtube.com/watch?v=kReeoKoOvZI.* A list of some prominent incidents and an explanation of why many experts feel misogyny should be formally acknowledged as an *"animating ideology for acts of mass violence in comparison to recognition of other ideologies"* can be found on: Wikipedia at: *https://en.wikipedia.org/wiki/Misogynist_terrorism.*

- ***InfoSecurity Magazine:*** Probably the most generalist, comprehensive website for cyber security professionals and well worth subscribing to the weekly bulletins if you are a non-technical security risk manager too. Events, podcasts, white papers and a company directory available online too.
  Website: *https://www.infosecurity-magazine.com/.*
  Twitter (now X): *https://Twitter.com/InfosecurityMag.*
- **Information Systems Security Association (ISSA):** US-based association with a global reach of cyber security professionals. According to ISSA's mission statement: *"ISSA is a nonprofit organization for the information security profession committed to promoting effective cyber security on a global basis.*
  Being a respected forum for networking and collaboration.
  Providing education and knowledge sharing at all career lifecycle stages.
  Being a highly regarded voice of information security that influences public opinion, government legislation,

education and technology with objective expertise that supports sound decision-making" (ISSA: 2023).
Website: *https://www.issa.org/*.

- **International Centre for Counter Terrorism (ICCT):** Headquartered in The Hague, Netherlands, the ICCT is an independent think-and-do tank providing multidisciplinary policy advice and practical support focused on prevention, the rule of law and current and emerging threats – three important parts of effective counter-terrorism work. ICCT's work stretches internationally, and focuses on countering violent extremism, criminal justice sector responses, and human rights related aspects of counter-terrorism.
  Website: *https://www.icct.nl/*.

- **International Organization for Standardization (ISO).** Headquartered in Geneva, Switzerland, the ISO is an international standard development organisation composed of representatives from the national standards organisations of member countries. For more information on the ISO/IEC 27000 series of standards go to:
  https://www.iso.org/standard/27001.

A proposed ISO international standard (ISO/IEC: 27090) – *Cybersecurity Artificial Intelligence: Guidance for addressing security threats to artificial intelligence systems* – is presently being drafted and due for release in 2025 (ISO website: 2023).

For more information on computer incident response and ISO 27035: 2020-2023:

https://www.iso27001security.com/html/27035.html.

- **JihadoScope:** Monitors jihadist activity across the web and social media. Tweets are in English and French. It is open to direct messaging. The website is a work in progress but JS's Twitter feed carries lots of up-to-date, relevant snippets and reports for security and organisational resilience people.
  Twitter (now X): *https://Twitter.com/JihadoScope*.

- **Middle East Media Research Institute (MEMRI):** According to the institute's website, MEMRI explores *"the Middle East and South Asia through their media, MEMRI bridges the language gap between the West and the Middle East and South Asia, providing timely translations of Arabic, Farsi, Urdu-Pashtu, Dari, Turkish, Russian, and Chinese media, as well as original analysis of political, ideological, intellectual, social, cultural, and religious trends. Founded in February 1998 to inform the debate over U.S. policy in the Middle East, MEMRI is an independent, nonpartisan, nonprofit, 501(c)3 organization. MEMRI's main office is located in Washington, DC, with branch offices in various world capitals"*. Its full news article service is subscription based.

  MEMRI's Cyber Terrorism and Jihad Lab can be accessed at:
  Website: *https://www.memri.org/cjlab*.
  Twitter (now X):
  https://Twitter.com/MEMRIReports?ref_src=twsrc%5 Egoogle%7Ctwcamp%5Eserp%7Ctwgr%5Eauthor.

Since MEMRI's cyber terrorism and jihad lab monitoring service began, dozens of their in-house research articles have explained just how terrorists are targeting humanity via broadcasts hosted on YouTube. Just a small sample can be found at the following "Testing YouTube's Terrorism-Flagging Feature" link: *https://www.memri.org/cjlab/categories/testing-youtubes-terrorism-promoting-flagging-feature*.

- **MITRE ATT&CK®:** Based in Virginia, US, MITRE describes itself as a *"globally-accessible knowledge base of adversary tactics and techniques based on real-world observations"*. At the time of writing, the website's front page provided a comprehensive *"attack matrix for enterprise"* that identifies the ten techniques used for hostile reconnaissance. MITRE's attack blog covers incisive, up-to-date vulnerabilities across the most widely used enterprise operating systems (OS) and popular mobile products.
  Website: *http://attack.mitre.org/*.
  Attack blog: *https://medium.com/mitre-attack*.
  Twitter (now X): *https://Twitter.com/MITREattack*.

- **National Cyber Security Centre, Ireland (NCSC IE):** Founded in 2011. Useful for a weekly media summary of cyber incidents and stories from around the world. The NCSC is, in its own words, *"responsible for advising and informing Government IT and Critical National Infrastructure providers of current threats and vulnerabilities associated with network information* *security"*. The website front page provides an incident report link.

Website: *https://www.ncsc.gov.ie/*.

Twitter (now X): *https://Twitter.com/ncsc_gov_ie*.

- **National Cyber Security Centre UK (NCSC):** The UK government's cyber security centre was established to protect UK businesses from cyber attacks as well as to advise on technical security standards. NCSC's Cyber Security Toolkit for Boards includes a good range of basic-level advice from conducting risk assessments to sample scripts and considerations for board meetings, available in its 'Tool Box' link.

  Website: *https://www.ncsc.gov.uk/collection/board-toolkit*.

  The latest NCSC threat reports can be found or signposted at the following website URL:

  https://www.ncsc.gov.uk/section/keep-up-to-date/threat-reports?q=&defaultTypes=report&sort=date%2Bdesc.

- **National Institute of Standards and Technology (NIST):** NIST's mission is to *"promote U.S. innovation and industrial competitiveness by advancing measurement science, standards, and technology in ways that enhance economic security and improve our quality of life"*. NIST states that its core competencies are *"measurement science, rigorous traceability"*, and the *"development and use of standards"* (NIST: 2022).

The NIST SP-800 series reports on the IT laboratory research at NIST and its guidelines. All SP-800 series reports can be accessed at:
https://csrc.nist.gov/publications/sp800.
All SP computer security guidance, including draft publications, can be found at the NIST Computer Security Resource Center, accessed at:
https://csrc.nist.gov/publications/sp#800-94.

- **Open Worldwide Application Security Project (OWASP):** In its own words, OWASP is a "vendor-neutral", independent *"nonprofit foundation that works to improve the security of software"*. OWASP runs more than 250 chapters worldwide and boasts tens of thousands of members.
  Website: *https://owasp.org/*.
  Twitter: *https://Twitter.com/owasp*.

- **Pool Re:** Born out of businesses suffering large and often irretrievable financial losses during 'The Troubles' in the UK and Northern Ireland, Pool Re was established with UK government support, and soon became the UK's leading terrorism reinsurer. Pool Re's mission is to *"provide financial protection from the impact of terrorism, and in so doing, improve the UK's resilience"*. Pool Re's Vulnerability Self-Assessment Tool (VSAT) is their free-to-use security risk management assessment tool that *"helps organisations to benchmark their risk maturity against UK best practice for terrorism mitigation"* (Pool Re: 2023). Pool Re's VSAT can be accessed and completed at:

Website: *https://www.poolre.co.uk/vsat/.*

- **Reddit and 'subreddits':** According to digital marketing guru Neal Schaffer, *"Reddit is a social network where registered members can vote [upon] content and discuss them. It is made up of millions of collective niche forums or groups called Subreddits. To put it differently, Reddit is a social platform comprised of subreddits".* Subreddits are *"a powerful network of niche communities that collectively define reddit"* says Schaffer. Reddit's monthly active users have spiralled since 2020 from around 613 million people to a projected 2.3 billion for 2024, making it one of our planet's most popular digital media platforms (bankmycell.com: 2023). Reddit is headquartered in San Francisco, California.
  Corporate website: *https://www.redditinc.com/.*
  Moderator Code of Conduct URL:
  https://www.redditinc.com/policies/moderator-code-of-conduct.

- **SANS Institute:** Popularly known as the acronym 'SANS', this for-profit organisation's full-name is SysAdmin, Audit, Network, and Security. The institute sponsors the 'SANS Storm Center' – an Internet monitoring system and the 'SANS Reading Room' – a research archive and infosec policy support hub. Visit the website and social media feeds to sign up for very useful bulletins:
  Website: *https://www.sans.org/uk_en/.*
  Twitter (now X): *https://Twitter.com/SANSInstitute.*

Twitter for Storm Center:
https://Twitter.com/sans_isc.

- **START:** Administered by the University of Maryland, START runs the Global Terrorism Database (GTD). The GTD is an open-source database including information about terrorism events around the world from 1970 up until 2020, with annual updates posted thereafter.
  Website: *https://www.start.umd.edu/gtd/*.

- **Tech Against Terrorism (TAT):** TAT is working on behalf of the UN Counter Terrorism Executive Directorate (CTED) to support the global tech industry to tackle terrorist exploitation of their technologies. TAT also formed to support smaller tech companies with guidance of best practice in protecting their users and reputation.
  https://www.techagainstterrorism.org/.

- **The Cyber Security Hub:**
  A very comprehensive, up-to-date and threat-information-rich Twitter feed that cites a barebones Linktree website.
  Website: *https://linktr.ee/thecybersecurityhub*.
  Twitter (now X):
  https://Twitter.com/thecybersechub?lang=en.

- ***The Hacker News***: Popular publication for breaking cyber security and hacking news, insights and analysis for information security professionals.
  Website: *https://thehackernews.com/*.

Twitter (now X):
https://Twitter.com/TheHackersNews.

- **West Point Combating Terrorism Center (CTC). Based at the famous military academy,** the Combating Terrorism Center at West Point *"is a national resource for the objective study of terrorism & policy-relevant research"*. CTC publishes the monthly *CTC Sentinel*, a high-quality, publication of journal articles that leverages the Center's impressive international network of scholars and practitioners.

  Website: *http://www.ctc.westpoint.edu/*.
  Twitter (now X): *https://Twitter.com/CTCWP*.

APPENDIX B: TERRORISM GROUPS

- **Al-Qaeda (AQ):** Founded in Peshawar, Pakistan, around 1988, AQ is a Sunni pan-Islamist terrorism organisation who self-identify as a religious military elite whose mission it is to accelerate Muslim world unification and the creation of a global caliphate (Klausen: 2021). After a merger with some Egyptian Islamic Jihad leaders, AQ maintained a strong central command structure (AQ Central) at least until it carried out the 9/11 atrocities. AQ then enabled and/or supported the development of powerful regional commands such as AQAP (Arab Peninsula), AQI (Iraq) and AQIM (Islamic Maghreb). Superseded by ISIS during the 2010s as the Western world's most lethal terror threat, AQ conducted fewer direct attacks in Europe and the US. The January 2015 murders of 11 employees and police at French satirical magazine *Charlie Hebdo*, followed up with attacks and sieges across the Ile-de-France region by the two sibling perpetrators, kept AQ in international news headlines. Its most recent leader Ayman Al-Zawahiri was reportedly killed by a US drone strike in Kabul in 2022.
- **Ansar Allah Movement (the Houthis):** Based in Yemen. An Islamist armed political group that led the removal of the US and Saudi-backed governments of former Yemeni president, **Ali Abdullah Saleh**. The Houthi movement is predominantly a Zaidi Shia force

but for operational purposes has often coordinated or tolerated operations by Al-Qaeda in the Arab Peninsula. The group is virulently hostile to the USA, Israel and allies and mirrors much of the same 'death to America' rhetoric commonly found within other revolutionary Iran-backed armed groups. Houthi fighters have been repeatedly identified by human rights monitors as shelling civilian areas and using child soldiers (Human Rights Watch: 2015).

- **Aryan Brotherhood (AB):** The AB was originally a California-based prison gang that was formed in the California prison system during the 1960s. There are now various networks and affiliates based usually on state boundaries (US Department of Justice: 2012). According to court documents, previously, the AB was primarily concerned with the protection of white inmates and white supremacy/separatism. Over time, the AB has expanded its criminal enterprise to include illegal activities for profit. Many activists have fomented political movements and recruited far-right, white supremacist and activists.

- **Aryan Nations (AN):** According to Encyclopedia.com, the AN *"acts as a paramilitary hate group and is one of America's most predominant and active white supremacist and anti-Semitic organizations"*. Based in Idaho, AN *"strongly advocates the establishment of a white state with the exclusion of all other races"* (Encyclopedia.com: 2023).

- **Aum Shinrikyo (Supreme Truth):** Aum Shinrikyo's ultimate goal was to encourage or create, through nuclear war between the US and Japan, a global Armageddon that would be necessary to cleanse the world. The cult wanted to take control of the Japanese government and defence forces by means of a military coup. This millenarian new religious movement, renamed 'Aleph' in 2000, was led by messianic despot Asahara Shoko (original name Matsumoto Chizuo). Asahara and six other AUM members were condemned to death and executed in 2018 (Atkins and McKay).

- **Feuerkrieg Division group (FKD):** According to the UK's Counter Terrorism Policing centre, *"the FKD is a small, international neo-Nazi organization that follow a white supremacist ideology and also advocates 'accelerationism' – which is the use of violence and acts of terrorism to bring about a 'race war' and the fall of existing social and political systems".* The third neo-Nazi group to be proscribed within the UK by 2020, FDG *"promote their ideology online through the sharing of violent white supremacist propaganda, commonly using social media platforms to target young people aged between 13 and 25"* (Counter Terrorism Policing: 2020).

- **Hamas:** The 'Islamic Resistance Movement' is a Palestinian Sunni Islamic Fundamentalist political and military organisation. Hamas's military organisation is known as the 'Izz ad-Din al-Qassam Brigades' and the political organisation is the de facto governing authority within the Gaza Strip. Hamas has conducted some of the largest volumes of lethal terrorism and counter-insurgency operations during contemporary times and has allies within the following two regions: Turkey and Qatar. Hamas has engaged in effective cyber warfare activities since 2012. Established in 1987, the group's charter calls for establishing an Islamic Palestinian state in place of Israel and rejects all agreements made between the PLO and Israel. HAMAS's strength is concentrated in the Gaza Strip and areas of the West Bank (US Director of National Intelligence: 2014).

- **Hizbullah:** According to the US Department for National Intelligence (DNI), Hizbullah was formed in 1982 and is a Shia-dominated political group that conducts terrorist operations. The US DNI cites mass casualty attacks and kidnappings of US troops, government and civilian personnel during the 1980s and 1990s. Israeli interests – particularly troops, government and settlers – feature as principle threat targets. The US Marine bombings (1983), the hijacking of TWA 847 (1985) and the lethal Khobar towers attack in Saudi Arabia (1996) are part of a forty-year timeline of armed operations by Hizbullah armed units. Hizbullah's main national sponsors are Iran and Syria (DNI website: 2023).

- **ISIS:** Founded in 2013. The Islamic State, also known as the Islamic State of Iraq and the Levant, Islamic State of Iraq and Syria, and by its Arabic acronym Da'ish or Daesh, is a transnational militant Islamist terrorist group and former unrecognised quasi-state that follows the Salafi jihadist branch of Sunni Islam. Its founder and leader Ibrahim Awad Ibrahim al-Badri, commonly known as Abu Bakr al-Baghdadi, was an Iraqi-born theologian who became one of the world's most notorious terror leaders. Baghdadi reportedly killed himself and his children by detonating a suicide bomb in 2019 as US forces closed in to capture him. His number two, Syrian-born Taha Sobhi Falaha, known as Abu Muhammad al-Adnani al-Sham, was killed in 2016 by (either) a Russian or US coalition airstrike depending, on the news reports you read.

- **Ku Klux Klan (KKK):** Commonly shortened to KKK or 'the Klan', this is the umbrella name for several historical and present American white supremacist, anti-immigrant hate groups. Since its inception during the American civil war in the 1860s, this secret membership organisation has conducted ethnicity motivated murders and bombings against most non-white American target communities, as well as leftists, atheists and abortion providers. Many Klan groups continue to crop up today and recruit members via public websites. As of 2016, the Anti-Defamation League puts total KKK membership at 3,000 (Levin: 2003) (Anti-Defamation League: 2016). One splinter group emerged in Kentucky called 'Elders Blood-NBlood Out Knights' (EBBOK) and on its website espouses Neo-Nazi operational tactics: *"We are a Christian hate group. We are a group unlike other groups. We accept all Nazis and skin heads (sic) cause* *we have the same beliefs.*" During the same year, two similar Klan groups also formed: based in Alpena, Michigan, the 'Great Lake Knights', and the 'Pacific Coast Knights' of Spokane, Washington (ADL: 2016).

- **Mujahideen Shura Council (in the environs of Jerusalem) (MSCEJ):** MSCEJ was subordinated to Al-Qaeda in the Sinai Peninsula. Salafist Jihad in mindset, the group believes that violence against Jewish citizens is a religious obligation that brings its followers closer to God. MSCEJ is not the same as the former 'Mujahideen Shura Council', a coalition of six terror groups (circa 2006) that essentially served as the precursor organising committee to Islamic State in Iraq. Although affiliated, the latter group attempted to coordinate and resource the insurgency against the US-led coalition within Iraq. MSCEJ was largely based in Gaza and conducted anti-Israel operations in Egypt's Sinai and inside disputed Israel/Palestinian territories (Long War Journal: 2012).

- **National Action (NA):** Formed in 2013, based in Warrington, UK, NA became the first neo-Nazi group in England to be proscribed as a terrorism organisation under the Terrorism Act (2000); this designation occurred during 2016. According to the UK's Home Office: *"The group's online propaganda material, disseminated via social media, frequently features extremely violent imagery and language. National Action also promoted and encouraged acts of terrorism after Jo Cox's murder"* (Home Office: 2016).

- **National Strike Force:** Is an offshoot of 'Ayran Strikeforce' (ASF), a mainly UK group that is dedicated to attacks against Muslims and Jews, among others. Followers are typically *Mein-Kampf*-reading Hitlerites who believe in white racial supremacy and the establishment of apartheid policies in their domestic countries. Its leader was imprisoned at Newcastle Crown Court for manufacturing chemical weapons (ricin) during 2010. ASF is thought to sustain around 3-400 members via, principally, online mobilisation (Reuters: 2010).
- **Symbionese Liberation Army (SLA):** The SLA are widely regarded by US law enforcement as the first domestic terrorist group associated with the political far left. Active mainly in California between 1973 and 1975, the group murdered a black police superintendent, and carried out kidnappings and bank robberies in supposed pursuit of a political manifesto (Caldwell, *New York Times*: 1974).

APPENDIX C: GLOSSARY

- **4chan:** Began life in 2003 as an 'imageboard', a type of chat forum that focuses on the posting of images, typically alongside text and discussion. 4chan hosts discussion and comment boards dedicated to a wide variety of topics, mainly non-political. 4chan's platform has been widely used to host diverse, radical and (sometimes) extreme views as well as to share images associated with toxicity and violence such as weapons. Because registration is not available, users tend to post anonymously, leading many researchers to describe it as a hub for subcultures and edgy topics. Other analysts feel 4chan's own users self-police the platform effectively and that the most extreme users flush themselves out for investigation merely by posting in the first place (Trammell: 2014).

- **8kun:** Formed in 2013, previously called 8chan, Infinitechan or Infinitychan, before being recently rebranded as 8kun, this platform is an imageboard website composed of user-created message boards. An owner moderates each board, with negligible intervention from site administers. The subtext to this platform is that it is dedicated to free speech and user anonymity, thus becoming a magnet for perpetrators of violence and extremism. Such individuals or groups considering or planning attacks are often keen to publicise themselves and their cause, yet also careful to avoid the intensifying constraints and detection tools implemented by larger digital media platforms. According to the BBC: Although there are hundreds of topic areas, the site is most notorious for its "/pol/" board, short for "politically incorrect". Moreover, *"8chan /pol/ was a crucial meeting ground for activists behind the anti-feminist campaign known as GamerGate, and more recently spawned QAnon – a conspiracy theory popular with some supporters of President Donald Trump"* (BBC website: 2019). The platform itself doesn't seem to shirk off this reputation. Its front page logo states boldly: *"Welcome to 8chan, the Darkest Reaches of the Internet"*. Perhaps the strongest description for 8chan has been described for us by Robert Evans, a Bellingcat journalist:

8chan is a large website, which includes a number of different discussion groups about everything from anime to left-wing politics. /pol/ is one particularly active board on the website, and it is best described as a gathering place for extremely online neo-Nazis. The overarching goal of /pol/, held by most of its members, is to radicalize their fellow anons to "real-life effortposting," i.e. acts of violence in the physical world. This goal is well embodied by a post I found in a discussion of the [April 2019] *Poway Synagogue shooting* (Bellingcat: 2019).

- **Asymmetric warfare:** Warfare that is between opposing forces that differ greatly in military power and that typically involves the use of unconventional weapons and tactics, such as those associated with guerrilla warfare and terrorist attacks (Merriam-Webster).

- **Brushing:** An online scam usually perpetrated by marketeers to boost the profile and ratings of their website. According to reporter Marty McCarthy, the scam proliferated during COVID-19 homeworking. McCarthy writes: *"Brushing is when people receive cheap, unsolicited packages in the mail from an online marketplace, such as Amazon. But the actual seller – the individual or company that sent you the item – is usually a third party that uses those websites to sell its products [...] The third-party seller writes a fake, five-star review of the product it has just 'sold' and sent to you, using your name as the author"* (McCarthy: 2020).

- **Catfishing:** Is the creation of a fake, attractive online identity used to ensnare victims into embarrassing behaviour as well as to capture their movements and data. The attackers' spoof accounts are maintained at an active, plausible level, with the fake identity joining user groups and posting updates that encourage interaction.

- **Christian Democratic Union of Germany (CDU):** Is one of the two mainstream national political parties within modern Germany, and previously West Germany. A moderate centre-right-leaning mass-membership organisation, whose previous leaders have included chancellors Angela Merkel and Helmut Kohl, the CDU has been the most successful political party in terms of winning national general elections since the Second World War.

- **Clickfarms:** A click farm is a form of misrepresentation where a large group of people are hired to click on paid advertising links for the click fraudster (click farm master or click farmer). The workers click the links, surf the target website for a period of time, and possibly sign up for newsletters before clicking another link (Munson: 2007). Fake likes generating from click farms are essentially different from those arising from bots, where computer programs are written by software experts.

- **Compounds:**   When atoms of more than one type develop and form together in a fixed ratio, they form compounds.

- **Credential stuffing:** The UK National Cyber Security Centre states that *"Credential stuffing takes advantage of people reusing username and password combinations across different accounts. By fraudulently gaining valid combinations for one site, and successfully using them on other sites, an attacker can access legitimate accounts. The primary motivation is financial, but it can lead to identity theft".*
  Source: *https://www.ncsc.gov.uk/pdfs/news/use-credential-stuffing-tools.pdf.*

- **Cyber security posture:** 'Posture' refers to the overall preparedness and readiness to identify, recover and respond from security threats and risks. According to cyber security firm, *Bitsight*, your posture could be low and out of step within hours of conducting your latest cyber security risk assessment. *"Identifying and managing security posture requires clear [and continued] visibility into the risks and threats within your digital ecosystem as well as the performance of security programs designed to address them,"* writes Bitsight's website team (Bitsight: 2023).

- **Cyber threat intelligence (CTI):** According to the Bank of England, CTI is knowledge, skills and experience-based information concerning the occurrence and assessment of both cyber and physical threats and threat actors that is intended to help mitigate potential attacks and harmful events occurring in cyberspace (Bank of England: 2016).

- **Data scraping:** A technique whereby a computer program extracts data (usually on a large scale) from human readable output coming from another program.

- **Disinformation:** Refers to false information that is spread with the specific intent of misleading or deceiving people (Dictionary.com).

- **Disorder:** Used principally by gamers, Disorder is an online VoIP and instant messaging platform. Founded in 2015, this popular chat app is available in around 30 different written languages and hosts around 150 million monthly active users and 350 million accounts (Metro: 2022).

- **False flag:** According to the BBC, a false flag is a political or military action carried out with the intention of blaming an opponent for it. Nations have often done this by staging a real or simulated attack on their own side and saying the enemy did it, as a pretext for going to war.

- **GDPR:** The General Data Protection Regulation is a regulation in EU law on data protection and privacy in the EU and the European Economic Area. The GDPR is an important segment of EU privacy law and of human rights law. It covers all EU citizens and their personal data, whether the data rests within the EU or outside the bloc.

- **Hawala:** 'Havaleh' in Persian. Trusted network of hawaladars (money brokers) who operate through a system of trust and honour. Cash is informally transferred from one hawaladar to another without physical money necessarily changing hands. Hawala systems remain popular in Asiatic and Islamic communities.

- **Health Insurance Portability and Accountability Act (1996) – HIPAA:** US Only. HIPAA is a US federal law that required the development of national standards to safeguard sensitive patient health information from being disclosed without the patient's consent or knowledge. Equivalent data in the UK is covered by the GDPR and the Data Protection Act (DPA) (2018).

- **Honeypot:** According to cyber security firm Kaspersky, a 'honeypot' appears *"like a real computer system, with applications and data, fooling cybercriminals into thinking it's a legitimate target. For example, a honeypot could mimic a company's customer billing* *system – a frequent target of attack* for criminals who want to find credit card numbers" (Kaspersky: 2023).

- **Internet of Things (IoT):** According to computer technology corporation Oracle, *"IoT describes the network of physical objects – 'things' – that are embedded with sensors, software, and other technologies for the purpose of connecting and exchanging data with other devices and systems over the internet. These devices range from ordinary household objects to sophisticated industrial tools."*
  Source: *https://www.oracle.com/uk/internet-of-things/what-is-iot/.*

- **IP address:** an Internet service provider (ISP) or network administrator assigns an Internet Protocol (IP) address. Associated with the TCP/IP protocol, an IP address helps identify a device connected to a network.

- **Jailbreaking (or Rooting):** These terms both refer to removing software security restrictions that are intentionally put in place by the device manufacturer. This process opens a 'back door' within an electronic device to install software – perhaps to eavesdrop, manipulate or exfiltrate data – from the system.

- **KYC:** 'Know your customer' due diligence undertaken by a vendor to verify the identity, legality and appropriateness of their potential customer or service user.

- **MAC address:** A media access control (MAC) address is a hardware identifier that uniquely identifies each device on a network

- **Misinformation:** False information that is communicated and disseminated , regardless of whether there is an intention to mislead

- **Multifactor authentication (MFA):** MFA *s an computer-user authentication method that requires the end-user to provide two or more verification factors to gain access to a system. Extra layers of security controls lessen the likelihood of experiencing a successful cyber-attack.*

- **The Payment Card Industry Data Security Standard (PCI DSS):** Is a widely accepted set of policies and procedures intended to enhance the security of credit, debit and cash card transactions and protect cardholders from having their money and personal data stolen. Originally a voluntary standard formed by the four major international credit card firms back in 2004, compliance to some or all the latest standards tend to be mandatory within the UK, US and many other advanced economies.

- **Pinterest:** Founded in 2010, headquartered in San Francisco, Pinterest is an image-sharing social media forum that helps users to upload content such as images and videos onto pinboards. The platform wields an international monthly active user base totally more than 460 million people as of April 2023 (CNBC: 2023).

- **Prompt engineering:** Prompt Engineering is the practice of users refining the manner in which they ask a question to an AI chatbot system. Prompt engineering can be abused to bypass content moderation restrictions on chatbots – such as ChatGPT - to produce potentially harmful content.

- **QAnon:** A conspiracy theory and emerging, amorphous online political movement that explores and promotes the idea that the US has been taken over by a cabal of extreme-left-leaning satanists, who use their power to indulge in sexual crimes and financial corruption (Crossley: 2021). Many QAnon subscribers and followers took part in the January 2021 Capitol Hill riots.

- **Securitisation:** The inclination and development of (principally) public-sector agencies to treat emerging social risks as phenomena to be 'managed' by risk mitigation tactics and strategies that are increasingly oriented towards security controls. Thus, over time, this process ushers in the securitisation of communities and societies (unless the 'process' is successfully challenged and counter-acted by other influencers and policy makers.

- **Snapchat:** Founded in 2011, based in Santa Monica, California, 'Snap' (colloquial) is an image-sharing social media app. Snapchat boasts 750 million monthly active users (TechCrunch: 2023). Initially designed for private person-to-person photo sharing (images disappeared after a period of time), the app's features are wide-ranging, including video distribution and video live chat.

- **Steam:** Founded in 2003, headquartered in Bellevue, Washington, Steam is a video game digital distribution service and storefront from Valve, a US-based corporation. Client functions include direct messaging, Cloud storage and in-game overlay functions. Steam is global, operates in 28 languages, and more than 50,000 games are located in the US catalogue alone. By 2023, Steam had hosted more than 120 million monthly active users worldwide, growing 30% since 2020 (backlinko.com: 2023).

- **Steganography:** According to cyber security firm Kaspersky, *"Steganography is the practice of concealing information within another message or physical object to avoid detection. Steganography can be used to hide virtually any type of digital content, including text, image, video, or audio content. That hidden data is then extracted at its destination."*

- **Synthetic media:** According to AI experts Synthesia, media content (text, image, sound, video) *"that has been fully or partially generated using AI"*. Synthetic media is developed in the digital world by AI algorithms while non-synthetic media is created in the physical environment by humans (Synthesia Media: 2023).

- **Threat and vulnerability assessments or reviews (TVA/TVR):** TVAs/TVRs can be written in many ways but are usually presented within a table/matrix that explicitly define the threat, vulnerability (weakness), likelihood of occurrence and potential organisational impact. A further table column might include security controls (mitigation). Likelihood and Impact are usually rated with a score between one (very low) and five (very high).

- **Twitch:** Founded in 2011 as a spin-off from Justin.TV, Twitch is a general-interest streaming channel. It is an American live streaming service that focuses on video game live streaming in addition to offering esports, live sports and music broadcasts in "real-life" streams. Twitch Interactive was acquired by Amazon in 2014. As with YouTube and other video streaming websites, streamers with large amounts of followers receive revenue from subscriptions (50% at the time of writing). Twitch opened a Safety Advisory Council in 2020, after the Halle, Germany, terror attacks. By 2023, Twitch had 140 million active monthly users and received content from 8 million unique streamers every month (Demandsage.com: 2023).

- **Wiper malware:** A wiper is a type of malware deployed by the attacker, typically with a single goal in mind: to erase end-user data beyond recoverability. Usually when deploying wiper malware, attackers attempt to conceal their digital forensic tracks by leaving erroneous evidence such as complex layers of cover-ups and/or 'false flag' clues.

APPENDIX D: BIBLIOGRAPHY

- @abdirahimS on Twitter (2019). Accessed on 24/07/2023 at: *https://twitter.com/abdirahims/status/1117770998957387776*.
- @MinaLami (2019). Twitter commentary accessed and downloaded on 24/07/2023 at: *https://twitter.com/Minalami/status/11091433877462466657*.
- ABC News (2004). "American Al-Qaeda Unmasked?". 9/11/2004. Accessed and downloaded on 28/07/2023 at: *https://abcnews.go.com/WNT/story?id=239727*.
- ABC Rural (2021). "JBS cyber attack grinds biggest meat producer to a halt, causing livestock trade tumult". 01.06.2021. Accessed and downloaded on 13/04/2023 at: *https://www.abc.net.au/news/rural/2021-06-01/jbs-cyber-attacks-biggest-meat-processor-halt-livestock-trade/100180702*.
- Abu Saada, M and Turan, Y (2021) "Israeli-Palestinian Cyber Conflict", Eskişehir Osmangazi Üniversitesi İİBF Dergisi, 16(1), pp186–204.
- Adams, A (2023) "Cyber Security Strategic Leadership" presentation to CSARN Global Cyber Academy on 21/02/2023.

- Adshead, G and Horne, E (2022). *The Devil You Know. Encounters in Forensic Psychiatry*. London. Faber & Faber.
- Al-Fahd, Nasir bin Hamid (2003). "A Treatise on the Legal Status of Using Weapons of Mass Destruction Against Infidels". Posted to: *www.ilmway.com/site/maqdis/MS_860* (May 2003). Website no longer publicly available.
- Almutairi, A (2017). "Social Media As A Recruitment Tool For ISIS". John Carroll University. *Carroll Collected*. Accessed and downloaded on 08/03/2023 at: *https://collected.jcu.edu/cgi/viewcontent.cgi?article=1081&context=mastersessays*.
- AlSarayreh, A (2020): "How ISIS use social media for recruitment". *Canadian Forces College.* Accessed on 07/11/2022 and available at: *https://www.cfc.forces.gc.ca/259/290/22/305/AlSarayreh.pdf*.
- American Civil Liberties Union website (2023). Accessed and downloaded on 09/05/2023 at: *https://www.aclu.org/other/patriot-act-sunsets*.
- American Psychological Association (2021). "How can we minimize Instagram's harmful effects?". Zara Abrams citing Adam Alter. 02/12/2021. APA Monitor. Vol. 53. No.2. Accessed and downloaded on 28/07/2023 at: *https://www.apa.org/monitor/2022/03/feature-minimize-instagram-effects*.

- American Society for Industrial Security (ASIS). "Workplace Violence Prevention and Intervention" (WVPI) 2011. Protection of assets manuals. *ASIS International.*

- Amman, M and Meloy, R (2022). "Incitement to Violence and Stochastic Terrorism: Legal, Academic and Practical Parameters for Researchers and Investigators". *Terrorism and Political Violence.* 19/12/2022. Accessed and downloaded on 08/02/2024 at: *https://www.tandfonline.com/doi/abs/10.1080/0954655 3.2022.2143352.*

- Anti-Defamation League (ADL) (2016). "Tattered Robes: The State of the Ku Klux Klan in the United States". 05/11/2016. Accessed and downloaded on 15/07/2023 at: *https://www.adl.org/resources/report/tattered-robes-state-ku-klux-klan-united-states.*

- Associated Press (2017). "Docs: Bomb threats suspect offered services on dark net". Gurman, S. 08/08/2017. Accessed and downloaded on 15/05/2023 at: *https://apnews.com/article/5ef71ebdb5244b99ae4ce40 5f9d0ab3f.*

- Associated Press (2022). ''Buffalo shooter targeted black neighborhood, officials say". 15/05/2022. Thompson, C and Balsamo, M. Accessed and downloaded on 19/07/2023 at: *https://apnews.com/article/buffalo-shooting-0475a5bd971d23a4e0a13ef840650bb1.*

- Atkins, I and McKay, J (ND): Accessed and downloaded on 01/06/2023 at: *https://scalar.usc.edu/works/aum-shinrikyo/major-goals*.
- Atwan, AB (2015). *Islamic state: The Digital Caliphate*. Oakland: University of California Press. Accessed and downloaded on 29/03/2023 at: *https://www.ucpress.edu/book/9780520289727/islamic-state*.
- Awan, I (2017). "Cyber Extremism: Isis and the Power of Social Media". *Social Science and Policy*, Vol 54. Pp138–149. Accessed and downloaded on 29/03/2023 at: *https://link.springer.com/article/10.1007/s12115-017-0114-0*.
- Azani, E (2014). International institute for counter-terrorism newsletter. Herzliya: Cyber-Terrorism Desk.
- Backlinko.com (2023). "Steam Usage and Catalogue Stats for 2023". Accessed and downloaded on 24/07/2023 at: *https://backlinko.com/steam-users*.
- Baele, S, Brace L and Coan T (2021). Variations on a Theme? Comparing 4chan, 8kun and Other chans' Far Right "/pol" Boards. Perspectives on Terrorism. Vol. 15. Issue 1. Accessed and downloaded on 24/07/2023 at: *https://www.jstor.org/stable/26984798?seq=1*.
- Bakier, AH (2014). "IS Spokesman Issues Appeal to End the Inter-Jihadist Rivalry." Jamestown Foundation. 10/10/2014. Accessed and downloaded on 25/07/2023 at: *https://www.refworld.org/docid/543f97c24.html*.

- Bandura. A, (1998). *Mechanisms of moral disengagement in Origins of Terrorism: Psychologies, Ideologies, Theologies, States of Mind.* Woodrow Wilson Center for International Scholars. (ed) Walter Laquer.
- Bankmycell.com (2023). "How Many Users Does X (Formerly Twitter) Have?" (July 2023). Accessed and downloaded on 26/07/2023 at: *https://www.bankmycell.com/blog/how-many-users-does-twitter-have#section-4*.
- Bank of England (2016). "CBEST Intelligence Led Testing. Understanding Cyber Threat Intelligence Operations". Version 2.0. Accessed and downloaded on 13/04/2023 at: *https://www.bankofengland.co.uk/-/media/boe/files/financial-stability/financial-sector-continuity/understanding-cyber-threat-intelligence-operations.pdf*.
- Barquin, R (1992). "In Pursuit of a 'Ten Commandments' for Computer Ethics". Accessed and downloaded on 29/07/2023 at: *https://computerethics.institute/publications/ten-commandments-of-computer-ethics/*.
- BBC (24/10/2017). "IS Foreign Fighters: 5,600 have returned home – report" accessed and downloaded on 26/10/2022 at: *https://www.bbc.co.uk/news/world-middle-east-41734069*.
- BBC (2019). "Molly Russell: Coroner demands social media firms turn over account data". Crawford, A.

20/11/2019. Accessed and downloaded on 03/06/2023 at: *https://www.bbc.co.uk/news/uk-england-london-50490998*.

- BBC Monitoring (2019). "Analysis: Islamic State's experiments with the decentralised web". Peter Kind. 22/03/2019. Accessed and downloaded on 24/07/2023 at: *https://monitoring.bbc.co.uk/product/c200paga*.
- BBC News (2018). "[Name redacted] convicted over gay pride attack plot". 05/08/2023. Accessed and downloaded on 17/07/2023 at: *https://www.bbc.co.uk/news/uk-england-cumbria-42944925*.
- BBC News (2019). "Europol disrupts Islamic State propaganda machine". BBC Monitoring. 25/11/2019. Accessed and downloaded on 24/07/2023 at: *https://www.bbc.co.uk/news/world-middle-east-50545816*.
- BBC News (2021). "Incels: A new terror threat to the UK?". Casciani, D and De Simone, D. 13/08/2021. Accessed and downloaded on 11/07/2023 at: *https://www.bbc.co.uk/news/uk-58207064*.
- BBC News (2023). "Right Wing Terrorist Plotter [Name Redacted] Jailed". 11/07/2023. Accessed and downloaded on 17/07/2023 at: *https://www.bbc.co.uk/news/uk-england-tyne-66163679*.
- BBC News: Business (2023). "Elon Musk: Australia threatens to fine Twitter over online hate". Peter Hoskins. 22/06/2023. Accessed and downloaded on

27/07/2023 at: *https://www.bbc.co.uk/news/business-65981699*.

- BBC Technology (2017). "IS-linked propaganda outlet moves to Instagram". 12/05/2017. Accessed and downloaded on 12/04/2023 at: *https://www.bbc.co.uk/news/technology-39883233*.
- BBC Website (2019). "What is 8chan?" 05/08/2019. Accessed and downloaded on 13/07/2023 at: *https://www.bbc.co.uk/news/blogs-trending-49233767*.
- Beebom (2023). "25 Best ChatGPT Alternatives in 2023". Sharma, U. 21/04/2023. Accessed and downloaded on 30/04/2023 at: *https://beebom.com/best-chatgpt-alternatives/*.
- Belfer Center (2022). "National Cyber Power Index". Accessed and downloaded on 29/07/2023 at: *https://www.belfercenter.org/sites/default/files/files/publication/CyberProject_National%20Cyber%20Power%20Index%202022_v3_220922.pdf*.
- Bellingcat (2019). "Ignore the Poway Synagogue Shooter's Manifesto: Pay Attention to 8chan's /pol/ Board". Evans, R. 28/04/2019. Accessed and downloaded on 18/07/2023 at: *https://www.bellingcat.com/news/americas/2019/04/28/ignore-the-poway-synagogue-shooters-manifesto-pay-attention-to-8chans-pol-board/*.
- Bellingcat (2019). "The El Paso Shooting and the Gamification of Terror". Evans, R. 04/08/2019. Accessed and downloaded on 18/07/2023 at:

*https://www.bellingcat.com/news/americas/2019/08/04
/the-el-paso-shooting-and-the-gamification-of-terror/*.

- Bharade, A. (03/05/2023). Accessed and downloaded
  on 03/05/2023 at:
  *https://www.businessinsider.in/international/news/touri
  sts-in-hawaii-followed-their-gps-and-drove-their-car-
  straight-into-a-harbor-pretty-sure-that-was-not-
  supposed-to-happen/articleshow/99957238.cms*.
- Bilton, N (2017). *American Kingpin: The Epic Hunt
  for the Criminal Mastermind Behind the Silk Road*.
  Edmonton. Portfolio.
- Bingley, R (2003). *Terrorism Just the Facts*. London:
  Heinemann.
- Bingley, R (2022). "Your computer and smartphone
  have become Putin's weapon of choice". *Sunday
  Express*. 27/02/2022. Accessed and downloaded on
  14/04/2023 at:
  *https://www.express.co.uk/comment/expresscomment/1
  572753/cyber-attack-hack-russia-putin-war-richard-
  bingley*.
- Bitsight website (2023). "Security Posture Meaning.
  The True Meaning and Value of Security Posture".
  Accessed and downloaded on 12/06/2023 at:
  *https://www.bitsight.com/glossary/security-posture-
  meaning*.
- Blockchain ConsultUs (2019). "Terrorists Use of
  Cryptocurrencies". Casadei Bernardi, S. London.
  Accessed and downloaded on 16/05/2023 at:
  https://www.blockchainconsultus.io/wp-

content/uploads/2019/08/3191-BCU-Crypto-Terrorist.pdf.

- Bloomberg (2021). "Facebook Says It Has Spent $13 Billion on Safety, Security". Kurt Wagner. 21/09/2021. Accessed and downloaded on 27/06/2023 at: *https://www.bloomberg.com/news/articles/2021-09-21/facebook-says-it-has-spent-13-billion-on-safety-security*.

- Bonanno, GA and Jost, JT (2006). "Conservative shift among high-exposure survivors of the September 11th terrorist attacks". *Basic and Applied Social Psychology*. 28(4), pp311–323.

- Bosch, T (2011). "Jared Lee Loughner's Worldview a Conspiracy Theory Laundry List". 10/01/2011. Accessed and downloaded on 19/07/2023 at: *https://web.archive.org/web/20110111165941/http://www.aolnews.com/2011/01/10/jared-lee-loughners-worldview-a-conspiracy-theory-laundry-list/*.

- Broder, J and Tucker, E (2012). *Risk and the Security Survey*. Fourth Edition. Oxford. Butterworth-Heinemann

- Bumiller, E and Shanker, T (2012). "Panetta Warns of Dire Threat of Cyberattack on U.S.". *The New York Times*. Accessed on 11/10/2012 at: *https://www.nytimes.com/2012/10/12/world/panetta-warns-of-dire-threat-of-cyberattack.html*.

- Burke, J (2016). "The Age of Selfie Jihad: How Evolving Media Technology is Changing Terrorism". *CTC Sentinel*, Vol. 9: Issue 11. Accessed on 06/03/2024 at: *https://ctc.westpoint.edu/the-age-of-selfie-jihad-how-evolving-media-technology-is-changing-terrorism/*.

- Business Insider (2023). "Tourists in Hawaii followed their GPS and drove their car straight into a harbour: 'Pretty sure that was not supposed to happen'".
- Caldwell, E. *The New York Times* (1974). Accessed and downloaded on 01/06/2023 at: *https://www.nytimes.com/1974/02/23/archives/symbion ese-liberation-army-terrorism-from-left.html*.
- CBS News (1998). "Anthrax Plot Foiled by FBI". 19/02/1998. Accessed and downloaded on 01/06/2023 at: *https://www.cbsnews.com/news/anthrax-plot-foiled-by-fbi/*.
- CBS News (2011). "Researchers Show How a Car's Electronics Can Be Taken Over Remotely". Markhoff, J. 10/03/2011. Accessed and downloaded on 09/05/2023 at: *https://www.cnbc.com/2011/03/10/researchers-show-how-a-cars-electronics-can-be-taken-over-remotely.html*.
- CBS News (2022). "New Secret Service report details growing incel terrorism threat". Sganga, N. 15/03/2022. Accessed and downloaded on 10/07/2023 at: *https://www.cbsnews.com/news/incel-threat-secret-service-report/*.
- Channel News Asia (2021). "16-year-old Singaporean detained under ISA after planning to attack Muslims at two mosques". 27/01/2023. Mahmud, AH. Accessed

and downloaded on 19/07/2023 at:
https://www.channelnewsasia.com/singapore/16-year-old-singaporean-detained-isa-planned-attack-2-mosques-435241.

- Children's Online Privacy Protection Act (COPPA) 2018.
- Christian Science Monitor (1986). "The Terrorist Mentality' interview with Lord Chalfont". Kidder, R. 15/05/1986
- CISA (2021). "Cyber Security and Infrastructure Security Convergence Guide". Cybersecurity and Infrastructure Security Agency. 2020.
- *City Security Magazine* (2023). "How large venues can start preparing for Martyn's Law". Green, S. Issue 87. Spring 2023.
- CNBC (2023). "Pinterest shares slip on fourth-quarter revenue miss and weak forecast". Vanian, J. 10/02/2023. Accessed and downloaded on 27/07/2023 at: *https://www.cnbc.com/2023/02/06/pinterest-pins-earnings-q4-2022.html*.
- CNN (2011). "Loughner's dad feared he was out of control, neighbor says". 13/11/2011. Accessed and downloaded on 19/07/2023 at: *http://edition.cnn.com/2011/CRIME/01/12/arizona.shooting.suspect/*.
- CNN (2018). "Gunman in Florida yoga studio shooting made misogynistic comments on YouTube, NYT reports". Dakin And one and Artemis Moshtaghian. 03/11/2028. Accessed and downloaded on 10/07/2023

at: *https://edition.cnn.com/2018/11/03/us/tallahassee-shooting-yoga-studio/index.html*.

- CNN (2019a). "Facebook, Google and Twitter sign pledge to combat online extremism after New Zealand shooting". Fiegerman, S. 15/05/2019. Accessed and downloaded on 27/07/2023 at: *https://edition.cnn.com/2019/05/15/tech/tech-companies-christchurch-call/index.html*.

- CNN (2019b). "After US terrorism designation, Instagram begins banning some Iranian generals". O'Sullivan, D. 17/04/2019. Accessed and downloaded on 28/07/2023 at: *https://edition.cnn.com/2019/04/17/world/instagram-ban-iran-terrorism/index.html*.

- CNN (2021). "Ransomware gang that hit meat supplier mysteriously vanishes from the internet". Fung, B, Cohen, Z and Sands, G. *CNN Business*. 14/07/2021. Accessed and downloaded on 14/04/2023 at: *https://edition.cnn.com/2021/07/13/tech/revil-ransomware-disappears/index.html*.

- Cockburn, P (2014). *The Rise Of Islamic State: Isis And The New Sunni Revolution*. London. Verso.

- Congress.gov (2023). H.R. 821 "Social Media Child Protection Act". Accessed and downloaded on 27/06/2023 at: *https://www.congress.gov/bill/118th-congress/house-bill/821*.

- ConsultDTS.com (2023). "NIST Vs ISO: Which one is right for your organization?" Accessed and

downloaded on 19/06/2023 at:
https://consultdts.com/article/nist-vs-iso-27001/.

- Council of Europe, Budapest Convention can be accessed at:
  https://www.coe.int/en/web/cybercrime/home.
- Council on Foreign Relations (2018). "Compromise of TV5 Monde". Accessed and downloaded on 15/04/2023 at: *https://www.cfr.org/cyber-operations/compromise-tv5-monde.*
- Counter Terrorism Policing (2018). "Together, We're Tackling Online Terrorism". Press Release. 19/12/2018. Accessed and downloaded on 26/07/2023 at: *https://www.counterterrorism.police.uk/together-were-tackling-online-terrorism/.*
- Counter Terrorism Policing (2020). "Feuerkrieg Division (FKD) proscribed as terrorist group". 17/07/2020. Accessed and downloaded on 17/07/2023 at: *https://www.counterterrorism.police.uk/fkd-proscribed/.*
- Counter Terrorism Policing (2021). "New stats reveal the number of children arrested for terrorism offences is highest since records began". Accessed and downloaded on 07/03/2023 at: *https://www.counterterrorism.police.uk/new-stats-reveal-the-number-of-children-arrested-for-terrorism-offences-is-highest-since-records-began/.*
- Counter Terrorism Policing website (2023). Accessed and downloaded throughout this research at: *https://www.counterterrorism.police.uk/.*

- CPS (2019). "Cybercrime – prosecution guidance". Accessed on 30/07/2023 at: *https://www.cps.gov.uk/legal-guidance/cybercrime-prosecution-guidance*.
- CPS (2023). Guidance on prosecting terrorism was accessed and downloaded throughout this research at: *https://www.cps.gov.uk/crime-info/terrorism*.
- Crenshaw, M (1998). "The logic of terrorism: Terrorist behaviour as a product of strategic choice" in Reich, W (ed) (1998) *Origins of Terrorism: Psychologies, Ideologies, Theologies, States of Mind*.
- Crossley, J (2021). "The Apocalypse and Political Discourse in an Age of COVID". *Journal for the Study of the New Testament*, Vol. 44. Issue 1. Accessed and downloaded on 30/07/2023 at: *https://journals.sagepub.com/doi/10.1177/0142064X21 1025464*.
- Crypto News (2023). "Today in Crypto". 28/04/2023. Accessed and downloaded on 16/05/2023 at: *https://cryptonews.com/news/today-crypto-binance-begin-japan-operations-millennials-are-dominant-crypto-enthusiast-group-canadian-police-issue-warnings-after-75m-scam-hamas-stops-crypto-donations.htm*.
- CSO Online (2015). "Paris attacks demand 'wake-up call' on smartphone encryption". CSO United Kingdom by Matt Hamblen. 17/11/2015. Accessed and downloaded on 12/04/2023 at: *https://www.csoonline.com/article/3005570/paris-*

attacks-demand-wake-up-call-on-smartphone-encryption.html.

- CST Blog (2020). Accessed and downloaded on 07/03/2023 at: *https://cst.org.uk/news/blog/2020/05/13/white-jihad-jack-renshaws-journey-from-a-far-right-student-to-would-be-terrorist*.
- CST Research Briefing (2020). "White Jihad: Jack Renshaw's journey from far right student to would-be terrorist". Accessed and downloaded on 07/03/2023 at: *https://cst.org.uk/news/blog/2020/05/13/white-jihad-jack-renshaws-journey-from-a-far-right-student-to-would-be-terrorist*.
- CTC Westpoint (2012). "Announcement of al-Shabab's al-Kata'ib Media Foundation". Accessed and downloaded on 28/07/2023 at: *https://ctc.westpoint.edu/militant-imagery-project/0325/*.
- *Cybercrime Magazine* (2020). "Cybercrime To Cost The World $10.5 Trillion Annually By 2025". Accessed and downloaded on 05/07/2023 at: *https://cybersecurityventures.com/hackerpocalypse-cybercrime-report-2016/*.
- Cymet, T and Kerkvliet, G (2004). "What is the true number of victims of the postal anthrax attack of 2001?" *The Journal of the American Osteopathic Association*. November 2004.
- *Daily Mirror* (2016). "ISIS warn London 'next to be attacked' as UK churches put on terror alert after

French priest murder". Scott Campbell. 26/07/2016. Accessed and downloaded on 12/04/2023 at: *https://www.mirror.co.uk/news/world-news/isis-warn-london-next-attacked-8500399.*

- Dataconomy.com (2022). "The War Never Ends On The Cyber Front". Accessed and downloaded on 02/11/2022 at: *https://dataconomy.com/2022/10/11/cyber-terrorism-definition-attacks/.*
- DataGuard (2023). "Strengthening cybersecurity through the EU's NIS2 Directive". Accessed and downloaded on 05/07/2023 at: *https://www.dataguard.co.uk/blog/strengthening-cybersecurity-through-the-eu-nis2-directive?.*
- DataReportal (2023). "Instagram Statistics and Trends". Accessed and downloaded on 12/04/2023 at: *https://datareportal.com/essential-instagram-stats.*
- DCMS (2019). "Online Harms White Paper". Accessed and downloaded on 01/06/2023 at: *https://www.gov.uk/government/consultations/online-harms-white-paper/online-harms-white-paper.*
- Dean, A (2018). *Nine Lives: My Time As MI6's Top Spy Inside Al-Qaeda.* London. Oneworld.
- Dearden, L (2021). "UK's youngest terror offender walks free from court after recruiting for Neo-Nazi group". *Independent.* 08/02/2021. Accessed and downloaded on 07/03/2023 at: *https://www.independent.co.uk/news/uk/crime/neo-nazi-uk-fkd-youngest-terror-offender-b1799103.html.*

- Delo, C (2012). "Facebook Moves To Wipe Out Fake 'Likes'. But Can't Do Anything About Fat Fingers". 31/08/2012. Accessed and downloaded on 05/07/2023 at: *https://adage.com/article/digital/facebook-moves-wipe-fake-likes-fat-fingers/236983*.
- Deloitte (2017). "Connecting the protected barrels: Cybersecurity for upstream oil and gas". Mittal, A, Zonneveld, P, and Slaughter, A. 26/06/2017. Accessed and downloaded on 15/04/2023 at: *https://www2.deloitte.com/tr/en/pages/energy-and-resources/articles/oil-and-gas-cybersecurity.html*.
- Demandsage.com (2023). "Twitch 2023 Statistics in Depth". Accessed and downloaded on 18/07/2023 at: *https://www.demandsage.com/twitch-users/*.
- DeNardo, J. (1985). *The Political Strategy of Protest and Rebellion*. New Jersey. Princeton University Press.
- Department for Transport (2018). "Aviation Cyber Security Strategy: Moving Britain Forward". Accessed and downloaded on 10/05/2023 at: *https://assets.publishing.service.gov.uk/government/uploads/system/uploads/attachment_data/file/917529/aviation-cyber-security-strategy-document.pdf*.
- De Standaard (2012). "Sharia4belgium stopt ermee". 8/10/2012. Accessed and downloaded on 28/07/2023 at: *https://www.standaard.be/cnt/DMF20121008_00326293?_section=60549815*.
- DHS Office of Intelligence and Analysis (2021). Unclassified. 19/04/2021. Accessed and downloaded

on 06/06/2023 at: *https://www.justsecurity.org/wp-content/uploads/2021/09/january-6-clearinghouse-dhs-ia-domestic-violent-extremists-dves-tiktok-april-19-2021.pdf.*

- Dino, D (2019). "E-Recruits: How Gaming is Helping Terror Groups Radicalize and Recruit a Generation of Online Gamers". Concentric. 17/03/2019. Accessed and downloaded on 21/07/2023 at: *https://www.concentric.io/blog/e-recruits-how-gaming-is-helping-terrorist-groups-radicalize-and-recruit-a-generation-of-online-gamers.*

- DNI website (2023). "Counter Terrorism Guide: Hizbullah". Accessed and downloaded on 06/09/2023 at: *https://www.dni.gov/nctc/groups/hizballah.html.*

- DW (2019). "German neo-Nazi doomsday prepper network uncovered". Knight, B. 29/06/2019. Accessed and downloaded on 17/07/2023 at: *https://www.dw.com/en/german-neo-nazi-doomsday-prepper-network-ordered-body-bags-made-kill-lists/a-49410494.*

- Electronic Frontier Foundation (EFF) (2021). "The Cryptocurrency Surveillance Provision Buried in the Infrastructure Bill is a Disaster for Digital Privacy". 02/08/2021. Accessed on 14/12/2022 at: *https://www.eff.org/deeplinks/2021/08/cryptocurrency-surveillance-provision-buried-infrastructure-bill-disaster-digital.*

- Encyclopedia,com (2023). "Aryan Nations". Accessed and downloaded on 01/06/2023 at:

https://www.encyclopedia.com/politics/legal-and-political-magazines/aryan-nations.

- EU Commission (2021). *Incels: A First Scan of the Phenomenon (in the EU) and its Relevance and Challenges for P/CVE*. EU Commission and Radicalisation Network Awareness Practitioners. European Union. Accessed and downloaded on 11/07/2023 at: *https://home-affairs.ec.europa.eu/system/files/2021-10/ran_incels_first_scan_of_phenomen_and_relevance_challenges_for_p-cve_202110_en.pdf*.

- EU Commission (2022). *The Gamification of (Violent) Extremism*. Lakhani, S, White, J and Wallner, C. Radicalisation Awareness Network. Accessed and downloaded on 25/07/2023 at: *https://home-affairs.ec.europa.eu/system/files/2022-09/RAN%20Policy%20Support-%20gamification%20of%20violent%20extremism_en.pdf*.

- EU Commission (2023). "EU Cyber Resilience Act". Accessed and downloaded on 05/07/2023 at: *https://digital-strategy.ec.europa.eu/en/policies/cyber-resilience-act*.

- Eurocontrol (2021). "Think Paper: Aviation under attack from a wave of cyber crime". (05/07/2021) Accessed and downloaded on 10/05/2023 at: *https://www.eurocontrol.int/publication/eurocontrol-think-paper-12-aviation-under-attack-wave-cybercrime*.

- Euronews (2022). "AI cyber attacks are a 'critical threat'. This is how NATO is countering them". Pascale Davies. 26/12/2022. Accessed and downloaded on 04/04/2023 at: *https://www.euronews.com/next/2022/12/26/ai-cyber-attacks-are-a-critical-threat-this-is-how-nato-is-countering-them*.

- European Council (2023). "Infographic – Terrorism in the EU: facts and figures". Accessed and downloaded on 27/07/2023 at: *https://www.consilium.europa.eu/en/infographics/terrorism-eu-facts-figures/*.

- Europol (2022). *European Union: Terrorism Situation and Trend Report 2022*. Accessed and downloaded on 27/07/2023 at: *https://www.europol.europa.eu/cms/sites/default/files/documents/Tesat_Report_2022_0.pdf*.

- Europol (2023). *ChatGTP: The Impact of Large Language Models on Law Enforcement*. Accessed and downloaded on 04/04/2023 at: *https://www.europol.europa.eu/publications-events/publications/chatgpt-impact-of-large-language-models-law-enforcement*.

- Evans, T; Milton, D; Young, J. (2020). "Choosing to Fight, Choosing to Die: Examining How ISIS Foreign Fighters Select Their Operational Roles". Oxford University Press on behalf of the International Studies Association. *International Studies Review*, Volume 23, Issue 3, September 2021, pp509–531. Abstract

Accessed and downloaded on 31/07/2023 at: *https://academic.oup.com/isr/article-abstract/23/3/509/5879006*.

- ExplodingTopics.com (2023). "How many gamers are there? 2023 statistics". Accessed and downloaded on 21/07/2023 at: *https://explodingtopics.com/blog/number-of-gamers*.

- Ferracuti, F, and Bruno, F (1981). "Psychiatric aspects of terrorism in Italy. From Mad, the Bad and the Different". Accessed and downloaded on 30/07/2023 at: *https://www.ojp.gov/ncjrs/virtual-library/abstracts/psychiatric-aspects-terrorism-italy-mad-bad-and-different-p-199-213*.

- Firstpost (2023). "AI is dangerous, can threaten national security, society needs to adapt, says Google CEO Sundar Pichai". (18/04/2023). Accessed and downloaded on 02/05/2023 at: *https://www.firstpost.com/world/ai-is-dangerous-can-threaten-national-security-society-needs-to-adapt-says-google-ceo-sundar-pichai-12469082.html*.

- Flashpoint (2017). "Cyber Jihadists Dabble in DDoS: Assessing the Threat". Flashpoint Blog. 13/07/2023. Accessed and downloaded on 07/04/2023 at: *https://flashpoint.io/blog/cyber-jihadists-ddos/*.

- Forbes (2023). "ChatGPT's Biggest Competition: Here Are The Companies Working On Rival AI Chatbots". Hart, R. 23/02/2023. Accessed and downloaded on 01/05/2023 at: *https://www.forbes.com/sites/roberthart/2023/02/23/ch*

atgpts-biggest-competition-here-are-the-companies-working-on-rival-ai-chatbots/?sh=4b149eb4216b.

- Forbes (2023). "Top Social Media Statistics And Trends Of 2023". Accessed and downloaded on 01/07/2023 at: *https://www.forbes.com/advisor/business/social-media-statistics/.*

- Fortinet (2022). "Recent Cyber Attacks". Accessed and downloaded on 27/06/2023 at: *https://www.fortinet.com/resources/cyberglossary/recent-cyber-attacks.*

- Fox News (2014). "'How to Make Bomb in Kitchen of Mom' Featured in Al-Qaida's 1st English News magazine". NewsCore. 17/11/2014. Accessed and downloaded on 28/07/2023 at: *https://www.foxnews.com/world/how-to-make-bomb-in-kitchen-of-mom-featured-in-al-qaedas-1st-english-magazine.*

- Freedom House (2022). "[Internet] Freedom in the World 2022". Accessed and downloaded on 09/05/2023 at: *https://freedomhouse.org/country/united-kingdom/freedom-world/2022.*

- Freedom House (2023). "[Internet] Freedom in the World 2023". Accessed and downloaded on 12/04/2024 at: *https://freedomhouse.org/country/united-kingdom/freedom-world/2023.*

- *Financial Times* (2023). "Terror attack on Vienna pride parade thwarted by Austria's intelligence agency". Jones, S. 18/06/2023. Accessed and downloaded on 17/07/2023 at: *https://www.ft.com/content/4fd671dc-9aee-4709-b081-059b0051640d.*
- Gerstel, D (2016). "ISIS and Innovative Propaganda". Swarthmore IR Journal. (ND). Accessed and downloaded on 24/07/2023 at: *https://works.swarthmore.edu/cgi/viewcontent.cgi?article=1004&context=swarthmoreirjournal.*
- Gillespie, T (2018). *Custodians of the Internet.* Yale. Yale University Press.
- Global Internet Forum to Counter Terrorism (GIFCT) website (2023). Accessed and downloaded throughout this authorship. The Hash Sharing Database, Incident Response and Content Incident Protocol content is particularly useful for understanding prevention and response. See: 'What We Do' drop down at: *https://gifct.org/#.*
- Global Terrorism Index (2022). Accessed and downloaded on 12/04/2024 at *https://www.isdglobal.org/digital_dispatches/global-terrorism-index-2022-key-findings-in-6-charts/.*
- Google Transparency Report (2023). "Featured Policies". Accessed and downloaded on 26/07/2023 at: *https://transparencyreport.google.com/youtube-policy/featured-policies/violent-extremism?hl=en.*
- GoHenry (2022). "How to set up Facebook parental controls". 09/09/2022. Accessed and downloaded on

26/06/2023 at:
https://www.gohenry.com/uk/blog/parental-controls/how-to-set-up-facebook-parental-controls.

- GOV.UK (2021). "Longer jail terms and stricter monitoring as new terror laws gain Royal Assent". 29/04/2021.
https://www.gov.uk/government/news/longer-jail-terms-and-stricter-monitoring-as-new-terror-laws-gain-royal-assent.

- Gustini, R (2011). "Report: FBI warns of Al-Qaeda 'hit list'". *The Atlantic*. 17/06/2011. Accessed and downloaded on 17/04/2024 at:
https://www.theatlantic.com/national/archive/2011/06/report-fbi-issues-warning-about-40-person-al-qaeda-hit-list/351879/.

- Guynn, J (2016). "Twitter suspends alt-right accounts". *USA Today*. Accessed and downloaded on 08/03/2023 at:
https://eu.usatoday.com/story/tech/news/2016/11/15/twitter-suspends-alt-right-accounts/93943194/.

- Guyonneau, R and Le Dez, A (2019). "Artificial Intelligence in Digital Warfare". *The Cyber Defense Review*, Vol. 4. No. 2 (Fall 2019) pp103–116.

- Hackernoon (2021). "ISO/IEC 27035: The Incident Security Incident Management Guide". 18/03/2021. By @gtmars.com. Accessed and downloaded on 15/06/2023 at: *https://hackernoon.com/isoiec-27035-the-incident-security-incident-management-guide-nt5v354n/*.

- Hackerone.com (2023). "Pentesting Certification: Why Certify and Top 6 Certifications". Accessed and downloaded on 30/07/2023 at: *https://www.hackerone.com/knowledge-center/pentesting-certification-top-6-certifications*.
- Ham-Kucharski, A (2022). "Respawning Jihadist: ISIS Recruiting Through Online Gaming Communities". Portland State University. Fall 2022. Accessed and downloaded on 21/07/2023 at: *https://pdxscholar.library.pdx.edu/cgi/viewcontent.cgi?article=1001&context=is_student*.
- Hamm, M and Spaaj, R (2015). "Lone Wolf Terrorism in America: Using Knowledge of Radicalization Pathways to Forge Prevention Strategies". US Department of Justice. p3. Accessed and downloaded on 09/03/2023 at: *https://www.ojp.gov/pdffiles1/nij/grants/248691.pdf*.
- Harper, P and Micallef, C (2022). "Child's Play: How old do you have to be to have a Facebook and Instagram account? Social media age restrictions explained". *The Sun*. 08/06/2022. Accessed and downloaded on 27/06/2023 at: *https://www.thesun.co.uk/tech/4136922/age-restrictions-facebook-snapchat-twitter-instagram/*.
- Harvard Business Review (2021). "Are We Entering a New Era of Social Media Regulation?" Ghosh, D. 14/01/2021. Accessed and downloaded on 09/05/2023 at: *https://hbr.org/2021/01/are-we-entering-a-new-era-of-social-media-regulation*.

- HMG Legislation website (2023). "Counter-Terrorism and Sentencing Act (2021)". Accessed and downloaded n 07/05/2023 at: *https://www.legislation.gov.uk/ukpga/2021/11/contents/enacted*.
- HMG Prevent Strategy (2011). *Prevent Strategy*. Accessed and downloaded on 01/06/2023 at: *https://assets.publishing.service.gov.uk/government/uploads/system/uploads/attachment_data/file/97976/prevent-strategy-review.pdf*.
- Hoffman, B; Shapiro, E; Ware, J (2022). "Assessing the Threat of Incel Violence". *Studies in Conflict and Terrorism*. Accessed and downloaded on 11/07/2023 at: *https://research-repository.st-andrews.ac.uk/bitstream/handle/10023/24162/Hoffman_2020_SCT_Assessingthreat_AAM.pdf*.
- Homeland Security US (2023). "Podcast Duo Convicted of Terrorism Offenses". 10/07/2023. Accessed and downloaded on 17/07/2023 at: *https://www.hstoday.us/subject-matter-areas/counterterrorism/podcast-duo-convicted-of-terrorism-offenses/*.
- Home Office (2016). "National Action becomes first extreme right-wing group to be banned in UK". 16/12/2016. Accessed and downloaded on 17/07/2023 at: *https://www.gov.uk/government/news/national-action-becomes-first-extreme-right-wing-group-to-be-banned-in-uk*.

- Home Office (2023). "Counter-terrorism Strategy". 18/07/2023. Accessed and downloaded on 19/07/2023 at: *https://www.gov.uk/government/publications/counter-terrorism-strategy-contest-2023/counter-terrorism-strategy-contest-2023-accessible*.

- Home Office (2023a). "Review of the Computer Misuse Act: consultation and response to call for information". 20/02/2023. Accessed and downloaded on 30/07/2023 at: *https://www.gov.uk/government/consultations/review-of-the-computer-misuse-act-1990/review-of-the-computer-misuse-act-1990-consultation-and-response-to-call-for-information-accessible*.

- Human Rights Watch (2015). "Q&A on the conflict in Yemen and International Law". 06/04/2015. Accessed and downloaded on 28/07/2023 at: *https://www.hrw.org/news/2015/04/06/q-conflict-yemen-and-international-law*.

- IFP (2021). "5 Famous Outages That Lost Businesses Millions (and What You Can Learn From Them)". 25/11/2021. Accessed and downloaded on 16/04/2023 at: *https://www.insightsforprofessionals.com/it/leadership/famous-business-outages*.

- *InfoSecurity Magazine* (2022). "PressReader Suffers Cyber-Attack". Coble, S. 07/03/2022. Accessed and downloaded on 15/04/2023 at:

https://www.infosecurity-magazine.com/news/pressreader-suffers-cyber-attack/.

- *InfoSecurity Magazine* (2023). "Cyber-Attacks in the Media Industry Making Headlines". Coker, J (ND). Accessed and downloaded on 15/04/2023 at: *https://www.infosecurity-magazine.com/news-features/cyber-attacks-media-industry/*.
- *InfoSecurity Magazine* (June 2023). "US Military Personnel Warned of Malicious Smartwatches". Mascellino, A. 23/06/2023. Accessed and downloaded on 26/06/2023 at: *https://www.infosecurity-magazine.com/news/us-military-warned-malicious/*.
- *InfoSecurity Magazine* (May 2023). "SpinOk Trojan Compromises 421 Million Android Devices". Mascellino, A. 31/05/2023. Accessed and downloaded on 26/06/2023 at: *https://www.infosecurity-magazine.com/news/spinok-trojan-compromises-421m/*.
- Instagram (2023). "Community Guidelines". Accessed and downloaded on 28/07/2023 at: *https://help.instagram.com/477434105621119*.
- Internet Archive Wayback Machine (2023). "Conviction of former CompuServe Official in Munich Court". Accessed and downloaded on 09/05/2023 at: *https://web.archive.org/web/20040225201934/http://www.gseis.ucla.edu/iclp/fsomm.html*.
- Islam, T and Ryan, J (2016). "Vulnerability Assessment and Impact Analysis". *Science Direct*. Accessed and downloaded on 07/06/2023 at:

https://www.sciencedirect.com/topics/economics-econometrics-and-finance/vulnerability-analysis.

- ISO/IEC 27001:2013. "*Information technology – Security techniques – Information security management systems – Requirements*".
- ISO/IEC 27001:2022. "Information security, cybersecurity and privacy protection: Information security management systems". Accessed and downloaded on 16/04/2024 at: *https://www.iso.org/obp/ui/en/#iso:std:iso-iec:27001:ed-3:v1:en*.
- ISO/IEC 27035-2:2023. "Information technology: Information security incident management . Part 2: Guidelines to plan and prepare for incident response". Accessed and downloaded on 16/04/2024 at: *https://www.iso.org/standard/78974.html*.
- ISO/IEC 27037:2012. "Information technology Security techniques: Guidelines for identification, collection, acquisition and preservation of digital evidence". Accessed and downloaded on 26/04/2024 at: *https://www.iso.org/standard/44381.html*.
- ISO Docs (2022). "ISO 31000 RISK MANAGEMENT". 02/02/2022. Accessed and downloaded on 06/06/2023 at: *https://iso-docs.com/blogs/iso-concepts/iso-31000-risk-management*.
- ISO Security.com (2023). "ISO/IEC 27037. Information technology – Security techniques – Guidelines for identification, collection, acquisition

and preservation of digital evidence". Overview and discussion by unnamed author accessed and downloaded on 21/06/2023 at: *https://www.iso27001security.com/html/27037.html*.

- ISO Security Blog. (2023). ISO 27035 was first published during 2011 as a single standard. For more information, see: *https://www.iso27001security.com/html/27035.html*.

- ISO Website (2023). Proposed ISO standard ISO/IEC 27090 on addressing security threats to AI systems can be found at: *https://www.iso27001security.com/html/27090.html*.

- IT Governance (2023). "Why use an ISO/IEC 27000-series standard?" Accessed and downloaded on 16/04/2023 at: *https://www.itgovernance.co.uk/iso27000-family*.

- IT Governance B (2023). "ISO/IEC 27017 2015 Standard". Accessed and downloaded on 16/04/2023 at: *https://www.itgovernance.co.uk/shop/product/isoiec-27017-2015-standard*.

- IT Governance Blog (2023). "ISO 27001 Annex of Controls Explained". Irwin, L. 06/01/2023. Accessed and downloaded on 05/04/2023 at: *https://www.itgovernance.co.uk/blog/iso-27001-the-14-control-sets-of-annex-a-explained*.

- IT Governance C (2023). "ISO/IEC 27031 2011 Standard". Accessed and downloaded on 16/04/2023 at:

https://www.itgovernance.co.uk/shop/product/isoiec-27031-2011-standard.

- Jäger, H; Schmidtchen, G; Süllwold, L (eds) (1981). *Analyzen zum Terrorismus 2*: *Lebenslaufanalysen*. Darmstadt, Germany: DeutscherVerlag

- Jerusalem Post (2022). "Cyber attacks on hospitals can kill – here's why". 16/10/2021. Accessed and downloaded on 15/12/2022 at: *https://www.jpost.com/cybertech/cyber-attacks-on-hospitals-can-kill-heres-why-682057*.

- Jihadology (2018). "Member of Islamic State and al-Sham Leaks Unpublished Video Message from Adam Gadahn". Accessed article on 23/09/2022.

- Jihadoscope (2019). Jihadoscope monitors jihadist activity across the news and social media. Scroll down for it tweets at its Twitter feed. Accessed and downloaded on 17/07/2023 at: *https://twitter.com/jihadoscope?lang=en*.

- Kalmoe, N (2014). "Fueling the fire: Violent metaphors, trait aggression, and support for political violence". *Political Communication,* 31(4), pp545–563.

- Kaspersky (2023). "What is a honeypot?". Accessed and downloaded on 05/07/2023 at: *https://usa.kaspersky.com/resource-center/threats/what-is-a-honeypot*.

- Kaspersky (2023). "What is steganography? Definition and explanation". Accessed and downloaded on

11/04/2023 at: *https://www.kaspersky.com/resource-center/definitions/what-is-steganography*.

- Kent, M (2023). Interview with author on impact of terrorist speeches on Internet. Conducted on 06/07/2023 in London.
- Khatchadourian, R (2007). "Azzam the American: The making of an Al-Qaeda homegrown". *The New Yorker*.
- King, P (2019). "Islamic State group's experiments with the decentralized web". European Counter Terrorism Center. 09/04/2019. Accessed and downloaded on 24/07/2023 at: *https://www.europol.europa.eu/sites/default/files/documents/islamic_state_group_experiments_with_the_decentralised_web_-_p.king_.pdf*.
- Kirat, D; Jang, J; Stoecklin M (2018). "DeepLocker: Concealing Targeted Attacks with AI Locksmithing". IBM Research. Black Hat USA 2018. Accessed and downloaded on 07/04/2023 at: *us-18-Kirat-DeepLocker-Concealing-Targeted-Attacks-with-AI-Locksmithing.pdf (blackhat.com)* .
- Klausen, J (2021). *The Founder. Western Jihadism: A Thirty Year History*. Oxford. Oxford University Press.
- Klein, A (2019). "From Twitter to Charlottesville: Analyzing the Fighting Words Between the Alt-Right and Antifa". *International Journal of Communication*, Vol. 13 (2019), pp297–318.
- Kovacs, E (2020). "University Project Tracks Ransomware Attacks on Critical Infrastructure". *Security Week*. 12/09/2020. Accessed and downloaded

on 15/12/2022 at:
https://www.securityweek.com/university-project-tracks-ransomware-attacks-critical-infrastructure.
Other relevant *Security Week* articles about health sector attacks can be found at:

- o (Germany) *https://www.securityweek.com/german-hospital-hacked-patient-taken-another-city-dies*.
- o (France) *https://www.securityweek.com/french-hospital-cancels-operations-after-cyberattack*.
- o (Israel) *https://www.securityweek.com/israeli-hospital-targeted-ransomware-attack*.
- o (USA) *https://www.securityweek.com/us-hospitals-warned-imminent-ransomware-attacks-russia and https://www.securityweek.com/vermont-hospital-still-calculating-cost-ransomware-attack* and *https://www.securityweek.com/hacked-hospital-chain-says-all-250-us-facilities-affected*.

- Kovacs, E (2022). "Hamas Cyberspies Return With New Malware After Exposure Of Operations". *Security Week*. 09/02/2022. Accessed and downloaded on 06/12/2022 at: *https://www.securityweek.com/hamas-cyberspies-return-new-malware-after-exposure-operations*.
- Kreps, S and Schneider, J (2019). "Escalation firebreaks in the cyber, conventional, and nuclear domains: moving beyond effects-based logics". *Journal of Cybersecurity*
- Kuner (1998). "Judgment of the Munich Court in the 'CompuServe Case'". 15/07/1998. Accessed and

downloaded on 09/05/2023 at:
http://www.kuner.com/data/reg/somm.html.

- Kyber Security (2019). "3 Reasons to Align with the NIST Cybersecurity Framework". 19/04/2023. Accessed and downloaded on 12/06/2023 at: *https://kybersecure.com/3-reasons-to-align-with-nist-cybersecurity-framework/*.

- Lancashire Post (2022). "Preston teenager charged with sharing terrorist propaganda on Instagram". Matthew Calderbank. 21/10/2022. Accessed and downloaded on 28/07/2023 at: *https://www.lep.co.uk/news/crime/preston-teenager-charged-with-sharing-terrorist-propaganda-on-instagram-3889012*.

- Lee, C; Choi, K; Shandler, R; Kayser, C (2021). "Mapping Global Cyberterror Networks: An Empirical Study of Al-Qaeda and ISIS Cyberterrorism". *Journal of Contemporary Criminal Justice*, accessed and downloaded on 31/10/2022 at: *https://drive.google.com/file/d/1JjET6quQE_7-W0Z6Ihc1anp5rOuK80xV/vie*.

- Leuprecht C; Skillicorn, D; McCauley, C (2020). "Terrorists, radicals and activists: Distinguishing between countering violent extremism and preventing extremist violence, and why it matters", in von Hlatky, S (ed) *Countering violent extremism and terrorism: Assessing domestic and international strategies*. Montreal & Kingston, Canada. McGill-Queens University Press: pp18–46.

- Levin, B (2003). "Cyberhate: A Legal and Historical Analysis of Extremists' use of Computer Networks in America", in Perry, B (ed) *Hate and Bias Crime: A Reader*. Routledge. 2003.
- Lima A., et al (2016). "Towards Safe and Secure Autonomous and Cooperative Vehicle Ecosystems", Proceedings of the 2nd ACM Workshop on Cyber-Physical Systems Security and Privacy.
- *Long War Journal* (2012). "'Global Jihadists' overrun Egyptian army outpost on Israeli border". Roggio, B. 05/08/2012. Accessed and downloaded on 01/06/2023 at: *https://www.longwarjournal.org/archives/2012/08/global_jihadists_ove.php*.
- *Los Angeles Times* (2015). "Dylann Roof's manifesto resembles comments on neo-Nazi website, analysis finds". Lee, K. 22/06/2015. Accessed and downloaded on 19/07/2023 at: *https://www.latimes.com/nation/la-na-dylann-roof-web-20150622-story.html*.
- Mackey, R and Lee, M (2022). "Left-Wing Voices Are Silenced on Twitter as Far-Right Trolls Advise Elon Musk". *The Intercept.* 29/11/2022. Accessed and downloaded on 27/07/2023 at: *https://theintercept.com/2022/11/29/elon-musk-twitter-andy-ngo-antifascist/*.
- Macklin, G (2019). "The Christchurch Attacks: Livestream Terror in the Viral Video Age". *CTC Sentinel*. July 2019. Vol 12, Issue 6. Accessed and downloaded on 25/07/2023 at:

https://ctc.westpoint.edu/christchurch-attacks-livestream-terror-viral-video-age/.

- Mandiant FireEye Intelligence (2018). "TRITON Attribution: Russian Government-Owned Lab Most Likely Built Custom Intrusion Tools for Triton Attackers". Accessed and downloaded on 15/04/2023 at: *https://www.mandiant.com/resources/blog/triton-attribution-russian-government-owned-lab-most-likely-built-tools*.
- Margolin, H (2022). "The Top Platforms ISIS is Using in the Deep and Dark Web". Webz.io. 22/02/2023. Accessed and downloaded on 24/07/2023 at: *https://webz.io/dwp/the-top-platforms-isis-is-using-in-the-deep-and-dark-web/*.
- Markovic, I (2023). "How to use the risk assessment matrix to organize your project better". 08.03.2023. Accessed and downloaded on 02/06/2023 at: *https://tms-outsource.com/blog/posts/risk-assessment-matrix/*.
- Mashable.com (2020). "YouTube puts human content moderators back to work". Kraus, R. 20/09/2020. Accessed and downloaded on 26/07/2023 at: *https://mashable.com/article/youtube-human-content-moderation*.
- McCabe, D (2021). "How a Stabbing in Israel Echoes Through the Fight Over Online Speech". (24/03/2012). *The New York Times*.
- McCarthy, J (2016). "Americans cite cyber terrorism among top three threats to US Gallup". 10 February.

Accessed and downloaded on 31/10/2022 at: *https:// news.gallup.com/poll/189161/americans-cite-cyberterrorism-among-top-three-threats.aspx*.

- McCarthy, M (2020). "How online scam 'brushing' works and why COVID-19 is to blame for its resurgence". Accessed and downloaded on 27/06/2023 at: *https://www.abc.net.au/news/2020-08-27/what-is-brushing-why-is-it-on-rise-during-coronavirus-pandemic/12602084*.

- Medium.com (2014). "42 Quotes from Sam Altman on Later Stage Start Up Advice". Ragen Sanghvi. 05/12/2014. Accessed and downloaded on 08/06/2023 at: *https://medium.com/how-to-start-a-startup/42-quotes-from-sam-altman-on-later-stage-startup-advice-6c3d1cc4431d*.

- Meltwater.com (2023). "UK Social Media Statistics". Accessed and downloaded on 28/07/2023 at: *https://www.meltwater.com/en/blog/uk-social-media-statistics*.

- MEMRI (2016): "Bank Al-Ansar 'The Supporters Bank' – Supplies Jihadis with ready-to-use Facebook, Twitter accounts". Accessed and downloaded on 24/06/2023 at: *https://www.memri.org/cjlab/bank-al-ansar-the-supporters-bank-supplies-jihadis-with-ready-to-use-facebook-twitter-accounts*.

- MEMRI (2022a). "Large Pro-Islamic State (ISIS) Group Operating Openly on Facebook Shares ISIS Content, Recruits 'Media Fighters'". 15/11/2022.

Accessed and downloaded on 24/07/2023 at: *https://www.memri.org/jttm/large-pro-islamic-state-isis-group-operating-openly-facebook-shares-isis-content-recruits-media*.

- MEMRI (2022b). "Pro-ISIS Media Team Raid 'Brigade Calls' for Organized ISIS Media Dissemination As Most Important Means Of Support". 12/08/2022. Accessed and downloaded on 24/07/2023 at: *https://www.memri.org/jttm/pro-isis-media-team-raid-brigade-calls-organized-isis-media-dissemination-most-important-means*.
- MEMRI (2023). "ISIS Supporter Outlines How To Become Involved In Cyber Jihad". 09/03/2023. Accessed and downloaded on 24/07/2023 at: *https://www.memri.org/cjlab/isis-supporter-outlines-how-become-involved-cyber-jihad*.
- MEMRI (2023). "ISIS Supporter Offers Tips For Would-Be Programmers". 21/07/2023. Accessed and downloaded on 24/07/2023 at: *https://www.memri.org/cjlab/isis-supporter-offers-tips-would-be-programmers*.
- MEMRI (April 2023). "Global Network of Eco-Accelerationists Use Instagram To Share Violent Threats, Manifestos and Images of Industrial Sabotage". 25/04/2023. Accessed and downloaded on 28/07/2023 at: *https://www.memri.org/dttm/global-network-eco-accelerationists-use-instagram-share-violent-threats-manifestos-and-images*.

- MEMRI (May 2023). "Review of Twitter Account Of New Jihadi Group Tehreek-e-Jihad Pakistan (TEJ)". 18/05/2023. Accessed and downloaded on 27/07/2023 at: *https://www.memri.org/jttm/review-twitter-account-new-jihadi-group-tehreek-e-jihad-pakistan-tjp-which-warns-pakistani-army*.
- MEMRI (July 2023a). "Lebanese Hizbullah-Affiliated Accounts Active on Twitter". 03/07/2023. Accessed and downloaded on 27/07/2023 at: *https://www.memri.org/cjlab/lebanese-hizbullah-affiliated-accounts-active-twitter-despite-content-moderation-efforts*.
- MEMRI (July 2023b). "Jihadis Promote Their Accounts On Meta's Newly-Launched Threads App". Accessed and downloaded on 27/07/2023 at: *https://www.memri.org/cjlab/jihadis-promote-their-accounts-metas-newly-launched-threads-app-pro-isis-outlet-calls-using*.
- MEMRI (July 2023c). "ISIS Supporter Calls for Lone Wolf attacks Against 'Far-Right Extremists, Neo-Nazis and White Supremacists' in the West". 24/07/2023. Accessed and downloaded on 27/07/2023 at: *https://www.memri.org/jttm/isis-supporter-calls-lone-wolf-attacks-against-far-right-extremists-neo-nazis-and-white*.
- Merari, A, (1990). "The readiness to kill and die. Suicidal terrorism in the Middle East." In, Reich, W. et al. *Origins of Terrorism: Psychologies, Ideologies,*

Theologies, States of Mind. Washington DC. Woodrow Wilson Center Press. pp192–207

- Meta (2018). "An Update on Our Plans to Restrict Data Access on Facebook". 04/04/2018. Accessed and downloaded on 27/06/2023 at: *https://about.fb.com/news/2018/04/restricting-data-access/.*

- Meta (2018). The *State-by-State Breakdown of People Whose Facebook Information May Have Been Improperly Shared with Cambridge Analytica* bulletin was accessed and downloaded on 27/06/2023 at: *https://about.fb.com/wp-content/uploads/2018/05/state-by-state-breakdown.pdf.*

- Metro (2022). "What is Discord, the popular chat app used by gamers?" Sundaravelu, A. 16/11/2022. Accessed and downloaded on 17/07/2023 at: *https://metro.co.uk/2022/11/16/what-is-discord-the-popular-chat-app-used-by-gamers-17769256/.*

- Monterey Institute of International Studies (2001). "Chronology of Aum Shinrikyo's CBW Activities". Accessed and downloaded on 01/06/2023 at: *https://www.nonproliferation.org/wp-content/uploads/2016/06/aum_chrn.pdf.*

- Moses, D (2019). "White Genocide and the Ethics of Public Analysis". *Journal of Genocide Research*, Vol 21. No. 2. pp201–213.

- Munson, L (2007). "What is a Click Farm?" Security FAQs. 28/06/2015. Accessed on 26/06/2022.

- MyZine.com (2007). "Al-Qaeda video warning to US by American Adam Gadahn". 30/09/2007. Not retrievable but cited in CNN (2015) at: *https://edition.cnn.com/2015/04/23/world/adam-gadahn-al-qaeda/index.html*.
- National Cyber Security Centre (NCSC) (2023). "Cyber Security Toolkit for Boards". 30/03/2023. Accessed and downloaded on 12/06/2023 at: *https://www.ncsc.gov.uk/collection/board-toolkit/embedding-cyber-security-into-your-organisation*.
- NBC News (2004). "FBI still fears threat from crop-dusters". 22.04.2004. Accessed and downloaded on 11/04/2023 at: *https://www.nbcnews.com/id/wbna4808551*.
- NBC News (2015a). "Paris Kosher Supermarket Attacker, Amedy Coulibaly, Was Wearing GoPro". NBC News. 31/01/2015. Accessed and downloaded on 28/06/2022 at: *https://www.nbcnews.com/storyline/paris-magazine-attack/paris-kosher-supermarket-attacker-amedy-coulibaly-was-wearing-gopro-n297386*.
- NBC News (2015b). "Americans Warren Weinstein and Adam Gadahn killed in U.S. Drone Strikes". NBC News. 23/04/2015.
- NCSC (2023). The complete business toolkit can be accessed and downloaded at: *https://www.ncsc.gov.uk/files/NCSC_Cyber-Security-Board-Toolkit.pdf*.

- Netherlands National Coordinator for Counterterrorism (ND) (2007). "Jihadis and the internet". Accessed and downloaded on 28/07/2023 at: *https://irp.fas.org/world/netherlands/jihadis.pdf.*
- *New Delhi Times* (2014). "ISIS Supporters in France: The Jihadis Next Door?" 20/12/2014. Accessed and downloaded on 02/11/2022 at: *https://www.newdelhitimes.com/isis-supporters-in-france-the-jihadis-next-door123/.*
- *News-Herald* (2023). "Former Woodhaven student charged with threat of terrorism after Instagram Live rant". Martin, J. 19/05/2023. Accessed and downloaded on 28/07/2023 at: *https://www.thenewsherald.com/2023/05/19/former-woodhaven-student-charged-with-threat-of-terrorism-after-instagram-live-rant/.*
- New Net Technologies (2023). "Airbus Hit By Cyber Attacks On Multiple Suppliers". Accessed and downloaded on 10/05/2023 at: *https://www.newnettechnologies.com/airbus-hit-by-cyber-attacks-on-multiple-suppliers.html.*
- *New York Post* (2023) "British teen charged with terrorism was exploited, radicalized online: documentary". Land, O. O3/01/2023. Accessed and downloaded on 10/07/2023 at: *https://nypost.com/2023/01/03/british-teen-who-died-by-suicide-after-being-charged-with-terrorism-was-exploited-online-documentary/.*

- NIST (2020). "Protecting Controlled Unclassified Information in Nonfederal Systems and Organisations". NIST 800-171. Accessed and downloaded on 29/07/2023 at: *https://csrc.nist.gov/pubs/sp/800/171/r2/upd1/final*.
- NIST (2022a). Accessed and downloaded on 12/06/2023 at: *https://www.usa.gov/agencies/national-institute-of-standards-and-technology*.
- NIST (2022b). "About". Accessed and downloaded on 20/06/2023 at: *https://www.nist.gov/about-nist*.
- NIST (2023). "NIST Drafts Major Update to Its Widely Used Cybersecurity Framework". Accessed and downloaded on 25/04/2024 at: *https://www.nist.gov/news-events/news/2023/08/nist-drafts-major-update-its-widely-used-cybersecurity-framework*.
- NIST (2024). "NIST Releases Version 2.0 of Landmark Cybersecurity Framework". Accessed and downloaded on 25/04/2024 at: *https://www.nist.gov/news-events/news/2024/02/nist-releases-version-20-landmark-cybersecurity-framework*.
- NIST Computer Security Resource Center (2022). "Getting Started with the NIST Cybersecurity Framework: A Quick Start Guide". 19/04/2022. Accessed and downloaded on 12/06/2023 at: *https://csrc.nist.gov/Projects/cybersecurity-framework/nist-cybersecurity-framework-a-quick-start-guide*.

- NIST Privacy Framework (2020). Revision 5 comments accessed and downloaded on 29/07/2023 at: *https://www.nist.gov/privacy-framework/nist-sp-800-53*.
- NIST SP 800-61:2 (2012). "Computer Security Incident Handling Guide". August 2012. Accessed and downloaded on 08/06/2023 at: *https://nvlpubs.nist.gov/nistpubs/specialpublications/nist.sp.800-61r2.pdf*.
- NIST SP 800-86 (2006). "Guide to Integrating Forensic Techniques into Incident Response". Accessed and downloaded on 21/06/2023 at: *https://nvlpubs.nist.gov/nistpubs/Legacy/SP/nistspecialpublication800-86.pdf*.
- NIST SP 800-94 (2007). "Guide to Intrusion Detection and Prevention Systems". Accessed and downloaded on 21/06/2023 at: *https://nvlpubs.nist.gov/nistpubs/Legacy/SP/nistspecialpublication800-94.pdf*.
- Noguchi, M and Ueda, H. (2019). "An analysis of the actual status of recent cyberattacks on critical infrastructures". *NEC Technical Journal*, Special Issue Cybersecurity, Vol. 12. No. 2, pp19–24.
- Norman, J (2018). "North Korea, Cyberterrorism Top Threats to U.S." Accessed and downloaded on 22/06/2023 at: *https://news.gallup.com/poll/228437/north-korea-cyberterrorism-top-threats.aspx*.

- NPR (2017). "Long Island Woman Charged With Using Bitcoin To Launder Money To Support ISIS". Wamsley, L. 15/12/2017. Accessed and downloaded on 16/05/2023 at: *https://www.npr.org/sections/thetwo-way/2017/12/15/571099023/long-island-woman-charged-with-using-bitcoin-to-launder-money-to-support-isis.*

- NSIS Norway Presentation (2014). Accessed and downloaded on 18/07/2023 at: *https://rm.coe.int/1680305d01.*

- Office of Justice Programs (2002). "Computer Crimes and the USA PATRIOT Act". Ellen Podgor. *Criminal Justice*, Vol 17. Issue 2. Summer 2002. pp61–63, 69. Accessed and downloaded on 30/07/2023 at: *https://www.ojp.gov/ncjrs/virtual-library/abstracts/computer-crimes-and-usa-patriot-act.*

- Oil and Gas IQ (2022). Davis, D. "5 Big Cyberattacks in Oil and Gas". 11/01/2022. Accessed and downloaded on 15/04/2023 at: *https://www.oilandgasiq.com/digital-transformation/articles/5-big-cyber-security-attacks-in-oil-and-gas.*

- OODALOOP (2021) "Security Analysis Clears TikTok of Censorship, Privacy Accusations". Accessed and downloaded on 16/04/2024 at: *https://www.oodaloop.com/briefs/2021/03/24/security-analysis-clears-tiktok-of-censorship-privacy-accusations/.*

- Ortiz de Gortari, A, cited in VentureBeat.com (2014). "Seeing things: When Gaming messes with reality – and your brain". Crawley, D. 28/01/2014. Accessed and downloaded on 24/07/2023 at: *https://venturebeat.com/games/when-gaming-messes-with-reality/*.

- OSCE and ODIHR (2007). "Countering Terrorism, Protecting Human Rights". OSCE Office for Democratic Institutions and Human Rights (ODIHR). Warsaw, 2007. Accessed and downloaded on 30/07/2023 at: *https://www.osce.org/files/f/documents/d/6/29103.pdf*.

- PALs Guidance (2023). "Publicly accessible locations (PALs) guidance CCTV". Accessed and downloaded on 12/04/2024 at *https://www.protectuk.police.uk/cctv*.

- Perlmutter, P (1999). *Legacy of Hate: A Short History of Ethnic, Religious, and Racial Prejudice in America*. New York. Routledge.

- Petro, D and Morris, B (2017). "Weaponizing Machine Learning: Humanity was Overrated Anyway". *DefCon*. Accessed and downloaded on 07/04/2023 at *https://www.defcon.org/html/defcon-25/dc-25-speakers.html#Petro*.

- Post, J (1998). "Terrorist psycho-logic: Terrorist behavior as a product of psychological forces". In *Origins of terrorism: Psychologies, ideologies, theologies, states of mind*, (ed) Reich. pp25–40. Washington, DC. Woodrow Wilson Center Press.

- Post, J; Ruby; Shaw (2000). "From Car Bombs To Logic Bombs: The Growing Threat from Information Terrorism". Accessed and downloaded on 10/10/2022 at: *https://www.researchgate.net/publication/254268342_From_Car_Bombs_to_Logic_Bombs_The_Growing_T hreat_from_Information_Terrorism*.
- PhoenixNAP (2019). "Upgrade your Security Incident Response Plan (CSIRP)". 10/03/2019. Accessed and downloaded on 16/06/2023 at: *https://phoenixnap.com/blog/cyber-security-incident-response-plan*.
- PhoenixTS (2013). "Car Hacking Just Got Deathly Serious". Neu, A. 27/06/2013. Accessed and downloaded on 08/03/2024 at: *https://phoenixts.com/blog/car-hacking-thought-to-be-cause-of-michael-hastings-death/*.
- Politico (2023). "How UK's Online Safety Bill fell victim to never-ending political crisis". Scott, M and Dickson, A. 28/02/2023. Accessed and downloaded on 09/05/2023 at: *https://www.politico.eu/article/online-safety-bill-uk-westminster-politics/*.
- Pool Re (2022). "Protect Duty Hub". Accessed on 20/10/2022 and available at: *https://www.poolre.co.uk/protect-duty/*.
- Press Reader (2022) "Girl groomed by neo-Nazis killed herself in care home". Accessed and downloaded on 15/04/2024 at: *https://www.pressreader.com/uk/the-sunday-telegraph/20221023/282664691315386*.

- Project Management.com (2022). "5 Phases of Project Management Life Cycle you need to know". Donato, H. 17/10/2022. Accessed and downloaded on 12/06/2023 at: *https://project-management.com/project-management-phases/*.
- Rand Corporation (2019). "Terrorist Use of Cryptocurrencies". 27.03.2019. Accessed and downloaded on 15/12/2022 at: *https://www.rand.org/pubs/research_reports/RR3026.html*.
- Reich, W. et al (1990). *Origins of Terrorism: Psychologies, Ideologies, Theologies, States of Mind.* Washington DC. Woodrow Wilson Center Press.
- Reuters (2010). "British white supremacist jailed for making ricin". 14/05/2010. Accessed and downloaded on 17/07/2023 at: *https://www.reuters.com/article/us-britain-supremacist-idUSTRE64D4IY20100514*.
- Rise to Peace (2022). "Black Pill Ideology: What is Incel Extremism?" Accessed and downloaded on 11/07/2023 at: *https://www.risetopeace.org/2022/04/14/black-pill-ideology-what-is-incel-extremism/risetopece/*.
- Rodriguez, A (2023). "Why Project management is Essential in Cyber Security and Information Security". 02/05/2023. Accessed and downloaded on 12/06/2023 at: *https://www.linkedin.com/pulse/why-project-management-essential-cyber-security-adrian-rodriguez/*.

- Rose, H and AC (2021). *"We are Generation Terror!": Youth-on-youth Radicalisation in Extreme-right Youth Groups.* International Centre for the Study of Radicalisation (ICSR) and Community Security Trust (CST) accessed and downloaded on 07/03/2023 at: *https://icsr.info/wp-content/uploads/2021/12/ICSR-CST-Report-We-are-Generation-Terror-Youth%E2%80%91on%E2%80%91youth-Radicalisation-in-Extreme%E2%80%91right-Youth-Groups.pdf.*
- S&P Global Insights (2022). "Cyberattacks on oil surge as hackers target commodities". Accessed and downloaded on 15/04/2023 at: *https://www.spglobal.com/commodityinsights/en/market-insights/latest-news/oil/021822-cyberattacks-on-oil-surge-as-hackers-target-commodities.*
- Sageman, M (2017). *Turning To Political Violence: The Emergence of Terrorism.* Philadelphia. University of Pennsylvania Press.
- Scapolo, F (2021). "Twitter Permanently Bans Donald Trump. What Does That Mean For Us?" Institute for Internet & the Just Society. 10/01/2021. Accessed and downloaded on 08/03/2023 at: *https://www.internetjustsociety.org/twitter-permanently-bans-donald-trump-what-does-that-mean-for-us.*
- Schmid, A (2004). "Terrorism – The Definitional Problem". *Case Western Reserve Journal of International Law.* Vol. 36. Issue 2. Accessed and

downloaded on 31/07/2023 at:
https://scholarlycommons.law.case.edu/cgi/viewcontent
.cgi?article=1400&context=jil.
- SearchEngineJournal.com (2022). "The Top 10 Social
  Media Sites & Platforms". Accessed and downloaded
  on 01/07/2023 at:
  https://www.searchenginejournal.com/social-
  media/biggest-social-media-sites/#close.
- Segal, H, (Vimeo: 2015). Grid 15 Talk *Terrorism and*
  the Media. Accessed and downloaded on 07/06/2023
  at: *https://vimeo.com/138592737.*
- Shandler, R et al (2021). "Cyber Terrorism and Public
  Support for Retaliation – A Multi Country Survey
  Experiment". *British Journal of Political Science..*
- Sky News (2018). "Can you buy chemical weapons on
  the dark web?" 20/03/2023. Accessed and downloaded
  on 01/06/2023 at: *https://news.sky.com/story/can-you-*
  buy-chemical-weapons-on-the-dark-web-11297819.
- Smart Home Fox (2023). "Tik Tok Statistics in the
  UK". Accessed and downloaded on 06/06/2023. For a
  top-20 list of Tik Tok users worldwide go to:
  https://www.smart-home-fox.co.uk/tiktok-user-
  statistics.
- Smith, A (2018). "There's an open secret about
  Cambridge Analytica in the political world: It doesn't
  have the 'secret sauce' it claims". 21/03/2018. Business
  Insider.
- SocialShepherd.com (2023). "23 Essential Twitter (X)
  Statistics You Need to Know in 2023". Jack Shepherd.

16/05/2023. Accessed and downloaded on 26/07/2023 at:
https://thesocialshepherd.com/blog/twitter-statistics.

- Soufan, A (2012). *The Black Banners: Inside the Hunt for Al-Qaed*a. London. Penguin.
- START Global Terrorism Database (2023). University of Maryland. National Consortium for the Study of Terrorism and Responses to Terrorism. Accessed and downloaded at: *https://www.start.umd.edu/gtd/about/*.
- Statista (2023). "Number of internet and social media users worldwide as of April 2023". Accessed and downloaded on 03/06/2023 at:
https://www.statista.com/statistics/617136/digital-population-worldwide/.
- Statista (2023a). "Facebook – Statistics & Facts". Accessed and downloaded on 27/06/2023 at:
https://www.statista.com/topics/751/facebook/#topicOverview.
- Statista (2023b). "Number of X (formerly Twitter) users worldwide from 2019 to 2024". Accessed and downloaded on 26/06/2023 at:
https://www.statista.com/statistics/303681/twitter-users-worldwide/.
- Statista (2023c). "Share of internet users worldwide who play video games on any device as of 3rd quarter 2022 by age group and gender". Accessed and downloaded on 21/07/2023 at:
https://www.statista.com/statistics/326420/console-gamers-gender/.

- Statista (2024). "Number of Tik Tok users worldwide from 2020 to 2025 in millions". Accessed and downloaded on 23/04/2024 at: *https://www.statista.com/statistics/1327116/number-of-global-tiktok-users/*.
- Statoil (2013). "Publication of the investigation report on the In Amenas terrorist attack". Accessed on 17/04/2024, the report can now be viewed at: *https://www.equinor.com/news/archive/2013/09/12/12S epInAmenasreport*.
- Stephenson Harwood (2022). "Aviation is facing a rising wave of cyber-attacks in the wake of Covid". 08/08/2022. Accessed and downloaded on 10/05/2023 at: *https://www.shlegal.com/insights/aviation-is-facing-a-rising-wave-of-cyber-attacks-in-the-wake-of-covid*.
- Stern, J and Berger, JM (2015). "Thugs wanted – bring your own boots: how ISIS attracts foreign fighters to its twisted utopia". *The Guardian*. 09/03/2015. Accessed and downloaded on 08/03/2023 at: *https://www.theguardian.com/world/2015/mar/09/how-isis-attracts-foreign-fighters-the-state-of-terror-book*.
- Stern, J and Berger, JM (2015). *ISIS: The State of Terror*. New York. Harper Collins.
- Stevenson, R and Anthony, J (2019). "'Thousands' of Christchurch shootings videos removed from YouTube, Google says" (16/03/2019). *https://www.stuff.co.nz/business/111330323/facebook-working-around-the-clock-to-block-christchurch-shootings-video*.

- Stijelja, S and Mishara, BL (2022). "Psychosocial Characteristics of Involuntary Celibates (Incels): A Review of Empirical Research and Assessment of the Potential Implications of Research on Adult Virginity and Late Sexual Onset". *Sexuality & Culture* (2022). Accessed on 01/03/2024 at: *https://doi.org/10.31234/osf.io/9mutg*.

- Stop Autonomous Weapons (2017). "Slaughterbots" video. 12/11/2023. Accessed and downloaded on 11/04/2023 at: *https://www.youtube.com/watch?v=9CO6M2HsoIA*.

- Suskind, R (2006). *The One Percent Doctrine: Deep Inside America's Pursuit of Its Enemies Since 9/11*. London. Simon & Schuster UK. pp. 180 and 195–8.

- Synthesia Media (2023) "What is synthetic media?". Accessed and downloaded on 17/04/2024: *https://www.synthesia.io/glossary/synthetic-media*.

- Syracuse University (2023). "What Is the Decentralized Web? 25 Experts Break it Down". Accessed and downloaded on 24/07/2023 at: *https://onlinegrad.syracuse.edu/blog/what-is-the-decentralized-web/*.

- Taylor, M. (2010). "Is Terrorism a Group Phenomenon?" *Aggression and Violent Behavior*, Vol 15. Issue 2. pp121–9; Taylor, M and Horgan, J. "A Conceptual Framework for Addressing Psychological Process in the Development of a Terrorist". *Terrorism and Political Violence*, (2006). pp585–601.

- Tech Against Terrorism (2019). "Analysis: ISIS use of smaller platforms and the DWeb to share terrorist content – April 2019". 29/04/2019. Accessed and downloaded on 24/07/2023 at: *https://www.techagainstterrorism.org/2019/04/29/anal ysis-isis-use-of-smaller-platforms-and-the-dweb-to-share-terrorist-content-april-2019/*.
- Tech Against Terrorism (2022). "Strategy Paper: Responding To Terrorist Operated Websites". July 2022. Accessed and downloaded on 06/06/2023 at: *https://www.techagainstterrorism.org/wp-content/uploads/2022/07/TAT-TOW-Mitigation-Strategy-July-2022.pdf*.
- TechCrunch (2023). "Snapchat announces 750M monthly active users". Perez, S. 16/02/2023. Accessed and downloaded at: *https://techcrunch.com/2023/02/16/snapchat-announces-750-million-monthly-active-users/?*.
- TechTarget (2023). "What is North American Electric Reliability Corporation Critical Infrastructure Protection (NERC CIP)?" Accessed and downloaded on 29/07/2023 at: *https://www.techtarget.com/searchsecurity/definition/N orth-American-Electric-Reliability-Corporation-Critical-Infrastructure-Protection-NERC-CIP*.
- Tenet, G (2007). *At the Center of the Storm: The CIA During America's Time of Crisis*. New York. Harper Collins.

- Terba, S (2018). "An Assessment of Violent Extremism Use of Social Media Technologies". *RealClear Defense.* 05/02/2018. Accessed and downloaded on 05/04/2023 at: *https://www.realcleardefense.com/articles/2018/02/05/an_assessment_of_violent_extremist_use_of_social_media_technologies_113015.html*.

- Terba, S (2019). "Does Rising Artificial Intelligence Pose a Threat?" *RealClear Defense.* 18/02/2019. Accessed and downloaded on 06/04/2023 at: *https://www.realcleardefense.com/articles/2019/02/18/does_rising_artificial_intelligence_pose_a_threat_114192.html*.

- *The Atlantic* (2015). "Why Join ISIS? How Fighters Respond When You Ask Them". Tucker, P and Defense One. 09/12/2015. Accessed and downloaded on 03/02/2023 at: *https://www.theatlantic.com/international/archive/2015/12/why-people-join-isis/419685/*.

- *The Guardian* (2015). "Thugs wanted – bring your own boots. How ISIS attracts foreign fighters to its twisted utopia". 09/03/2015. Stern, J and Berger, JM. Accessed and downloaded on 02/01/2023 at: *https://www.theguardian.com/world/2015/mar/09/how-isis-attracts-foreign-fighters-the-state-of-terror-book*.

- *The Guardian* (2018). "Fitness tracking app Strava gives away location of secret US army bases". Hern, A. 28/01/2018. Accessed and downloaded on 26/06/2023 at:

https://www.theguardian.com/world/2018/jan/28/fitnes s-tracking-app-gives-away-location-of-secret-us-army-bases.

- *The Guardian* (2019). "Norway Mosque Attack Suspect inspired by Christchurch and El Paso Shootings". Burke, J. 11/08/2023. Accessed and downloaded on 18/07/2023 at: *https://www.theguardian.com/world/2019/aug/11/norw ay-mosque-attack-suspect-may-have-been-inspired-by-christchurch-and-el-paso-shootings*.
- *The Guardian* (2020) "Prosecutors open homicide case after cyber-attack on German hospital". Accessed and downloaded on 16/04/2024 at: *https://theguardian.com/technology/2020/sep/18/prose cutors-open-homicide-case-after-cyber-attack-on-german-hospital*.
- *The New York Times* (1974). "Symbionese Liberation Army: Terrorism from the Left". 23/02/1974.
- *The New York Times* (2015). "Dylan Roof Photos and a Manifesto found are posted on Website". 20/06/2015. Accessed and downloaded on 19/07/2023 at: *https://www.nytimes.com/2015/06/21/us/dylann-storm-roof-photos-website-charleston-church-shooting.html*.
- *The New York Times* (2016). "Twitter suspends 235,000 more accounts over extremism". Benner, K. 18/08/2023. Accessed and downloaded on 27/03/2023 at: *https://www.nytimes.com/2016/08/19/technology/twitte r-suspends-accounts-extremism.html*.

- *The New York Times* (2018). "Cyberattack Disrupts Printing of Major Newspapers". Sanger, D, and Perlroth, N. 30/12/2018. Accessed and downloaded at: *https://www.nytimes.com/2018/12/30/business/media/los-angeles-times-cyberattack.html*.
- *The New York Times* (2022). "Before the Massacre: Erratic Behavior and a Chilling Threat". 17/05/2022. Accessed and downloaded on 19/07/2023 at: *https://www.nytimes.com/2022/05/15/nyregion/gunman-buffalo-shooting-suspect.html*.
- *The New York Times* (2023). "'The Godfather of AI' Leaves Google and Warns of Danger Ahead". Accessed and downloaded on 01/05/2023 at: *https://www.nytimes.com/2023/05/01/technology/ai-google-chatbot-engineer-quits-hinton.html*.
- Tracxn. (2023). "Chatbots Startups in Russia". Accessed and downloaded on 17/04/2024 at: *https://tracxn.com/d/explore/chatbots-startups-in-russia/__29l1kO6m5kDbgW4PiR8YWO87dSBIYmJIb7koHPiqnKM/companies*.
- TrustRadius (2023). User Rating Blog. Accessed and downloaded on 12/04/2023 at: *https://www.trustradius.com/products/telegram/reviews*.
- Twitter Help Center (2023). "Perpetrators of Violent Attacks". Safety and cybercrime. February 2023. Accessed and downloaded on 27/07/2023 at: *https://help.twitter.com/en/rules-and-policies/perpetrators-of-violent-attacks*.

- UN CTED (2021). United Nations Security Council Counter-Terrorism Committee Executive Directorate. Information and Communications Technologies. May 2021. Accessed and downloaded on 05/07/2023 at: *https://www.un.org/sites/www.un.org.securitycouncil.ct c/files/ctc_cted_factsheet_ict_may_2021.pdf*.
- University College Dublin (UCD) (2013). *MANAGING A DIGITAL INVESTIGATION UNIT: A Handbook for Senior Law Enforcement Officers*. Genoe, R. *Centre for Cybersecurity and Cybercrime investigation.*
- United Nations Office of Counter Terrorism (2018). *The protection of critical infrastructures against terrorist attacks: Compendium of good practices.* Accessed and downloaded on 13/04/2023 at: *https://www.un.org/securitycouncil/ctc/sites/www.un.or g.securitycouncil.ctc/files/files/documents/2021/Jan/co mpendium_of_good_practices_eng.pdf*.
- United Nations Office on Drugs and Crime UNODC (2012). "The use of the Internet for terrorist purposes". Accessed and downloaded on 11/04/2023 at: *https://www.unodc.org/documents/frontpage/Use_of_I nternet_for_Terrorist_Purposes.pdf*.
- United Nations Office on Drugs and Crime UNODC (2017). *Handbook on Children Recruited and Exploited by Terrorist and Violent Extremist Groups*. Accessed and downloaded on 02/06/2023 at: *https://www.unodc.org/documents/justice-and-prison-reform/Child-Victims/Handbook_on_Children_Recruited_and_Explo*

ited_by_Terrorist_and_Violent_Extremist_Groups_the _Role_of_the_Justice_System.E.pdf.

- UPI (2017) "Twitter announces stricter policy on abusive, violent accounts". Accessed and downloaded on 15/04/2024 at: *https://www.upi.com/Top_News/US/2017/12/18/Twitter -announces-stricter-policy-on-abusive-violent- accounts/9161513644616/*.

- US Department of Justice (2012). "Aryan Brotherhood of Texas Gang Leader Sentenced". Accessed and downloaded on 10/07/2023 at: *https://www.justice.gov/opa/pr/aryan-brotherhood- texas-gang-leader-sentenced-houston-violent-crimes- aid-racketeering*.

- US Department of Justice (2014). Awareness Brief: "Twitter and Violent Extremism". Accessed and downloaded on 06/03/2024 at: *https://portal.cops.usdoj.gov/resourcecenter/RIC/Publi cations/cops-w0741-pub.pdf*.

- US Department of Justice (2022). "Four Defendants Charged with Conspiring to Provide Material Support to ISIS". Department of Justice Press Release. 15/12/2022. Accessed and downloaded on 16/05/2023 at: *https://www.justice.gov/opa/pr/four-defendants- charged-conspiring-provide-material-support-isis*.

- US Department of Justice (2023). "High-Level Member of ISIS Sentenced to Life in Prison for Material Support to a Foreign Terrorist Organization Resulting in Death". Department of Justice Press

Release. 14/07/2023. Accessed and downloaded on 24/07/2023 at: *https://www.justice.gov/opa/pr/high-level-member-isis-sentenced-life-prison-material-support-foreign-terrorist-organization.*

- US Department of Justice Forfeiture Complaint (2017). 20/07/2017. p27. Accessed and downloaded on 15/05/2023 at: *https://www.justice.gov/opa/press-release/file/982821/download.*
- US Director of National Intelligence (2014). "Counter Terrorism Guide". Accessed and downloaded on 13/07/2023 at: *https://www.dni.gov/nctc/groups/hamas.html.*
- US Secret Service (2022). *Hot Yoga Tallahassee: A Case Study of Misogynistic Extremism.* Accessed and downloaded on 11/07/2023 at: *https://www.documentcloud.org/documents/21417518-secret-service-2018-yoga-class-shooting-case-study.*
- Verve (2022). "How to Efficiently and Effectively Achieve NERC CIP Compliance". John Livingston. 18/10/2022. Accessed and downloaded on 29/07/2023 at: *https://verveindustrial.com/resources/blog/what-are-the-nerc-cip-standards-in-ics-security/.*
- Victoroff, J (2005). "The Mind of the Terrorist: A Review and Critique of Psychological Approaches in Journal of Conflict Resolution". Vol 49. No. 1. pp3–42, 33.
- VoxPop.eu (2019). "ISIS affiliated Nashir News Agency on Koonekti". 05/07/2019. Accessed and downloaded on 24/07/2023 at:

https://www.voxpol.eu/isis-use-of-smaller-platforms-and-the-dweb-to-share-terrorist-content/isis-affiliated-nashir-news-agency-on-koonekti/.

- Ward, A (2018). "ISIS's Use of Social Media Still Poses a Threat to Stability in the Middle East and Africa". Accessed and downloaded on 26/10/2022 at: *https://www.rand.org/pubs/commentary/2018/12/isiss-use-of-social-media-still-poses-a-threat-to-stability.html.*

- Warner, B (2010). "Segmenting the Electorate: The Effects of Exposure to Political Extremism Online". *Communication Studies.* Vol 61. Issue 4. pp430–444.

- *Washington Post* (2015). "Driver follows GPS off a demolished bridge, killing wife, police say". Holley, P. 31/03/2015. Accessed and downloaded on 03/05/2023 at: *https://www.washingtonpost.com/news/morning-mix/wp/2015/03/31/driver-follows-gps-off-demolished-bridge-killing-wife-police-say/.*

- *Washington Post* (2018). "In fight against ISIS's propaganda machine, raids and online trench warfare". Warrick, J. 19/08/2023. Accessed and downloaded on 24/07/2023 at: *https://www.washingtonpost.com/world/national-security/in-fight-against-isiss-propaganda-machine-raids-and-online-trench-warfare/2018/08/19/379d4da4-9f46-11e8-8e87-c869fe70a721_story.html.*

- *Washington Post* (2019). "New Zealand suspect allegedly claimed 'brief contact' with Norwegian mass murderer Anders Breivik". Taylor, A. 15/03/2019. Accessed and downloaded on 18/07/2023 at: *https://www.washingtonpost.com/world/2019/03/15/ne w-zealand-suspect-allegedly-claimed-brief-contact-with-norwegian-mass-murderer-anders-breivik/.*

- *Washington Post* (2021). "Ransomware Attack Might Have Caused Another Death". 01/10/2021. Accessed and downloaded on 07/04/2023 at: *https://www.washingtonpost.com/politics/2021/10/01/r ansomware-attack-might-have-caused-another-death/.*
- Web Archive (1985). "Man charged in Library Shooting Testifies He Wanted to Shoot Women". Kropko, MR. 11/06/1985. Accessed and downloaded on 10/07/2023 at: *https://web.archive.org/web/20230512205404/https://a pnews.com/article/be4b2f5204ad2b4f31b30d3eaca0de 90.*
- WebDeveloperNotes.com (2023). Quote accessed and downloaded on 30/07/2023 at: *https://www.webdevelopersnotes.com/ensure-security-dont-own-a-computer.*
- Weimann, G (2018). "Competition and Innovation in a Hostile Environment: How Jabhat Al-Nusra and Islamic State Moved to Twitter in 2013–2014". *Studies in Conflict and Terrorism.* Vol 42. Issue 1–2.
- Weiss, J (1974). 'Suicide' in *American Handbook of Psychiatry*, 2nd ed. (ed) Arieti, S. New York. Basic Books. (1974). Vol 3. Pp743–65.

- West Sussex County Council (2015). "In Amenas Inquest Hearing transcripts". Accessed and downloaded on 22/05/2023 at: *https://www.westsussex.gov.uk/births-ceremonies-and-deaths/deaths/in-amenas-inquest-hearing-transcripts/*.
- Wigan Council (2023). "Cyber Terrorism: What is Cyber Terrorism?". Accessed and downloaded on 29/07/2023 at: *https://www.wigan.gov.uk/Resident/Crime-Emergencies/Counter-terrorism/Cyber-terrorism.aspx*.
- *Wired* (2019). "When Algorithms Think You Want to Die". Gerrard, Y and Gillespie, T. 21/02/2023. Accessed and downloaded on 03/06/2023 at: *https://www.wired.com/story/when-algorithms-think-you-want-to-die/*.
- *Wired* (2022). "Get Ready for Cyber-Attacks on Global Food Supplies". Emily Orton. 15/02/2022. Accessed and downloaded on 13/04/2023 at: *https://www.wired.co.uk/article/cyber-security-global-food-supply*.
- *Wired* (2023). "How You Can Tell the AI Images of Trump's Arrest Are Deepfakes". Rogers, R. 21/03/2023. Accessed and downloaded on 03/05/2023 at: *https://www.wired.com/story/how-to-tell-fake-ai-images-donald-trump-arrest/*.
- Wood, G (2017) "The American Climbing The Ranks of ISIS." Accessed and downloaded on 16/04/2024 at: *https://www.theatlantic.com/magazine/archive/2017/03/the-american-leader-in-the-islamic-state/510872/*.

- World Population Review (2023). "Telegram users by country 2023". Accessed and downloaded on 12/04/2023 at: *https://worldpopulationreview.com/country-rankings/telegram-users-by-country*.
- World Population Review (2024). "Instagram Users by Country (2024)". Accessed and downloaded on 19/04/2024 at: *https://worldpopulationreview.com/country-rankings/instagram-users-by-country*.
- Your MentalHealthPal.com (2023). "10 Possible Reasons Why I Can't Trust Anyone". Baweja, S. 10/04/2023. Accessed and downloaded on 03/05/2023 at: *https://yourmentalhealthpal.com/why-cant-i-trust-anyone/*.
- YouTube website (2023). Accessed and downloaded on 26/07/2023 at: *https://www.youtube.com/jobs/*.
- Zand, B (2022). UNTOLD: "The Secret World of Incels". Channel 4 Documentaries. (47.15). 07/11/2022. Accessed and downloaded on 06/06/2023 at: *https://www.youtube.com/watch?v=kReeoKoOvZI*.
- Ziegele, M (9/10/2019). "Zwei Tote bei Schießerei in Halle - Video des Täters bestätigt rechtsextremistisches Motiv". *Frankfurter Rundschau* (in German). Accessed and downloaded on 17/07/2023 at: *https://www.fr.de/politik/terroranschlag-halle-synagogentuer-wird-gedenkens-zr-13083592.html*.

APPENDIX E: CYBER CRIME TYPES AND RELATED CYBER-DEPENDENT/CYBER-ENABLED OFFENCES

For the latest information on Cybercrime Prosecution Guidance, please visit:

- *https://www.cps.gov.uk/legal-guidance/cybercrime-prosecution-guidance*.

FURTHER READING

IT Governance Publishing (ITGP) is the world's leading publisher for governance and compliance. Our industry-leading pocket guides, books and training resources are written by real-world practitioners and thought leaders. They are used globally by audiences of all levels, from students to C-suite executives.

Our high-quality publications cover all IT governance, risk and compliance frameworks and are available in a range of formats. This ensures our customers can access the information they need in the way they need it.

Other publications you may find useful include:

- *Artificial intelligence – Ethical, social, and security impacts for the present and the future* by Dr Julie E. Mehan, *www.itgovernance.co.uk/shop/product/artificial-intelligence-ethical-social-and-security-impacts-for-the-present-and-the-future*
- *ISO 22301:2019 and business continuity management – Understand how to plan, implement and enhance a business continuity management system (BCMS)* by Alan Calder, *www.itgovernance.co.uk/shop/product/iso-223012019-and-business-continuity-management-understand-how-to-plan-implement-and-enhance-a-business-continuity-management-system-bcms*

- *IT Governance – An international guide to data security and ISO 27001/ISO 27002, Eighth edition* by Alan Calder and Steve Watkins, *www.itgovernance.co.uk/shop/product/it-governance-an-international-guide-to-data-security-and-iso-27001iso-27002-eighth-edition*

For more information on ITGP and branded publishing services, and to view our full list of publications, visit *www.itgovernancepublishing.co.uk*.

To receive regular updates from ITGP, including information on new publications in your area(s) of interest, sign up for our newsletter at *www.itgovernancepublishing.co.uk/topic/newsletter*.

Branded publishing

Through our branded publishing service, you can customise ITGP publications with your company's branding.

Find out more at

www.itgovernancepublishing.co.uk/topic/branded-publishing-services.

Related services

ITGP is part of GRC International Group, which offers a comprehensive range of complementary products and services to help organisations meet their objectives.

For a full range of resources on cyber security visit *www.itgovernance.co.uk/shop/category/information-security*.

Training services

The IT Governance training programme is built on our extensive practical experience designing and implementing management systems based on ISO standards, best practice and regulations.

Our courses help attendees develop practical skills and comply with contractual and regulatory requirements. They also support career development via recognised qualifications.

Learn more about our training courses and view the full course catalogue at *www.itgovernance.co.uk/training*.

Professional services and consultancy

We are a leading global consultancy of IT governance, risk management and compliance solutions. We advise businesses around the world on their most critical issues and present cost-saving and risk-reducing solutions based on international best practice and frameworks.

We offer a wide range of delivery methods to suit all budgets, timescales and preferred project approaches.

Find out how our consultancy services can help your organisation at *www.itgovernance.co.uk/consulting*.

Industry news

Want to stay up to date with the latest developments and resources in the IT governance and compliance market? Subscribe to our Weekly Round-up newsletter and we will send you mobile-friendly emails with fresh news and features about your preferred areas of interest, as well as unmissable offers and free resources to help you successfully start your projects. *www.itgovernance.co.uk/weekly-round-up*.

EU for product safety is Stephen Evans, The Mill Enterprise Hub, Stagreenan, Drogheda, Co. Louth, A92 CD3D, Ireland. (servicecentre@itgovernance.eu)

www.ingramcontent.com/pod-product-compliance
Lightning Source LLC
Chambersburg PA
CBHW050803270326
41926CB00025B/4519